RADICAL *Review*
HISTORY

Issue | 122

T0369891

Queering Archives: Intimate Tracings

QUEERING ARCHIVES

REFLECTION

Editors' Introduction

Queering Archives: Intimate Tracings

In the longer introduction of *Radical History Review*'s two thematic issues "Queering Archives," we frame the archive as an evasive and dynamic space animated by the tensions of knowledge production, absence, and presence. As Jeffrey Weeks argued in *RHR* in 1979, "The evolution of sexual meanings and identities that we have traced over the past hundred years or so are by no means complete."[1] Fragments of information float unfixed—historically unraveled—and we form archives when we pull the fragments into the orbit of efforts to know. Yet the business of knowing is unsteady, as scholars of sexuality and gender have amply demonstrated. Between the fraught and necessary practices of historicization, anachronism, interpretation, bias, and partial readings that propel historical scholarship, archival fragments fall in and out of the frame of an easily perceptible knowledge. Queer historical knowledge thus is evasive—like a coin dropped in the ocean and for which one grasps, reaching it only for it to slip away again, rolling deeper into the beyond. To say that the knowledge work of animating queer historical fragments is marked by such slipperiness is to underline how the archive negotiates the decomposition and recomposition of knowledge's materials. We pull and push at the fading paper, the fraying fabric, the photographs bleaching into their backgrounds, and manipulate technologies on their way to obsolescence, all as part of some suturing effort of one kind or another.

While archives are stages for the appearance of life, this life is always reconstituted, and the efforts of reconstitution that give the archive distinguishable form are always dramatized by the fragility not only of the documented life but of both the materials themselves and the investigative desire giving rise to their discovery.

Radical History Review
Issue 122 (May 2015)   DOI 10.1215/01636545-2849486
© 2015 by MARHO: The Radical Historians' Organization, Inc.

It is this compounding of fragility, of contingent expression, that yields "the labile real of the archive."[2] Under the pressure of the investigator's desire, fragments are drawn together to sing of such—or point to this desire's misgivings. This tension of knowledge production in the archive—this dialectical drama of intimate tracing and historical unraveling—is what produces the archive as a compelling time and space for witnessing the mechanics of queer knowledge production.

This second issue represents an elaboration on the meditation on historical unravelings in the first issue of "Queering Archives." Through the optics of *intimate tracings*—visualized both figuratively and metaphorically through the fragmented bodies in Mundo Meza's 1979 pen-and-ink sketch, reproduced here on the cover—this issue provides a sustained engagement with notions of the intimate, with practices that constitute a tracing of the body, and with the amalgamation of these notions and practices in the joined context of sexuality, gender, and the archive. Insofar as the archive sponsors contests over historical meaning, interpretive and signifying practices of tracing and unraveling characterize the push and pull of knowledge work in the archive: the detective's pursuit and the concomitant assembly, the loose threads and the exposed moments revealing that the whole does not hold together. Understanding "intimacy" as denoting the personal, the proximate, and the sexual, we mobilize *intimate tracings* here to draw together and triangulate a set of practices: experiences of being *in* the archive, methodological reflections on using archival materials, and efforts to map the contours of sexual life through archival sources. Our notion of "intimate tracings" alludes partly to "the very processes through which the bodies and desires of others [and of ourselves] come to be archived in the first place and thereby enter historicity."[3]

The contributors to this issue reflect on archival knowledges by tracing their own scholarly narratives through archives. In various ways, the contributions delineate how archives have been mobilized to perform intimate labors and evince how intimacy itself has been naturalized as an affective relation with the archive. Indeed, the sentimental figuration of the archive as an exemplary intimate site—a space and time for secrets of the most personal and sexual kind—is necessarily inverted by the history of lesbian, gay, bisexual, and transgender (LGBT) community archives, which were partly founded on the premise of making private sexual histories public knowledge. With these histories in mind, this issue, taken as a whole, invites critical reflection on the twinned disciplining relationship between the intimate and the archival, fostering a frank tracing of the affordances and excesses of intimate knowledge and of the notion that the histories of sexuality and gender might be apprehended by recourse to the intimate knowledges of the archive.

This issue's first section, "On Being in the Archive," brings together critical reflections on the political, methodological, and theoretical significance of being *in* the archive, as both archival subject and visitor. In the opening essay, "Minor Threats," Mimi Thi Nguyen, drawing on the queer experience of unexpectedly confronting her own zines in the archive, grapples with the stakes of incorporating queer knowledge in mainstream archives. Through her reflections on being archived, and being invited into the institutional desire to archive "minor threats," Nguyen fashions a queer archival politics of refusal, one that resists the imperative "to discipline objects or signs to perceive what is being lost in conventional fantasies of progress or perfectibility" (21).

Picking up this thread, Jack Jen Gieseking reflects on being in the archive in an ethnographic sense in "Useful In/stability: The Dialectical Production of the Social and Spatial Lesbian Herstory Archives." In one of this issue's several pieces on the Lesbian Herstory Archives (LHA)—in many ways an exemplary queer archiving case study for contemporary theory and practice—Gieseking meditates on refusal, disorder, and intelligibility through her fieldwork observations of the LHA as an archive that commits to "flux *in place*, creating a stable space from which to remain in that state of flux" (34). Gieseking calls this "useful in/stability." Self-consciously seeing herself in the archive within her ethnographic view—"the dyke detective at the dining room table" (35)—Gieseking offers a useful segue into Jeanne Vaccaro's essay, "'Look More at the Camera than at Me': Susan and the Transgender Archive," which offers a critical discussion of how subjects are produced through archival documents. Studying documentary efforts to bestow archival legibility on a queer subject, Vaccaro examines documentary archival film's reliance on "an aesthetics of intimacy [as a] manipulation of the proximate" (39). Closing this section, Robert Summers traces similar concerns through recollected field notes of visiting archives of a different order, in "Queer Archives, Queer Movements: The Visual and Bodily Archives of Vaginal Davis." Here Summers reflects on the fragmented and queer archival styling of Vaginal Davis's studios, performative arts, and body.

The essays in the issue's second section, "Piecing Together Historical Traces," explore different approaches to the renarration of queer historical life via the archival. As recollections of the sometimes illicit and offensive aspects of sexual history, these pieces raise a range of questions: What can one do with archival knowledge when that knowledge is gained in questionable ways? How is one to engage with a queer archive that prompts unease, disgust, or ethical uncertainties?

Kwame Holmes, focusing on the collecting practices of archivists and oral historians of the "black LGBT" subject in twentieth-century Washington, DC, exposes the archive as an architecture of state power that both collects and produces political realities. To this end, he asks how an act of gossip—an archive that resists recognition and institutionalization—might encourage us to reexamine projects that purport to recover and give voice to those "lost," "hidden," or "closeted" historical subjects? By juxtaposing the Frank Kameny papers housed in the Library of Congress, a CD-ROM with scanned PDFs of *Blacklight* (a Washington, DC, "publication for the Black gay community" that ran from 1979 to 1983), and largely unarchivable pieces of gossip, Holmes explores and critiques the pathways through which black queer sexuality enters the public record. Robb Hernández's contribution, "Drawn from the Scraps: The Finding AIDS of Mundo Meza," pursues these concerns regarding the estranged relationship between archival practices and queer knowledge by offering a "queer detrital analysis" (71) of the legacy of Meza, a Tijuana-born, Los Angeles–based artist. Playing on "the double meaning of finding aids as both a technology for (re)search, retrieval, and description and a navigational system of AIDS cultural memory" (72), Hernàndez argues that queer history demands archival methods and practice that are attentive to this history's reliance on residue, fragments, and debris.

Rüstem Ertuğ Altınay examines nation building and the politics of historiography in Turkey through the archival practice of popular historian Reşad Ekrem Koçu, who dedicated much of his life to authoring the *İstanbul ansiklopedisi* (*The Encyclopedia of Istanbul*), a massive project he started in 1944 and continued until his death in 1975. Koçu's melancholic and eroticized relation with the Ottoman past is partly evidenced and retraced through his focus on the many "queer" subjects of empire: the male "lovers of facial beauty," same-sex prostitutes, androgynous boys, and transgender belly dancers, among others. Altınay notes, "In all these stories that Koçu loved to read, collect, and retell, there was an element of pleasure that informed (and was informed by) the history he constructed through his archival practice," but it is an archival practice that is ambiguous and can be put to conflicting nationalist, historiographical, and queer archival ends (98). Barry Reay's "Sex in the Archives: David Louis Bowie's New York Diaries, 1978–1993" also examines the archival practice of one individual, whose collection is housed at the New York Public Library. This contribution points to the fetishistic and ritualistic nature of archiving and collecting. At the level of archival description of the description of racialized and sexualized bodies within the diaries themselves, the stakes of representation become clear. Bowie's regular use of racialized terminology to describe his sex partners, for example, points to the problematics of archival representation and the essentializations used to classify bodies and desires. For Bowie, it seems, writing, documenting, and archiving came to be inextricable from sex. In this sense, archiving and sex become one and the same.

The section "Doing Archives" explicitly draws our attention to questions confronting contemporary queer archival practice. In "Body, Sex, Interface: Reckoning with Images at the Lesbian Herstory Archives," Cait McKinney returns us to the LHA through a meditation on the dilemmas for digitization and classification posed by an "unprocessed 'porn' box" and "vernacular photographs of nonfamous lesbians engaged in everyday contexts" in the archive's collection (117). Echoing Gieseking's analysis of the LHA as a site of "useful in/stability," McKinney provides an account of the archives as a "mediated space in transition," characterized by "its willfully provisional, improvisational, and self-critical approach to digitization" (126). As grassroots LGBT archives established in the 1970s age, they are confronted by shifting technological contexts as well as by changing expectations and circumstances with regards to who can access things that have been preserved. Elaborating McKinney's reflections on digitization through a discussion of open access to oral histories, Elise Chenier, in her essay "Privacy Anxieties: Ethics versus Activism in Archiving Lesbian Oral History Online," navigates the ethical and political challenges—and opportunities—prompted by new technologies and the inheritance of queer archival materials collected in times so markedly different from the contemporary moment. Proposing emerging practices for archiving oral histories online, Chenier elucidates how "as collections shift to online environments, the politics of the personal must be rethought anew" (139).

Digitization, open access, and the ethical treatment of queer archival materials are, as our contributors make clear, concerns that go beyond narrow questions regarding good records management. Practices of preservation, circulation, exhibition, and access explicitly raise questions about archival confidence. Insofar as every instance of archival donation is an expression of faith in the archive, every moment of archival reception is a moment in which the archive puts its bona fides on the line: What does it mean to keep the faith in a queer archive? What faith is being kept, and what is queer archiving endeavoring to be faithful to? Recalling the a priori or natural significance routinely accorded to the intimate in the queer archive—personal sexual ephemera is gathered together in faith that its accumulation adds up to something—questions about the character of that faith seem inevitable. When tomorrow's archives collect our contemporary queer residue, what will their efforts need to look like in order for us to regard them as faithful? Can we even imagine that anything approaching a consensus could be assembled around such a question? Is faithfulness a virtue? Taking up this line in "Faithful Histories" and running it in a divergent direction, K. Mohrman and Anthony M. Petro raise some of the contestable theoretical, methodological, and political implications for identifying queer archives within Mormon and Catholic traditions. Observing the charged historical and signifying relationship between sexuality and religion, Mohrman, in "Queering the LDS Archive," maps out ways in which the intimate traces within the already queer Mormon archive reveal how "queerness was, and is, contingent on and complicit with dominant formations" (147). Petro, in "Beyond Accountability: The Queer Archive of Catholic Sexual Abuse," argues that BishopAccountability.org—a website that documents and publishes material related to sexual abuse in the United States—evokes queer readings that "augment the rhetorical and political power of exposé by moving from the scandal of cover-up toward the difficult stories beneath" (161). Together, these essays argue that queer histories and the fragmented histories of the Mormon and the Catholic Churches overlap in irrevocable ways.

The section "Queer Archival Generations" comprises interview-style encounters and conversations—between archivists, scholars, activists, and artists—who reflect on techniques and practices of queer archiving over time. K. J. Rawson interviews Ben Power Alwin, curator of the Sexual Minorities Archives (founded in Chicago and now maintained in Alwin's home in western Massachusetts) since 1977. The SMA's method of grassroots archiving, fund-raising, and open access contrasts with many institutional archives of LGBT sexuality and gender that universities and historical societies maintain. The interview explores the 1992 decision to shift the archive's early focus from "the history and literature that was being collected by lesbians, for lesbians" to a diverse array of *sexual minorities*, marking a radical departure very much informed by Alwin's transition from female to male (179). As Rawson points out, "as Ben lives in the collection, his transgender body has become an everyday part of the archive and the archive has become an everyday part of his body" (178–79).

The intersections of the body and the archive are enacted in ways that are simultaneously modeled on and resist the modes of archiving put forth by previous generations of queer collectors, archivists, activists, and scholars. In "'Queering the Trans° Family Album,'" Elspeth H. Brown and Sara Davidmann share their experiences researching, writing, documenting, and photographing queer and trans° communities (including cis and trans° partners of trans° men) in the United Kingdom, Canada, and the United States. Their conversation stages some of the ethical issues at stake in the photographing and archiving of queer subjects, and both Brown and Davidmann pay close attention to how the subjects of their research and photography can maintain control over the ways that they come to be represented textually, visually, and aurally.

Riffing on the material histories of aging that now structure LGBT community archives in many parts of the world, this section draws attention to generational perspectives on the queer archiving project. The importance of archival engagements across generations for the generation of knowledge about sexuality, gender, life, and history is discussed in Peter Edelberg's interview with Karl Peder Pedersen, an archive activist involved with the Danish Gay and Lesbian Archive. As a reflection on the foundational relationship between the queer archive and the "source deficit" of queer history, this interview closes this section with a cautionary reflection on the historical fragility of the transfer of "archival material from generation to generation" (208). Archives, suggests Pedersen, are queers' children: in lieu of offspring, archives have been fashioned as agentic sites for passing on and handing down queer history.

Queer archives, thus rendered, not only reproduce memories of past queer life but stand in for hitherto impossible queer children. As an unruly set of progeny, what might the future hold for contemporary queer archives? "Queering Archives: A Roundtable Discussion"—the penultimate section of this issue—picks up this query in a broader conversation about the career of the queer archival, as both intellectual project and political practice. In particular, this discussion focuses on developments and limits within North American queer studies of the archive, which emerges as a central object of analysis and is itself archived in a way within the terms of the discussion.

The roundtable discussion provides a sustained critical engagement with the profile of the queer archive as a site for the repetitive, radical defamiliarization of knowledge: "I have never really deviated from the formative impression Foucault gave," writes Tavia Nyong'o, "that what I should expect from the archive is the estrangement of myself and others and that I could call that estrangement queer" (216). As Regina Kunzel makes clear in her contribution, the queer estrangement offered by archival knowledge exposes the ways in which histories of sexuality and gender residing in archives exceed the interests of historical projects that are legibly "LGBT" in orientation. Bringing subjects who are "reluctant," "unpalatable," and "unheroic" to the front of the stage, queer views of the archive bring into focus what Kunzel calls "a history of disavowal—a kind of strategic disaffiliation that might result from the promptings of gay activists to conceive of homosexuality beyond the mental hospital and psychiatrist's office and by historians who often followed suit" (230).

In a similar vein, Anjali Arondekar maps out the enduring efficacy of a queer approach to archives that "reaches beyond the grammar of failure and loss." Arondekar reflects on "how the absence and/or presence of archives secures historical futurity, and what proceeds from an unsettling of that attachment, from a movement away from the recursive historical dialectic of fulfillment and impoverishment" (216). These reflections suggest that queer archiving as a project is marked by routine, habituated reflections on its own limitations. Christina B. Hanhardt in her contribution reflects on related concerns, asking "how the idealization of recovery in LGBT social movements and archival projects functions not only as a bringing into visibility but also as a normalizing aspiration to the healthy and self-realized self" (230). Hanhardt continues: "What analytics and methods, then, might the logic of nonrecovery offer?" (231).

The relations between the archive and lived experience are developed in Susan Stryker's remarks. Thinking queerly beside pathologized models of knowledge, Stryker, following feminist and postcolonial critics and activists, explores how the queer archival fuses together "the archives and the body . . . as commensurable material expressions of assembled knowledges" (212). Through this focus on particular instances of knowledge being put together—certain bodies and archives at specific points in time and place—queer engagements with the archive incessantly recall the limits of these endeavors as well as those of their orienting institution or collection. This self-consciousness triggers a reflection on the politics of memory work and preservation so crucial to discussions of the queer archive. Ann Cvetkovich, for example, asserts that "indigenous frameworks that question notions of open access or the paper document and how the archive is embedded in property, ownership, and land claims have important implications for queer archives. The archival turn ultimately requires the thorough rethinking of what counts as knowledge and method. Approaching the land as living archive, transforming schools, and embracing the digital, indigenous resurgence is actively creating new cultures from the archive rather than mourning past violence or lost traditions."

By foregrounding, carrying, or conveying people's gendered, desiring bodies, queer archival projects pulse, as bodies do. They cruise and seduce and are caressed and taken. They are evidentiary traces of queer desire and life, and they mark a determination—a rubbery one that changes from time to time and case to case—at that moment to give up something intimate that is somehow traceable. And the moment of archival revelation is always a risk, though the endurance of queer archiving endeavors speaks to risk's rewards. As Juana María Rodríguez suggests, this risk is especially apparent to communities of color, "so often under attack, marked as a collective hot mess of excessive, irrational, unorganized bodies and behavior." Despite this, Rodríguez demonstrates how the queer archiving project has assembled knowledges that exceed and evade these disciplinary injunctions. Recalling the "queers and queens" she wrote about in her first book, Rodríguez reflects on their desire "to leave a beautiful trace" and the success of such which is monumentalized in their archival legacy.

Given the inspirational role that Joan Nestle has played for queer archivists and scholars, it is fitting that the closing contribution comes from her. This collection opened with "a queer love song" by Nguyen to queer archival fragments "that render the past in the present as a wish or a wanting for a *something more*" (12). In her coda, Nestle traces back and forth an intimate public history of being in the archives, from living with the LHA in her Upper West Side apartment in the 1970s to becoming one of what she calls "the archived":

We asked no permissions to announce our desires for change; we had no
training except the lessons of life based on racial, gender, and class hierarchies,
but living on the borders of the acceptable had shown me the richness of
difference, the comradeship of the obscene. It was always the primacy of the
endangered body and then the question, how do you imagine a grassroots site
of appreciation for the shamed and the derided, for the defiant and the lustful?
(236)

Four decades after cofounding the LHA, Nestle, along with her contemporaries, now surveys a field in which queer, LGBT, and feminist archiving has become an expanded enterprise, reaching deep into new social technologies and hitherto hostile institutional settings. As Cvetkovich argues in this issue, in scholarship and in practice, there is now "a queer archives movement with tremendous vitality" (219). Is this the future Nestle and her peers imagined when they launched endeavors like the LHA in the early 1970s? Do they see their efforts then in the face of things that have since come to pass? Are words like *legacy* and *inheritance* useful to account for these queer labors—or might the histories of queer archives suggest that we need some other vocabulary or model of relation? As a valentine to queer archives of the future, Nestle offers counsel, noting that "queer archives of the future perhaps will give evidence that it is harder to live with a history than without one" and calling for the ongoing vitality of "the archiving of dissent," an endeavor that, among other things, promises "to keep alive the markings of the disappeared" (241–42).

Dim markings, ravels of history, intimate tracings: these are collateral relations within the shared heritage of queer history. The futures they are fashioning, as intimated by this issue's contributors, are reworking how we think of the queer and the archive and it is this situation of "estrangement," as Nyong'o argues, that continues to recommend the queer archive as a generative perspective for politics, practice, and scholarship.

The contributions to this volume, and its predecessor ("Queering Archives: Historical Unravelings"), provide a wide range of diverse perspectives on archives, occasionally making contentious claims which question the limits of queer archives and illustrate the paradoxical and contested ways that "evidence" itself functions and is made to function. Whether we are looking at art, photography, cultural ephemera, criminal allegations, diaries, eroticized (and exoticized) textual depictions of racialized bodies, or other forms of representation, contributions to this issue illustrate some of the precarious ways in which the archival is mobilized to generate knowledge. They are offered here as efforts that underline how evidence in all its forms is open to interpretation and how archival knowledge is framed by the specific interrogative contexts that produce and interpret evidence in the first place. Aspects of these contributions challenge our own recognition of the queer and the archival. They are not offered as a portrait for what a prescriptive queer or queering of the archive might look like but, instead, as a set of provocations designed to nourish the field by sponsoring debate and stimulating alternate readings.

The queer relationships between evidence, imagination, and estrangement are central to any queer archival endeavor. As María Elena Martínez wrote in the first issue of "Queering Archives," when doing queer archival and historical work, "The imagination can be explicitly summoned, recognized, and valued as a source and resource, and in performance the body can function as a kind of archive such as when acting, singing, or dancing serves to access and transmit knowledge."[4] Bodies write, read, act, feel, and produce queer archival knowledges, and María Elena Martínez's creative and smart work is evidence of the processes of queering archives that we envision here. We miss her and the queer archival scholarship and methodologies she embodies. Queering archives would not have been the same without her. We dedicate this issue to her.

—Daniel Marshall, Kevin P. Murphy, and Zeb Tortorici

Notes

We are very grateful for all of the work done by our reviewers and those at *Radical History Review* and Duke University Press who contributed to the production of the two volumes of *Queering Archives*.

1.   Jeffrey Weeks, "Movements of Affirmation: Sexual Meanings and Homosexual Identities," *Radical History Review*, no. 20 (1979): 178.

2.   Daniel Marshall, "Queer Breeding: Historicising Popular Culture, Homosexuality, and Informal Sex Education," *Sex Education* 13, no. 5 (2013): 601.

3.   Zeb Tortorici, "Visceral Archives of the Body: Consuming the Dead, Digesting the Divine," *GLQ* 20, no. 4 (2014): 408.

4.   María Elena Martínez, "Archives, Bodies, and Imagination: The Case of Juana Aguilar and Queer Approaches to History, Sexuality, and Politics," *Radical History Review* 168 (2014): 168.

Minor Threats

Mimi Thi Nguyen

In a column published in 2009 for punk magazine *Maximum Rocknroll*, musician and writer Osa Atoe wondered at the seeming disappearance of black and brown punks from only a few years before her own time. She writes of revisiting her collection to read again ten-, fifteen-year-old zines including *Race Riot, How to Stage a Coup, Slander, Quantify*, and *Mala* and how these helped her and other black and brown punks who came later to establish a genealogy and a touchstone: "What all of these early POC [people of color] punk zines did for me was put me in touch with other brown punk kids. I remember meeting this queer Asian girl, Celeste at a BBQ/B-day party because I saw a copy of *Race Riot* sticking out of her bag. Later, we started a Queer People of Color (QPOC) group together made up of about six brown queer kids." Atoe also wonders what happened to us, to the black and brown punk women who created communion where there had been none. "What was the point of putting out zines like *Race Riot* & *How to Stage a Coup*, if not to try to spawn some kind of change in the punk scene? Well here we are! The change (I hope) they wished to see in the world! People of color punks, empowered by the words and deeds of those who came before us, building community with each other, and ready to fuck shit up."[1]

What emerged for me from Atoe's brown study is how these objects describe a cluster of unpredictable encounters with others across times. When I brought together the imperfect, partial histories that made up *Race Riot*—the initial call for contributions (printed as flyers, pasted onto postcards) circulated in 1994, 1995—I could not then have anticipated how a copy of a copy of a copy belonging to a sis-

Radical History Review
Issue 122 (May 2015)   DOI 10.1215/01636545-2849495

ter of an older brother's best friend might find its way into the hands of a young punk, ten or twenty years later (as it does) and create connection through the chance encounter—for Atoe and Celeste, others I have met since and more I do not know (yet). To answer Atoe's question in part, some of us are still punk, others put punk behind them, while our objects continue to corroborate our presence as provocation even now. So it might be that an archive of minor threats (like *Race Riot*, our zines together) is an incitement to grasp more tightly a promise from the past to a future.[2]

But I have concerns, too, about what happens to us and our threats. Those minor objects that once circulated between us are now amassing in library collections and institutional archives, shared and sometimes scanned, reformatted, and uploaded on public and semipublic platforms, while academic studies and popular press anthologies republish images and passages alongside close readings and remembrances—the conditions for encountering our objects are radically changed years later.[3] Once my own zines began to figure in historiographical and archival discourses about punk cultures, especially as radically minor objects that stand in for a critical reckoning with a politics of race and gender (one collection named it a "race riot movement" in retrospect), I wondered what else is changed in the increasingly institutional encounter that narrates a history of minor threats as a productive site for archival accumulation and intellectual inquiry.[4]

This essay considers how radically minor objects that render the past in the present as a wish or a wanting for a *something more* and also a caution about the production of knowledge about those objects into what Roderick Ferguson calls the reorder of things.[5] While I focus on punk in the field of cultural politics (and, to be more specific, punk feminisms, women of color punk feminisms), I follow cues from transnational and postcolonial feminist studies and queer of color critique to take up methodological and epistemological questions about minor objects as entry points for disruption and discipline, especially where power's sphere of control and knowledge's realm of interference together aim to capture the minor object. Here the concept of *minor objects* describes those marginal forms, persons, and worlds that are mobilized in narrative (including archival) constructions to designate moments of crisis. By way of a minor object, exclusion and normativity might be laid bare (though perhaps in no straightforward manner), and the contingent quality of knowledge or other claims fold under scrutiny. Punk as one such minor object saved my life (as the saying goes), because it gave me words and gestures for once inchoate feelings about the cluster of promises (the state and capital are on your side! the ring on your finger is a sign of love and protection!) that constitute what Lauren Berlant calls a cruel optimism.[6] *The good life, fuck that.*

But while it can also describe the limits of a structure or practice and be met with clear violence, a minor object might also be recruited to manage or overcome those limits and their laying bare, especially through acts such as recognition and inclusion, reestablishing normative principles without necessarily being itself engaged directly.[7] Called on to provide presence (as a constitutive outside) and course correction (toward a more "complete picture"), even as a minor object might be brought to bear on the fractures of empire or "the good life," the negative integration or partial recognition or presence of some minor objects into major histories can be made to resolve the same. What happens to the brats, new bloods, poison girls, androids of Mu, persons unknown, or younger lovers when we are interpellated to fill a void, correct a partial claim, set straight a story?[8] How do the politics surrounding institutional discourses of a minor threat, especially at the crash with race or gender, displace or defuse that threat through its incorporation into a politics, history, or archive? How might the specific difference of the minor object be enlisted to enhance a normative principle, an already known unity? This query then is about minor objects becoming objects of knowledge, especially once marshaled in institutional histories and inquiries to achieve continuity, chronology, and correspondences, and about the consequences for minor objects and those who might wish otherwise for them.

Against fantasies of subjective restoration and historical coherence, against plentitude and a conceivable whole, and against expertise and other organs for legitimacy, I argue our minor objects need not cohere or collude with preconceived principles or political projects in order for us to be with them, and let them manifest what they will—including those dense, bright, marvelous, and impossible meetings with one another but also their evasive maneuvers and truancies.

Black Punk Zine That Never Happened

How do we reckon with the impossibilities of a history of race in punk cultures that is absent and also not, addressed by zines that never happened and some that did? What if the something missing is not to be found, having never been in the first place? These are personal questions about those minor objects I made (*Race Riot*, *Slander*), but also political questions about how our objects bear the burden of demonstrating, and yet also failing, what informs our attachment to them. Reading our zines steeped in romance, anger, and sorrow, Atoe wanted to know what happened to the black and brown punks who labored to create an incomplete archive of us and who then seemed to disappear. "If you found a home in punk because yr a super weird queer kid, if punk is something useful to you, if it's the way you make art and the way you were politicized, how do you just leave? Where do you go?"[9] What she has are her traces of where we had been at one moment—our zines, records, photographs—and then the gap between these minor objects and the promises, or presences, attached to them.

"A zine by & for Black PUNKS, QUEERS, MISFITS, FEMINISTS, ARTISTS & MUSICIANS, WEIRDOS and the people who support us," *Shotgun Seamstress* is a snapshot (or a developing negative) in which Atoe's relationships to the past, present, and future are performed without necessarily being resolved directly, or even completely. In six and a half issues scattered across the years, Atoe documented sometimes-haphazard traces of black punk presence in interviews, but also minor objects such as photographs, zines, and records. But the hope that something missing might yet be found is so often thwarted, because some events or persons have not been documented or archived (in any way we can access). In the second issue, Atoe describes a black-and-white photograph from *Banned in DC: Photos and Anecdotes from the DC Punk Underground (79–85)* that inspires a longing for a time and place she never knew.[10] In the photograph, "two black dudes [are] standing outside the Wilson Center (punk show space), and one of the guys is holding a sign that says, 'All Ages: PUNK THROWDOWN with Trouble Funk, Government Issue, and Grand Mal.'" Government Issue was an 1980s hardcore band, as Atoe notes, while Trouble Funk was a black go-go band that would appear on several other bills with hardcore bands, including Minor Threat. She continues: "Before seeing that picture, I'd never really imagined a punk show looking like that. I started fantasizing about what it must've been like to be a Black Punk in DC in the 80s instead of now." And she wishes that she could assemble a "black punk zine that never happened," interviewing and recording black punks in that long-gone time and place.[11]

In imagining a black punk zine that never happened, Atoe dreams of more complete documentation that might help this photograph register more clearly. The hope to narrate the stories of persons unknown and recover them as historical subjects is induced and denied at once. The photograph is a particularly rich scene for such desires, in form and content manifesting a presence that is at the same time diminishing from view.[12] Or as Laura U. Marks notes, "The photograph is a sort of umbilical cord between the thing photographed 'then' and our gaze 'now.'"[13] Atoe also wishes to be there herself, to be a conduit for assembling and transmitting this impossible archive. But objects and archives are not enough. We know this because the actual document—the photograph, reproduced in this collection—is unable to represent those persons and events to their fullest. The photograph carries forward evidence of the past, but more, the sense that something has passed—something that may not have then been understood as something to note—and we only now know its loss, once it is too late. We might say, then, that the replicability of the image (in this collection, in her zine) and its finitude as an ephemeral moment together constitute what is collective and personal about this partial presence.

Atoe's "nostalgia" (the name she gives to her queer attachments) is not a conservative impulse but an imaginative one. Even as the acknowledgment that archival recovery might be impossible—and even if we knew the particulars of these black punks, would that be enough to claim to know?—commingles with the recognition that documents and photographs imperfectly represent that past to us, such desire may become itself a historical document of the present and what might yet come into being. With her desire, she animates the photograph and provides a context—not a historical specificity, which would be not an escape but a further entrenchment in a unity, as I press in a moment—but a context made up of gaps in the record, which document not the past but its imperfect resonance in the present. These feelings, while individual and idiosyncratic, are also about our passage as persons unknown in public (or semipublic) cultures—about those alternate histories and possibilities for cohabitation across times as yet blocked and thwarted by our historical situation.

I grappled with the impossibility of such desire before I had the words I do now. When I began collecting words and images for *Race Riot* as a pissed-off twenty-year-old punk, I imagined this object as a fuck-you and farewell gesture to the scene that I had loved and then felt I had lost. There had to be more of us (I reasoned), and I sought to establish an informal record of our presence and a critique of those practices of absenting us, through neglect or through violence. And yet this compilation was also a record of our longing for a history or a record of it, whether or not one or the other ever existed. It is a desire that permits us to see what we have not been able to see—not just black and brown punks but the political and aesthetic economy that renders black and brown punks unseeable, untraceable—such that the past that disappoints us can be created in the present. Long after this unmethodical process, I preserved the hand-scrawled letters, embellished envelopes (with stamps covered in glue), and other materials I had gathered, because it was important that these messages so full of love and rage still exist somehow and somewhere, as evidence of our passage and our importance. In plastic bins in the guest room closet, I store the letters, the cut-and-pasted flats of completed zines and half-realized ones, the scribbled notes from our communications and encounters as young people growing into adulthood through or around punk. Like Atoe, I wished to claim the fractures of a discontinuous history, the black and brown "PUNKS, QUEERS, MISFITS, FEMINISTS, ARTISTS & MUSICIANS, WEIRDOS"—to acknowledge those who came before us and laid the foundations for our becoming punk, and those who were with us when we went through this (or that) moment together, and those who came after us who wonder where we are now.

Riot in the Archive

Questions of accumulation and accessibility are fraught especially when institutional forms turn toward minor objects as case studies or raw material. In gender and women's studies and queer studies, archivists and scholars have turned to one strain of punk feminisms, the 1990s phenomenon of riot grrrl, to articulate theories about gender and sexuality in minor cultures. Yet what Jacques Derrida called an "archive fever" for minor objects—for instance, as evidence of the importance of preserving and studying such objects to better grasp feminist movements that *did* happen—might actually prevent us from engaging with them.[14] And when and where absences in archives and historiographies are observed, for instance, the absence of women of color in oral histories or their objects in university collections, how supplemental materials are secured and reordered into an existing continuous history becomes a crisis.

The fractious nature of race in feminisms is one snarl in archives and historiographies that might aim to define unities, episodes, and totalities. Where the object consigned alongside "like" others is the abstract premise and concrete basis for the archive and the construction of history, how likeness and also difference are recognized (or not) and structured does not merely translate a reality but produces one.[15] It is now commonplace to observe that race denotes a crisis in feminist historiographies, and riot grrrl (which has become synonymous at times with something called third-wave feminism) is no exemption. *Crisis* describes that decisive point at which a norm or a principle appears to break down and, as Gayatri Chakravorty Spivak put so well, the "presumptions of an enterprise are disproved by the enterprise itself," and *crisis* also names the opportune moment for transformative action to recuperate that way of being, or a political project.[16] Elsewhere, I describe this coupling of crisis and recuperation as the irruption of a progressive time and also a course correction that shapes a return. *Theirs was an important intervention during a moment of crisis, and lessons have been learned thusly and thereafter.*[17] Crisis thus calls attention to narrative constructions of history, which then shape the forms or practices that aim to redress partisan or partial presence (such as the "not enough") or contingent claims. That usual forms for crisis resolution include recognition, inclusion, and closeness is no distant observation. In recent years, that these operations are turned toward my minor objects—the zines and columns I wrote and also some notion of me as a punk critic—to absorb them into this narrative construction of absence and presence, crisis and recuperation, is one part of the weirdness that informs this work. (Another part is that my critique of just these operations is just as easily absorbed, but here I go anyway.) In considering a number of such moments (some having to do with me and some not), what makes these incidents so revealing is that acknowledgment of the minor object offers a form for a seeming repair of the fractures within and between feminisms, even as the gesture of inclusion intensifies these historiographical (and necessarily political) cleavages.

If we consider the archive as more than an institution but also a social formation, after Ferguson, it is as a system and structure of enunciability that the archive does not merely express a correspondence or historical consciousness but actively renders one.[18] As Kate Eichhorn observes, "Documents act only insofar as they are put into order and put into proximity with other documents."[19] Through teleology and equivalence as forms that determine relations or components shared between them, each object after the other is recruited as a serial example of principles and types, together cohering a continuous history and cogent body of statements about a person or a world. Of course, any consignment of objects is an ambiguously secured ensemble, bound according to what Michel Foucault calls the "*a priori* of a history that is given, since it is that of things actually said."[20] And so the archive is now often acknowledged as contingent and partial. Yet these failures are not necessarily considered evidence of the impossibility of complete knowledge but instead are evidence of archival absence, which empiricism can resolve. When a crisis in an archive coalesces around an absent minor object, with which historical consciousness and constitutive presuppositions have failed to reckon, the hope, then, is to discover the something missing and to reorder things in their proper place.

It is easy to find an echoing absence in recent historiographies. For instance, Sini Anderson's 2013 documentary *The Punk Singer*, about Bikini Kill vocalist Kathleen Hanna, includes troubling commentary from pop feminist figure Jennifer Baumgardner, who describes feminist "waves" emerging as women inspired by abolitionist and civil rights movements "turned race consciousness on themselves"— a historiographical sketch that commits epistemic violence in replicating (among other problems) race and gender as distinct categories or structures, rewriting feminisms as already "race conscious" in their origins, while eliding the failures of successive feminisms to reckon with race and coloniality. At the same time, we also easily hear now that riot grrrls (like so-called second-wave feminists) should have tried harder to include women of color. This retrospective stance sometimes registers as embarrassed acknowledgment, expressed in understatements such as "Collaboration hasn't been a strong point for feminists throughout history."[21] Thus one story among many about the demise of riot grrrl (a hydra-headed story) locates race at the heart of the fracture.[22] How race is made visible, then, in riot grrrl or any other feminist historiographies, as absence and as crisis (whether as then contemporaneous or now archival crisis), corroborates what actions and discourses aim to control disturbance.

What to do with the observed absence is an epistemological and methodological quandary. Does one find the something missing, and what does that recuperation mean for crisis? Who is being recuperated, and from what disaster? At the behest of Daniela Capistrano from the POC Zine Project, in 2012 I donated some select materials (copies of my copies—zines, fliers) to the Riot Grrrl Collection in the Fales Library at New York University in order to "diversify" their holdings, in hurried anticipation of the publication of selected documents in a published collection.[23] That is to say, Capistrano narrated an archival absence as a crisis, a decisive historical moment that demanded mediation.[24] That institutional record seemed at the moment to perceive women of color as outsiders or, at best, latecomers to zines and to riot grrrl, but the donation proved troubling for me at the time (I included with my donation a lengthy, tortured statement, which is part of the library's holdings and this essay) and now after. What does it mean to make radically minor objects archivable, accessible, or legible? To what labors is the radically minor object recruited beyond what the mere facts of documentation, preservation, and circulation claim to do, especially in a narrative moment of crisis? What might be rendered missing in the act of "correcting" an absence, including the conditions of absence and the forms through which its seeming correction—as supplement, for instance—is pursued?

For these reasons I feel ambivalence about the donation. Posited as a solution, presence reverts to the ideal terms of the archive in the first place—as representational fullness and total intelligibility. Empiricism in the familiar form of inclusion thus provides a seemingly nonideological resolution to the fractures of history. Sara Ahmed in her work on institutional initiatives "on being included" observes: "If the movement becomes the action, or even the aim, then moving the document might be what stops us from seeing what documents are not doing. If the success of the document is presumed to reside in how much it is passed around, this success might 'work' by concealing the failure of that document to do anything."[25] Following from such an insight, if that moment Capistrano called me to put together a donation is the point during which the presumptions of the enterprise (to account for riot grrrl as a movement) are disproved by the enterprise itself (because of absences in the record), then inclusion is the movement and passage is the measure for the audit or assessment of an archive, or a historiography—and my intervening donation, then, manages the crisis.

In an otherwise triumphalist *Los Angeles Times* review of Lisa Darms's *The Riot Grrrl Collection*, rock journalist Evelyn McDonnell deals with riot grrrl troubles thusly:

> In her smart, personal introductory essay, Johanna Fateman, erstwhile creator of the zine "Artaud-Mania" and co-founder with Hanna of the band Le Tigre, recalls how "each girl's photocopied missive was a revelation" and also how failure to constructively address issues of race and class privilege mired the movement in recriminations. Critics still deride Riot Grrrl for being too white, as if white girls have no right to express their problems. In fact, this collection reveals that some of the most powerful writing came in zines by girls of color ("Bamboo Girl" and "Gunk").

The paragraph—the only paragraph in the review that deals with difference within riot grrrl—ends with a curt nod: "Queer voices were also integral and in your face."[26]

McDonnell's review straddles both exclusion and inclusion in response to the crises posed by minor threats—recrimination, because some critics (including myself, cited in Fateman's essay) sought to disintegrate feminist solidarity and kill feminist joy, and incorporation, in order to demonstrate that a course correction did occur and a continuous history (one in which riot grrrl did not fail but instead prevailed) can be restored thereafter. McDonnell's apparent irritation, found in the summation of critics' stance (as though we argued, baselessly and cruelly, that "white girls have no right to express their problems") attributes to critics a disproportionate, irrational response to race trouble.[27] Meanwhile, we are to suppose that her dismissal of the caricatured critique is entirely sensible, as she can easily point to the inclusion of (and herself include) women of color in the story of the riot grrrl movement. It is as such that an archive might not safeguard the minor object but instead secure a system for its enunciability, which can then curtail its critique.[28] The same can be said about queercore, which names another copresent scene with alternate investments and forms but is here reduced in a single sentence as a confrontational presence seamlessly integrated into a genealogy of subversive art making. This assimilation of differences into forms of resemblance (in which distinguishing features are transformed into signs of interiority) might yet negate the minor threat.

Where the problem is defined as an absence that blocks the full accounting of an event or phenomenon, inclusion becomes the empirical form through which commensurability (or justice) is presumably achieved. The history or archive that observes the absence of minor objects—and even acknowledges their critiques—becomes successful in its articulation of failure, and usable as a measure of accountability, without actual transformation of the presumably observable principles that describe a historical continuity or coherence. In this manner the minor object provides some value (whether as color or critique) but no structure to the economies that otherwise inscribe an aesthetic, a movement. She becomes the difference that makes no difference.

In *The Reorder of Things*, Ferguson argues, "If genealogy is a form of history that can account for the constitution of knowledges, discourses, domains of objects, now is the time to make genealogy into a form of history that can account for the institutionalization of knowledge, modes of difference, and critical agency." The institutionalization of even a partial history (of riot grrrl, for instance,) promises to minor objects a sense of permanence and the achievement of accessible knowledge, but in doing so sets the terms for those objects' enunciability.[29] Toward this end (in speaking about sexuality in the colonial archive), Anjali Arondekar poses a useful provocation: "The critical challenge is to imagine a practice of archival reading that incites relationships between the seductions of recovery and the occlusions such retrieval mandates. By this I mean to say: What if the recuperative gesture returns us to a space of absence? How then does one restore absence to itself? Put simply, can an empty archive also be full?"[30]

Nobody Gets Me

The institutional archive that presumes that its form at least might actualize Atoe's fantasy of a *black punk zine that never happened* also presumes that such a fantasy is only a wish for closure. But institutionalization can also foreclose and overdetermine the shape of the object, where basic presumptions about the minor threat as a constitutive outside might also structure that object's entry into a politics, history, or archive, and too narrowly prescribe consciousness, continuity, or convergence. *(Sex Pistols, so what?)* It is as such that Rey Chow usefully identifies how a systemic series of appropriations might enfold a minor object into an established unity, through which "X is often constructed negatively as what defamiliarizes, what departs from conventional expectations, what disrupts the norm, etc.—terms that are invested in inscribing specificity by way of differentiation, deferment, and resistance."[31] Hence the capture of the minor object might find it diminished as a *mere moment* of consciousness in a historical continuity, or coinciding with a *generic principle* for a political project. To put it another way, differentiation, deferment, and resistance are precisely the politics through which a minor object might be made intelligible as crisis *and* correction. Thus the ease with which a heterogeneous minor object is incorporated within a structure of enunciability as a negative idiom, as a functional or instrumental outside, is precisely the danger of capture.

Let us consider seriously the aversion to becoming intelligible, predictable, or otherwise accessible. Such an aversion might be a prophylactic against the easy contempt or even enthusiastic attachment that mark the limits of inclusion and incorporation, which assumes that its minor objects have nothing more to say than what is permissible under a managing principle, and that what words or gestures unfold from such objects are easily subsumed into crisis *or* continuity. I take my cue from a scene from *Ladies and Gentlemen, the Fabulous Stains*.[32] During what appears to be a disastrous first gig with her all-girl punk band at the local bar, the red-and-black-eyed teenaged malcontent Corinne Burns is taunted by a woman in the audience, who dismisses her performance as the idle noise of rebellious adolescence (as if this was nothing at all). Corinne turns her sarcasm upon her hecklers, flaying misogynist fantasies of romantic intimacy and sneering, "Sucker!" Corinne then tosses her trench coat to the side of the stage as the audience gasps. She appears (as though) vulnerable in black underwear, fishnet stockings, and a sheer red blouse, but she defiantly refuses intelligibility, accessibility. Grabbing the microphone, she snarls, "I'm perfect, but nobody in this shithole gets me, because I don't put out."

What is sometimes dismissed as teenaged intractability or punk secrecy ("Nobody gets me") might bear out as a more dense denial. As Ahmed and Sianne Ngai, among others, observe so well, ugly or backward feelings that appear to suspend action or refuse to say might yet yield diagnostics of power under the shadow of capture, or even the promise of achievement.[33] Why not, then, be an obstacle to the disciplinary closure that renders a minor threat as negative integration or supplemental outside in a chain of signification or a brief moment of consciousness in a long history about a culture or a world?[34] Consigned to an outside, sometimes construed as crude material for another's speech while occluded from inhabiting the same order of signification, the minor object might refuse the troubled politics of information retrieval and knowledge production by state and capital.[35] *What we do is secret* is not just an anthem, but an argument about incommensurability.

This is not to foreclose on refusal as an attachment to *"becoming minor,"* which might not lead us to any sort of recognizable, let alone radical, politics at all.[36]

(Punk is littered with jerks.) Nor is this to suggest that there are no costs to absence or exclusion, including "the psychological costs of racism and sexism" for some of the "PUNKS, QUEERS, MISFITS, FEMINISTS, ARTISTS & MUSICIANS, WEIRDOS."[37] It is to insist instead that presence (especially in the often narrow forms through which presence is recognized) is no guarantee. What are the costs of these customary forms for desiring presence and perfectible knowledge? Such an alteration in our emphases disputes the principles that inclusion, intelligibility, intimacy, and sympathetic identification are necessary social goods. Instead, we might allow their denial to tell us something about what the minor object refuses: when established as a predictable condition or generic principle (to borrow from Chow, when X is radically different or X resists), the minor object loses its specificity to instead be appropriated into an existing unity.

What does this leave us? This essay has tried to say some things about minor objects: that they might be nonnormative and even threatening without having a unified or prescriptive politics, that their integration into institutional forms of history and archive as negative definition describes a form of capture, and that we do not have to discipline objects or signs to perceive what is being lost in conventional fantasies of progress or perfectibility. Punk long ago disappointed my teenaged hopes for an obviously revolutionary politic, being a placeholder for institutionally improper craving but also immersed in the errors of all manner of dumbfuckery. But in its doing so, I learned something else: not to believe in those forms of political life—such as consensus, clarity, or closeness—as obligatory measures (or commands) for fashioning politics or life otherwise. *Nobody gets me* might actually bleed into an onto-epistemological critique of usable knowledge about minor objects, unsettling the question of *how to be political* without a necessary orientation toward expertise, efficiency, or ends.

How, then, do we make disturbance present and perceptible, without requiring clarity or coherence from our statements, or transformation or consensus in our actions, as measures for calculation and appraisal? Under what circumstances might queer attachments, epistemic absences, and deliberate obscurities, or the thorny passage into an archive (including no doubt some of the gestures I make here), be marshaled within the order of a continuous history, through a complicity between critical articulation and political utility? Can we yet be destroyers of the status quo? What would it mean for a politics of knowledge and as yet obscure possibility to say to each other, from one minor threat to another, *You are perfect. Don't let anyone in this shithole get you. You don't have to put out.*

Notes

This essay is informed by longer histories of encounter than I could possibly recount. That said, thanks to Jenna Brager, Jenna Freedman, Alana Kumbier, Yumi Lee, Fiona I. B. Ngô, Golnar Nikpour, Janice Radway, Sarah Roberts, Jami Sailor, Tobi Vail, Thera Webb, the special issue editors, and my anonymous reviewers.

1. Osa Atoe, *Maximum Rocknroll* (self-published), no. 313 (2009): n.p.
2. For further elaborations on queer and postcolonial temporalities, see Elizabeth Freeman, *Time Binds: Queer Temporalities, Queer Histories* (Durham, NC: Duke University Press, 2010); and Bliss Cua Lim, *Translating Time: Cinema, the Fantastic, and Temporal Critique* (Durham, NC: Duke University Press, 2009).
3. In 2011 Brager and Sailor, zinesters and librarians, published the first issue of *Archiving the Underground*, a zine exploring the tensions that accompany "the academic project of archiving and 'academicizing' the subcultural practices in which we [zinesters] participate." Brager and Sailor may consider this essay my belated response to their questions. Jenna Brager and Jami Sailor, *Archiving the Underground* (self-published), no. 1 (2011): 3.
4. The collection is Stephen Duncombe and Maxwell Tremblay, eds., *White Riot: Punk Rock and the Politics of Race* (New York: Verso Books, 2012), 256. I made my first zine in 1991 as a junior in high school. I've been publishing zines irregularly but continuously since. The zines and other punk writings that are most archived and discussed were produced between 1992 and 2005.
5. Roderick Ferguson, *The Reorder of Things: The University and Its Pedagogies of Minority Difference* (Minneapolis: University of Minnesota Press, 2012). The passages citing Barbara Christian are particularly relevant (ibid., 35).
6. Lauren Berlant, *Cruel Optimism* (Durham, NC: Duke University Press, 2011).
7. These dangers are familiar to me, having considered the refugee as a supplemental figure of liberal empire. Mimi Thi Nguyen, *The Gift of Freedom: War, Debt, and Other Refugee Passages* (Durham, NC: Duke University Press, 2012).
8. This list of characters includes the names of a number of punk bands and songs featuring women and people of color.
9. Osa Atoe, *Maximum Rocknroll*, no. 313 (2009): n.p.
10. Cynthia Connolly, Leslie Clague, and Sharon Cheslow, comps., Cynthia Connolly et al., eds., *Banned in DC: Photos and Anecdotes from the DC Punk Underground (79–85)* (Washington, DC: Sun Dog Propaganda, 1988).
11. Osa Atoe, "Black Punk Zine that Never Happened," *Shotgun Seamstress*, no. 2, (2007), n.p.
12. While I could cite many, I will only name two: Roland Barthes, *Camera Lucida: Reflections on Photography*, translated by Richard Howard (New York: Hill and Wang, 1981); and Tina M. Campt, *Image Matters: Archive, Photography, and the African Diaspora in Europe* (Durham, NC: Duke University Press, 2012).
13. Laura U. Marks, "Loving a Disappearing Image," *Cinémas* 8, nos. 1–2 (1997): 98.
14. Jacques Derrida, *Archive Fever: A Freudian Impression*, trans. Eric Prenowitz (Chicago: University of Chicago Press, 1996).
15. My apologies to archivists and librarians who might wish for more precision here.
16. Gayatri Chakravorty Spivak, *The Post-Colonial Critic: Interviews, Strategies, Dialogues*, ed. Sarah Harasym (New York: Routledge, 1990), 138–39. See also Janet Roitman, *Anti-Crisis* (Durham: Duke University Press, 2014).
17. Mimi Thi Nguyen, "Riot Grrrl, Race, and Revival," *Women and Performance: A Journal of Feminist Theory* 22, nos. 2–3 (2012): 173–96.
18. Ferguson, *Reorder of Things*, 19.

19. "Interview with Kate Eichhorn, Author of *The Archival Turn in Feminism*," by Hope Leman, Critical Margins, January 1, 2014, criticalmargins.com/2014/01/01/interview-kate -eichhorn-author-archival-turn-feminism.

20. Michel Foucault, *The Archaeology of Knowledge and the Discourse on Language*, trans. A. M. Sheridan Smith (New York: Pantheon Books, 1972), 127.

21. Leigh Kolb, "'The Punk Singer' and a Room of Her—and Our—Own," Bitch Flicks, December 2, 2013, www.btchflcks.com/2013/12/the-punk-singer-and-a-room-of-her-and -our-own.html. *The Punk Singer*, documentary, directed by Sini Anderson (2013, New York City).

22. See, for instance, Sara Marcus, *Girls to the Front: The True Story of the Riot Grrrl Revolution* (New York: Harper Perennial, 2010). The politics of race and riot grrrl historiography is discussed in Nguyen, "Riot Grrrl, Race, and Revival."

23. As an exception to the narrative construction of race as a crisis, the Barnard College Zine Library actively builds its collection around race as a primary story, soliciting donations and making purchases of zines by queers and women of color (trans-inclusive). Eichhorn discusses Barnard zine librarian Jenna Freedman's activism in Eichhorn, "Interview."

24. Of course, that some perceive no absence at all is another sort of problem.

25. Sara Ahmed, *On Being Included: Racism and Diversity in Institutional Life* (Durham, NC: Duke University Press, 2012), 97.

26. Evelyn McDonnell, "'The Riot Grrrl Collection' Spreads Girl Germs of the '90s Movement," review of *The Riot Grrrl Collection*, by Lisa Darms, ed., *Los Angeles Times*, June 6, 2013, www.latimes.com/features/books/jacketcopy/la-ca-jc-riot-grrrl-collection20130609 ,0,6674338.story.

27. As Sianne Ngai notes, to do so lays the burden on the racialized subject to produce a commensurable, measured response to racism. Sianne Ngai, *Ugly Feelings* (Cambridge, MA: Harvard University Press, 2007), 188.

28. Foucault, *Archeology of Knowledge*, 129.

29. On black holes and historiography, see Evelynn Hammonds, "Black (W)holes and the Geometry of Black Female Sexuality," *differences: A Journal of Feminist Cultural Studies*, 6, nos. 2–3 (1994): 127–45. Inspired by Hammonds, see Elizabeth Stinson, "Means of Detection: A Critical Archiving of Black Feminism and Punk Performance," *Women and Performance: A Journal of Feminist Theory* 22, nos. 2–3 (2012): 275–311. Roderick Ferguson, *The Reorder of Things: The University and Its Pedagogies of Minority Difference* (Minneapolis: University of Minnesota Press, 2012), 226.

30. Anjali Arondekar, *For the Record: On Sexuality and the Colonial Archive in India* (Durham, NC: Duke University Press, 2009), 1.

31. Rey Chow, *The Age of the World Target: Self-Referentiality in War, Theory, and Comparative Work* (Durham, NC: Duke University Press, 2006), 60–61.

32. *Ladies and Gentlemen, The Fabulous Stains*, directed by Lou Adler (1982, Los Angeles: Paramount Pictures).

33. Sara Ahmed, *The Promise of Happiness* (Durham, NC: Duke University Press, 2010); Ngai, *Ugly Feelings*.

34. Sarah Roberts observes that this essay's concerns about "anachronistic inclusion, knowledge-sharing and institutionalization of culture and knowledge" resonate with a field of research and practice from library information sciences known as "traditional cultural expression." She elaborates: "This has to do with scholars, practitioners and community members [such as indigenous peoples] pushing back on the constant impetus and demand from memory institutions for inclusion and the making public of various types of cultural materials and

knowledge. . . . This is especially good to think about in an era in which it has become a widely accepted radical principle to want to have and make available all information at all times." Sarah Roberts, personal correspondence with the author, January 6, 2014.

35. This refusal is also often dismissed as anti-intellectual. However, some punks observe that academic study of punk lacks rigorous review, because its historians and theorists are largely unaffiliated with the academy. Anna Vo, "Introduction," *Fix My Head* (self-published), no. 4 (2013): n.p.; Zack Furness, "Introduction: Attempted Education and Righteous Accusations," in *Punkademics: The Basement Show in the Ivory Tower*, ed. Zach Furness (New York: Minor Compositions, 2012), 5–24; Golnar Nikpour, *Fix My Head* (self-published), no. 4 (2013): n.p. Of the archival impulse, Tobi Vail observes: "For instance now everyone calls that whole time period of punk feminism 'riot grrl' and it has a much broader definition than it did back then. There is a market for 'riot grrl' history, so we have to be suspicious of that economic factor but we shouldn't let this stop us from documenting our own scenes." Tobi Vail, "In the Beginning There Was Rhythm!" *Jigsaw* (blog), September 28, 2010, jigsawunderground.blogspot.com/2010/09/in-beginning-there-was-rhythm.html.

36. See Daniel Traber, "L.A.'s 'White Minority': Punk and the Contradictions of Self-Marginalization," *Cultural Critique* 48, no. 1 (2001): 30–64.

37. Ngai, *Ugly Feelings*, 206.

Useful In/stability

The Dialectical Production of the Social and Spatial Lesbian Herstory Archives

Jen Jack Gieseking

When Marge McDonald left many of her belongings to the Lesbian Herstory Archives (LHA) upon her death in 1986, her homophobic family in Columbus, Ohio, sought to auction or destroy them. The LHA reached out to local lesbian groups in Columbus, which took as many materials as possible, including an entire bookcase, and drove these objects in a pickup truck to New York City, where they remain forevermore intact (see fig. 1).[1] I begin with McDonald's story because it is emblematic of the LHA as a social and spatial site of queer knowledge production, both stable in its physical form and unstable in its sociality.

Responding to similar threads of loss and continuation, queer theory's work toward justice refuses binaries that restrict and deny difference. When discussions of stability and instability emerge often in queer theory, the resultant approach calls for destabilizing the "stable" norms of unequal societies. However, queer theory's embrace of instability paints all stabilizing practices as normalizing and unjust. Rather than upholding a stance of opposition and refusal by championing instability alone, what can be gleaned for queer theory by unpacking this dialectic? In examining the social and spatial qualities of the LHA, I adhere to both stability *and* instability, or what I call "*in/stability*." The usefulness of in/stability—all at once together and in conflict—is the work toward justice that the LHA produces when it sits in

Radical History Review
Issue 122 (May 2015)   DOI 10.1215/01636545-2849504
© 2015 by MARHO: The Radical Historians' Organization, Inc.

Figure 1. Marge McDonald's bookcase of lesbian books, photos, and mementos is mentioned often at Lesbian Herstory Archives, pictured in the center. McDonald can be seen in photos on the third shelf from the top. Credit: Jack Jen Gieseking CC BY-NC 2013

this juxtaposition. The resultant practice of *useful in/stability* illuminates a turn in queer analyses by examining and sitting in queer struggles rather than succumbing to binarial mores.

The renowned LHA in Brooklyn, New York, functions as a sociospatial exemplar of in/stability: a fixed, owned property that is also an always-in-process archive. While many women's objects and documents have found a permanent home in this space, the archive, founded and solely run by volunteers, is almost exclusively funded by donations. Finding aids for many collections have yet to be written. Many records lack dates or location information, leaving the researcher's search for lesbian history fragmented and unstable. Many archives have backlogs and an all-volunteer staff—as is often the case in lesbian, gay, bisexual, transgender, and queer (LGBTQ) archives and activist archives generally—but the LHA especially and intentionally embraces a more flexible production of its archival structure *with* its donors and visitors. A sociospatial analysis of the current state of the LHA helps us rethink what the politics of in/stability offer practices and theories of queering.

My arguments draw on theorists who have reckoned with binaries rather than disposed of them. For example, the "disidentifications" José Esteban Muñoz traces in the dialectics between selfhood and the social that emerge when performers disidentify from the racial and sexual mainstream speak to this project.[2] Such disidentifications mind the gap between refusal and adoption. My analysis also extends Ann Cvetkovich's writing on the LHA, a space that she describes as an "archive of feelings": "the profoundly affective power of a useful archive, especially an archive of sexuality and gay and lesbian life, which must preserve and produce not just social knowledge but feeling."[3] I read this "useful archive" as derived not only from a space of knowledge and feeling but also from its materiality.

Lesbian activist and LHA cofounder Joan Nestle wrote, "For gay people, history is a place where the body carries its own story."[4] I, too, build on my own embodied experiences as the lesbian-queer-trans researcher in the archive to reveal the tension between the instability of its archival structure and its stable physicality. Informed by critical geographic studies and queer theories, I propose that the lack of traditional archival order and the LHA's location in a permanent physical property demonstrate a queer tension of in/stability. Through five accounts I share from my embodied experiences as a lesbian-queer-trans° person conducting research in the archive, I develop the idea of *useful in/stability*. This concept suggests a turn for queer theory: making use of the spatial and social life of the LHA in the tension of in/stability increases the work toward justice due queer life. Steve Pile, in his work on geographies of resistance, writes that "the subjects of resistance are neither fixed nor fluid, but both and more."[5] Pile's sentiment of "both and more" describes the resistance I outline here. By turning from a politics of refusal that dwells on instability, the LHA in its in/stability is a radically inclusive and useful space of growth and difference.

Conceptualizing In/stability

A relatively undertheorized set of concepts in social theory, the paired notions of stability and instability permeate the moral and value judgments of everyday life, sexually and otherwise. The association between in/stability and queering run deep. As critical geographers Kath Browne and Catherine J. Nash state, "Queer scholarship, then, in its contemporary form is anti-normative and seeks to subvert, challenge and critique a host of taken for granted 'stabilities' in our social lives."[6] While the two words appear often in queer and geographic theoretical work, I could find no formal definitions in major texts or dictionaries from these areas of study. Drawing from key deployments of the terms, I define *stability* as "resistance to change," "a state of constancy," or "a sense of dependability"; *instability* is its antithesis, characterized by "changeability," "inconstancy," and "unreliability."

Critical geography uses space as a method and lens of analysis to combat social exploitation and oppression. In this framework, space is not a fixed container but is constantly (re)produced in how it is perceived, conceived, and lived, from the scales of the intimate to the global. Critical geographers Michael Brown and Larry Knopp, in discussing their work forming a queer epistemological frame for mapping, write: "Queer theory is not simply about destabilizing epistemologies and ontologies. . . .

The tensions and conflicts that we describe here . . . were not simple or easy moments of harmony or reconciliation or commensuration."[7] While their article also does not seek "reconciliation," Brown and Knopp's work highlights how everyday life for LGBT people involves a much more complicated dance between tensions, such as in the stable and unstable space of the LHA.

In theorizing archives, queer theorists account for narratives, representations, memorials, documentaries, ethnographies, digitalia, allegories, and objects to trace productions of queer life.[8] In theorizing the production of space, geographers examine the embodied experiences of spatial and social contact as coproduced. Both types of work embrace what Judith Halberstam describes as "new models of queer memory and queer history capable of recording and tracing subterranean scenes, fly-by-night clubs, and fleeting trends; we need, in Jose Muñoz's words, 'an archive of the ephemeral.' "[9] Cvetkovich's work on the LHA describes the place as "a ritual space within which cultural memory and history are preserved."[10] Cvetkovich goes on to suggest that by making a space to collectively remember and evidence the trauma of gay and lesbian life that might otherwise disappear, the LHA rewrites what documents and whose bodies are deemed significant to the archival sphere. The question of what makes up an archive in general, then, and the LHA especially, holds a special place in the lesbian and queer imaginary that makes room for not only the ephemeral but also the affective and material.

The LHA can be read as solely a lesbian, feminist, and/or lesbian feminist project, as it continues to extol these politics and theories; indeed, the concept of "queer" as it stands today did not exist throughout half of the institution's existence. Yet to consider "queer" anachronistically unfitting erases the archive's contribution to queer theory today as well as its work as a predecessor and ancestor to queer ideas and concepts. The experience of the social and spatial LHA demonstrates what can be generated by holding a dialectic in tension while working firmly against the projects of heteronormativity and patriarchy.

Getting (Un)Situated in the Archive

In my research, I examined organizational and publication records from the LHA, the world's largest collection of materials by, for, and about lesbians (broadly and self-defined). The LHA uses the word *herstory* in its name to denote women's erasure from his-tory; I use *history* in this article to claim the place of lesbian and queer life within dominant narratives. The collections include anything any self-identified lesbian, dyke, gay, bisexual, homosexual, Sapphic sistah, and/or queer woman from anywhere in the world and from any time has ever touched, owned, or produced.[11] The archive encompasses over a dozen types of records and various ephemera, as discussed below. In my own research experiences in the LHA, this tension between the in/stability of locale, identity, and sex influenced my own interactions with finding aids (or lack thereof) and primary materials related to lesbian herstory.

Founded in 1974 in lesbian activist Nestle's apartment, the LHA now resides in a historic brownstone townhouse in Park Slope, Brooklyn, purchased and paid off primarily through donations.[12] The spatial fixity of the building is unlike the social production of the archive. The archive holds fast to its politics to remain independently funded and run by lesbians alone. The archive is completely volunteer-run and organized by "coordinators" who collect, save, and store these documents and ephemera. Every lesbian is welcome to come and coproduce the archive once that person has taken part in an orientation, and thus collections could be updated or reconfigured at any given time. Each *archivette*—an LHA term for coordinators as well as for more come-and-go volunteers—takes part in producing finding aids uniquely; only a handful of coordinators have possessed professional archival or library training.

This article on my time at the LHA draws from a larger historical geography of contemporary lesbian and queer society, culture, and economies in New York City. My overall study addresses the shifts in lesbians' and queer women's spaces in New York City from 1983 to 2008—that is, from the AIDS epidemic to the rise of the internationally syndicated television drama *The L Word*—in order to understand the associated shifts in these women's experiences of justice and oppression over time. I use both *lesbians* and *queer women* to encompass my research participants' own identifications as well as those of the women whose stories constitute my archival research. Along with a year's worth of continuous research in the LHA, the project included group interviews with forty-seven self-identified lesbians and queer women who came out during this period.

This essay concentrates on my experiences working with the LHA lesbian and queer organizational records, as the prioritization of activism and political work is a core component of lesbian and queer women's communities and identities.[13] These organizational records provide the detailed, often day-by-day, stories of lesbian and queer political upheaval, radical activisms, desirous socializing, and practices of fighting against and even taking part in unjust economic processes such as disinvestment and gentrification. I draw on my field notes and participant observations from my time doing research in the LHA. I use group interview transcripts as a lens to read the stories found in the archive.

In Situ: Five Instances of Embodied Contact between Research and Researcher
Lesbians have been deprived of virtually all knowledge of our past. This is
deliberate since it keeps us invisible, isolated and powerless.
—*Not a Passing Phase: Reclaiming Lesbians in History, 1840–1985*,
Lesbian History Group

The intentional invisibilization of lesbian history, to which the early 1990s British collective the Lesbian History Group attests in their quotation, makes finding any collected materials on the lesbian and queer past a difficult pursuit. Lesbians and queer women have been further silenced since their socialization as women in private spaces is marked as less visible or radical.[14] Poor women and women of color face extreme invisibilization of their spaces and experiences due to their having less access to power, money, respect, and rights.

Even with a strong understanding of such structural inequalities, I arrived at the LHA expecting to find all materials regarding all types of women organized, cataloged, and dated. What I found was very much otherwise. The five instances I examine here reveal my piecing together of the concept of useful in/stability through my own embodied interactions with the materials and space of the LHA.

1. Searching for a Stable History: The First Day

My first visit to the LHA in 2007 involved taking a tour, which is the way each visitor enters the space, that is, through the stories of another woman about the many women in the archive. The rooms, bathrooms, and closets burst with topic collections, fiction and nonfiction books, videos, photographs, personal collections, videos, T-shirts, comics, organizational records, biographies, stickers, artworks, geographic-specific materials, unpublished studies, buttons, biographies, audio recordings, a dildo, and a Gay Games medal. During my time there, piles of unsorted publications formed a two-foot-high mound in a corner of what was once a bedroom overlook-

Figure 2. The author at the original bathroom sink in the master bedroom in the Lesbian Herstory Archives. Credit: Jack Jen Gieseking CC BY-NC 2013

ing a tree-lined street. There are even hats, stickers, and buttons displayed next to and in the sink in the old, large bathroom (see fig. 2).

The coordinators recommended that I begin my research in the subject files in filing cabinets that line the living room wall, containing entrées into popular topics, including bars, celibacy, Disney World, dyke marches, libraries, queer activism, sports, tourism, and utopias. I chose "bars" since they were the only type of place listed and found in New York City. Over five days, I recorded the entry tickets, postcard advertisements, and flyers spanning four decades of a random assortment of lesbian bars and parties throughout the world. The last item in the folder was an ad about an Olivia cruise. When I asked a coordinator if she should move this flyer from the "bars" folder to another on "tourism," she told me, much to my surprise, that any lesbian (broadly defined) could help produce the archive. I could even place it there if I wished. Since permission is required for photographing many of the materials, what remains of this version of this file in this moment is my notes. Therefore, the construction of these files or of most collections was not static: I frantically scribbled in the following marginalia of my notes: "Did no one know everything that existed here? Was there no order to our history, even one of our own invention?"[15]

It is a common joke that those who are keen to work in archives are often energized by the order of the materials as much as by the materials themselves. While activist archives are notoriously underfunded and always in process, the LHA enacts a specific way of destabilizing what *archive* means. My social science researcher frame was set increasingly askew. The sensation of instability swam up to meet me.

That same week, I shared my situation with a white, male, heterosexual critical geographer, and my feeling of undoing grew even worse. He was ecstatic for me: "*This* is *queering*!" he said, clapping his hands. I twitched before I emoted in reply. While enlivening to my colleague, the project of destabilizing had its limits in that it constrained my ability to produce the most thorough historical geography possible. Working from or depending on instability alone would not be enough to make sense of my experiences in the LHA or of the LHA itself.

2. The Stability of a Building of One's Own

I was often cold in the LHA. Physically frozen actually. Most researchers are cold in archives, either from winter drafts or from blasting air-conditioning in summer. My mentioning to a coordinator that I was cold led to her telling me (again) about the history of the physical building of the LHA. It was also a key story I heard repeated as tours entered the small, back bedroom where I set up my computer. A coordinator would tell visitors about the purchase of the building in 1991, after almost a decade of fund-raising, and what it meant for lesbians to have a permanent place of their own. She would explain that the LHA is funded by small grants and donations to meet the needed $300,000 as part of a politics of controlling and owning a space of their own.[16] The building sits in the internationally renowned Park Slope neighborhood—known primarily because of its intense gentrification—and is now worth well over $2 million.

In my research, women repeated the story of the building's purchase, as did women in the minutes and flyers of organizational records, women in feature stories of publications, and women who wandered through the archive whispering to one another while holding hands and kissing. The LHA is a constant, materialized myth that lesbians keep telling, a set of rooms of their own that all lesbians share. Choosing to purchase a house, rather than a commercial space, in which to place the

LHA allows for the tension of useful in/stability to begin to form. The archivettes and LHA donors and visitors make use of the space of the home, a space where women often have been forced to remain. As such, the LHA founders purchased a historically feminized, disempowering, and therefore destabilizing space and reinvented it as a useful, stable space from which to collect and share lesbian histories. At 484 14th Street, Brooklyn, New York 11215, lesbians have physically evidenced their own existence on their own terms within the bounds of capitalist property ownership; what could be more stable in the neoliberal era than property ownership?

These are points of stability I experienced in the archive: the drafty or air-conditioned cold as a weathered constant of place, the reinvention of the meaning of home as a way to demonstrate women's refusal to be ignored or invisibilized, and the knowledge that the building and collections were permanent, material, and visible. When I bumped into the walls (often) or picked up my pen from the floor (more often), I would let my hand rest against the surfaces to remind me of this place and its rare claim to being real in a world that often seeks to deny LGBTQ people who they are. It was at these moments that the LHA as a material space of affect and knowledge production melted into one. I knew that something beyond stability or instability was possible.

3. Instability and Stability in Relation: Realizing the Space-Time of the Archives

As happy as I was with my daily cups of chamomile tea to keep me warm those first few weeks in the LHA, I soon experienced a more profound and staying state of shock: many of these materials lacked any mention of location and/or date, and almost all lacked an author. Such anonymity was sometimes intentional, sometimes unintentional, and always frustrating. Coordinators had no more information than I and so shared in my confusion and poured me another cup of tea. As I shared during a group interview with research participants:

What's interesting about the archives is that maybe a third or a quarter of the fliers I read [so far] don't have a date on them. So you have no idea *when* they happened. And then a lot of things don't say *where*, it's just a phone number. . . . They would check their answering machines first to see if you were, you know, coming to beat them up. It's like a timeless, spaceless archive up to a certain point. Or then people just forgot to put the years on. One flyer reads: "COME TO THE RALLY! FRIDAY!" And you're sitting there screaming to no one but yourself, "*Which* Friday are you talking about?!?!?!" *This* is our *history*!

After that discussion ended, one of my research participants asked me if I was really surprised. She had a good point. Even in creating an archive of lesbian history, those spaceless and timeless moments in the LHA speak to the very visible partiality of history generally and more lesbians and queer women especially. The depth of lesbian and queer invisibility never seemed so palpable as it did when I was sitting in that archive the next day. I knew that I could count on it to remain there while also recognizing the flummoxing effects of its constant flux not only on me but on generations past and those yet to come. My research revealed that sitting in the tension of the LHA's social and spatial in/stability is useful in deepening and broadening lesbian history.

Only records from more recent years consistently provided the *when* and *where* of their meetings. Threats to LGBTQ people's safety lessened somewhat over time, while the determination to be out increased. Being ambiguous was helpful in organizing groups, meetings, and activisms that could attract attention from those wishing to thwart these efforts or harm these women. Negotiating these roadblocks became central to the project of mapping a larger lesbian-queer history.

4. Identity Matters of and to In/stability

Lesbian-queer women continue to possess less support and access to record their history than men and heterosexuals, and this situation is only amplified for low-income women and women of color. In 1998, seven years after the archive moved into its building, lesbian activist, archivist, and coordinator Polly Thistlethwaite recorded that the institution was organized, supported, and dominated by a primarily white lesbian community constituency.[17] Critical geographer Joana Coppi writes that while founding the LHA in a "large apartment sidelined financial questions in the 1980s and allowed for an emphasis on cultural and political activism across race and class," by the 1990s the "building fund campaign made fundraising the primary concern of volunteers." This shift further sidelined the concerns and voices of working-class women and concerns of some women of color.[18]

One of my favorite notes to myself while in the archive reads, "Don't forget where you found Audre." This location refers to the top row of the bookshelves in the closet on the right in the back room. There sits the selection of papers that Audre Lorde left the LHA. Uncertainty, chaos, and disorder produce and affect women's raced and classed bodies and spaces in different ways. I stopped to marvel how you can climb on a chair, take down her boxes, and leaf through drafts of her poems, books, and letters on your own. I also considered what it took for Lorde to create this work and the labor necessary both to leave it behind and for me to find it. My whiteness has its limits to what it can connect to and what instability it comes to bear. Our races visibilize our difference—my whiteness, her blackness; it is that which binds us in the useful in/stability of lesbian-queer life that sits in LHA documents and materials. Her work and presence remind us that lesbians and queer women of color and lesbians without means dwell even more profoundly in the in/stability dialectic. In/stability works differently for different bodies. It is the chance to make use of that in/stability in partnership with the LHA that allows for collaborative work toward justice.

Inasmuch as *queer* is constantly in flux and unstable, it is also therefore untethered from normative modes of thought or practice. The LHA commits to this flux *in place,* creating a stable space from which to remain in that state of flux. To read the spaces and experiences of these women over time, I needed to mind the LHA's in/stability in my choice of research methods and analysis.

5. Stabilizing an Archive While Respecting Its Destabilizing Power
In my search to describe the changing landscape of lesbian and queer culture and spaces over time in New York City, I consulted organizational records and publications because they provided the only (mostly) consistently dated materials to trace over time. The LHA holds over 2,300-plus organizational records, which primarily include documents regarding social, political, or cultural organizations and groups. From my experience in other LGBTQ archives, such as the LGBT Community Center National History Archive of New York City and the New York Public Library Lesbian and Gay Collections, I believe this collection to be the largest and most comprehensive LGBTQ organizational history in existence. I wrote in my field notes after my first month at the LHA: "These are my only options. These options are amazing."

By first selecting only those 724 records with meetings or offices in New York City, I then identified all organizations that began in or after 1983, which totaled 382. Organizational interests as well as reasons for forming or disbanding were incredibly varied, from the renowned Lesbian Avengers, Queer Nation, and ACT UP to lesser-known, wide-ranging groups and organizations like the following:

- Gay Veterans Association, Inc.—nonprofit dedicated to full equality for service members and veterans (1985–98)

- Imperial Kings and Queens of New York—transgender and cross-dressing social and political organization (1968–present)

- Lesbian Sex Mafia—sex-positive group that organizes sex parties and sex education (1981–present)

- Orthodykes of New York—organization for Orthodox Jewish lesbians (1999–present)

- Shades of Lavender—part of the Brooklyn AIDS Task Force with a specific focus on lesbians with AIDS (1993–99)

- *STP* (also known as *Swing the Pussy*)—antiviolence and information-sharing broadsheet newsletter (1998–2002)

- USS Northstar NCC-10462—Star Trek fan club (1991–99)

- Women About (previously Hykin' Dykes)—outdoors socializing group (1988–present)

Around this point, I saw myself becoming the dyke detective at the dining room table in the back bedroom on the second floor. I made seemingly basic materials legible, weaving histories of thousands of women from one city together. By now, though, I knew that making stability out of instability was impossible. I could only seek to make the material as useful as possible. A sole dot-matrix printout from the Lavender Bytes Computer Club indicated a span of years when such printers worked at such-and-such quality to presume the group's existence at that time. The early statements from the LGBT Community Center announced that this group's meetings were to be held in such-and-such locale, thereby temporarily fixing space and location. But these were not always positive pursuits. For some organizations, only by researching which homophobic epithets different city council members screamed over the years was I able to determine when these groups formed. In recording this information, bridges are built to connect and grounding given from which to expand these once spaceless and timeless and now partial histories as some absences were filled in, file by file.

Discussion: Offering Up Useful In/stability

While queer theory has dwelled for decades in the possibilities and affordances of instability, stability in queer life, theory, and space is useful in other, complementary ways as evidenced in my experiences as a researcher in the LHA. The archive generates new spaces and practices of archiving. I even accidentally archived my own dissertation notebook. During breaks, I alternated between carefully reading an original *Wonder Woman*, volume 1, issue 4—which I poured over repeatedly for the chemistry she had with her nemesis, the vixen known as Cheetah—and a full set of Alison Bechdel's *Dykes to Watch Out For* (*DTWOF*) (see in figure 1, the top shelf of the bookcase to the right). After months of searching every nook and cranny, I eventually found my notebook between volumes of Bechdel. Relieved and ecstatic, I suddenly understood that it will be welcome to find its own in/stability there soon, too. As such, the seemingly normative aspects of the LHA's property ownership are queered, creating Muñoz's disidentifications in the tension of the political, geographic, and social project of Cvetkovich's useful archive within.

My larger project, a historical geography of contemporary lesbian and queer society, culture, and economies, is fed by the tension of in/stability. Beyond the material stability of physical space lies a production of space in online environments. After much deliberation, I put all of the archival data into one giant spreadsheet to make use of the tension of in/stability and bring all of this work into conversation on one page. The resultant schematic includes over two thousand nodes of where and when lesbians and queers were and what they did in their organizing. Information from physical boxes and drawers that left me giddy sometimes and, more often, crying was placed into digital, tabular form and thus generates larger narratives about these women, ordered according to the logics of my research prerogatives. Is it an injustice to seek stability and place into grids the stories and labors of queer bodies that made such efforts to upend heteropatriarchal structures? How else can I tell a history of queer life other than to queer the queer, to put it in "order" to make some semblance of a useful narrative so that we know who we are, when we were, where we were, and what the hell happened to get us to our various heres?

This is one way to work between the stability and instability of queer archival disorder and invisibility: finding at least one (physical or digital) place from which to record and see all of our stories all at once. In the end, my work at the LHA knits together as much of lesbian and queer commonality and difference from these records of social change and radical activism as was possible for me. I continue to develop a set of interactive data visualizations to reckon with this massive set of data, which can be found at the project's website, jgieseking.org/category/data-visualizations. Not only are these stories bound to the material archives; they will grow and be shared online to question the stability of history and archives generally.

My compulsion to order is not based (solely) on a need for stability inasmuch as it is a call to contribute to understanding narratives of lesbian and queer instability and, therefore, to bring stability and instability into conversation. There is also my own agitation to make sense of the unknown as a social scientist. This framing of queer research and lives affords ways to substantiate—while holding up for critical inspection—the binaries that queering often works against.

Useful in/stability then is the project of making use of queer refusal, flux, and instability alongside common-sense-making tactics of survival through stability. Excluding the useful aspects of stability ignores the ways of queering the binary of stability and instability as a dialectic. This usefulness extends from queer theorists to the lesbians and queers who make up the LHA. My examination of useful in/stability also points to other binary couplings that can be seen anew when addressed in tension, which can assist in the work toward justice by more fully accounting for difference. Embracing merely the instability and flux of the archive as it is socially and materially produced leaves out the effort toward permanence and remembrance that the founders and archivettes seek to support. In/stability is as interdependent as the stories and lives of those in the LHA. Queer archives, as the LHA demonstrates, partly come into being through their own useful in/stability for researchers, archivists, and archival subjects alike. Useful in/stability can be embraced even while we organize, categorize, and classify what lies within—and see where it takes us.

Notes

I am forever thankful to the past, present, and future archivettes of the Lesbian Herstory Archives for creating and sustaining a space for all, as well as to my colleagues Joana Coppi, Rachel Corbman, and Margaret Galvan, my comrades in lesbian archival theorization and adoration. I am especially grateful to Naomi Adiv and the editors of this issue for their thoughtful and exciting comments.

This research was supported by the following fellowships and awards for which I remain deeply grateful: Woodrow Wilson Dissertation Fellowship in Women's Studies; Center for Place, Culture, and Politics; Joan Heller-Diane Bernard Fellowship from the Center for Lesbian and Gay Studies; and the CUNY Graduate Center Proshansky Dissertation Award.

1. Joan Nestle, "Historical Musings: The Kiss, 1950s–1990s," OutHistory, 2008, www .outhistory.org/exhibits/show/historical-musings/the-kiss.

2. José Esteban Muñoz, *Disidentifications: Queers of Color and the Performance of Politics* (Minneapolis: University of Minnesota Press, 1999).

3. Ann Cvetkovich, *An Archive of Feelings: Trauma, Sexuality, and Lesbian Public Cultures* (Durham, NC, Duke University Press, 2003), 241.

4. Joan Nestle, *A Restricted Country: Essays and Short Stories* (New York: Rivers Oram, 1988), 9–10.

5. Steve Pile, "Introduction: Opposition, Political Identities, and Spaces of Resistance," in *Geographies of Resistance*, ed. Steve Pile and Michael Keith (New York: Routledge, 1997), 30.

6. Kath Browne and Catherine J. Nash, "Queer Methods and Methodologies: An Introduction," in *Queer Methods and Methodologies: Intersecting Queer Theories and Social Science Research*, ed. Kath Browne and Catherine J. Nash (Burlington, VT: Ashgate, 2010), 7.

7. Michael Brown and Larry Knopp, "Queering the Map: The Productive Tensions of Colliding Epistemologies," *Annals of the Association of American Geographers* 98, no. 1 (2008): 55.

8. See Elizabeth Freeman, "Packing History, Count(er)ing Generations," *New Literary History* 31, no. 4 (2000): 727–44; and Elizabeth A. Povinelli, "The Woman on the Other Side of the Wall: Archiving the Otherwise in Postcolonial Digital Archives," *differences* 22, no. 1 (2011): 146–71.

9. Judith Halberstam, *In a Queer Time and Place: Transgender Bodies, Subcultural Lives* (New York: New York University Press, 2005), 161.

10. Cvetkovich, *Archive of Feelings*, 241.

11. Lesbian Herstory Educational Foundation, Inc., *Lesbian Herstory Archives Newsletter*, 1975–2003, LHA, Brooklyn, NY.

12. Ibid.

13. Julie Abraham, *Metropolitan Lovers: The Homosexuality of Cities* (Minneapolis: University of Minnesota Press, 2009).

14. Maxine Wolfe, "Invisible Women in Invisible Places: The Production of Social Space in Lesbian Bars," in *Queers in Space: Communities, Public Places, Sites of Resistance*, ed. Anne-Marie Bouthillette and Yolanda Retter (Seattle: Bay, 1997), 300–324.

15. For a humorously parodic version of the LHA's disorder and magic, see *The Watermelon Woman*, directed by Cheryl Dunye (New York: First Run Features, 2000).

16. Deborah Edel, interview by the author, LHA, Brooklyn, NY, July 16, 2008.

17. Polly Thistlethwaite, "Building 'A Home of Our Own': The Construction of the Lesbian Herstory Archives," in *Daring to Find Our Names: The Search for Lesbigay Library History*, ed. James V. Carmichael Jr. (Westport, CT: Greenwood, 1998), 160–62.

18. Joana Coppi, "Historicizing Identity: The Lesbian Herstory Archives and the Production of Space" (master's thesis, Humboldt University of Berlin, 2012), 69–70.

"Look More at the Camera than at Me"

Susan and the Transgender Archive

Jeanne Vaccaro

In 1992 photographer Brian Weil began an intensive video documentation of "Susan," a transsexual woman and military special operative in St. Louis, Missouri. Weil made a chronicle of Susan in transition—retiring her military service to the United States Army, presiding at a theatrical "Irish wake" mourning the symbolic death of her male identity and commemorating her legal transition to female, and undertaking the physical and emotional contours of hormone therapy and gender-confirmation surgeries at Theda Clark Medical Center in Neenah, Wisconsin. Weil and Susan became acquainted as part of a social network of Midwestern support meetings for gender nonconforming people as he began a project to interview transwomen for a narrative documentary about the nascent movement for transgender equality. In his visits between 1992 and 1995 Weil generated hundreds of hours of videotape of Susan and they forged a genuine friendship, but his accidental death of a heroin overdose in 1996 abruptly and inconclusively halted the project and documentation of Susan's story. However, because of the first monographic retrospective of Weil's photographic practice from 1979 on, exhibited at the Institute of Contemporary Art (ICA) at the University of Pennsylvania in Philadelphia (February 6–March 31, 2013), there is both renewed interest and opportunity to consider Weil's oeuvre and how his aesthetic style and philosophy of image making contest and remake the relationship between authenticity and documentary.

I got to know Susan on a single-channel installation at ICA, watching some

Radical History Review

Issue 122 (May 2015)   DOI 10.1215/01636545-2849513

© 2015 by MARHO: The Radical Historians' Organization, Inc.

moments of her life unfold on repeat. Clad in a 1980s suit jacket with shoulder pads and Sally Jessy Raphael lookalike glasses, Susan tells the camera "how this all began." The early 1990s, when Weil undertook his study of gender identity, mark a pivotal nexus of burgeoning visibility for transgender as a social, political, *and* intellectual category, a coalescence and circulation that historian Susan Stryker identifies as transgender beginning to function as "an adjective rather than a noun."[1] Weil's focus on the Midwestern participants offers a counter to urban bias in gender and sexuality studies, but in many ways Susan is an ambivalent figure to mobilize, in part because of the ethical precarity of her position in an unfinished archive of which she is not in custody. Although the archive of Weil's unedited tapes of Susan and several other unidentified transwomen he interviewed is incomplete and we can't anticipate how he intended to intervene on, edit, or display the visual material he collected, in this short essay I explore how Weil's artistic practice and photographic method shape Susan's story to form a living archive of transgender politics.

"You'd Never Be Able to See What I See"
In his practice of participant-observation photography Weil cultivated an intense connection to diverse objects, ideas, and communities. He tediously labored to infiltrate marginal and difficult-to-access spaces. As a result of his self-disciplined method of working he created images that indulge, rather than dissolve, the tension between art object and maker, yielding an aesthetics of intimacy in his manipulation of the proximate. Stamatina Gregory, curator of the ICA show, observes that "one gets the sense that the act of photography is only tangentially relevant to the larger task of knowing: of forming relationships and expanding one's worldview, and developing social consciousness—what Weil tended to refer to as *being in the world*."[2] Weil was known to orchestrate scenes, and he intervened on his print negatives; he cut, burned, and overexposed film; and he bled light onto and overexposed the fleshy contours of the bodies he photographed. Intervening on negatives made his images richly dense and textured, yet it gave them a strange sense of absence as well as a representational (and archival) impossibility. Weil regularly worked with a motion camera as a means to his photographic process—shooting on Super 8 film and making photographs out of film stills—but the transgender project was his first foray into video as an end in itself, and it was also his only use of color.

Weil was a participant in ACT UP New York (the AIDS Coalition to Unleash Power) and founder of New York City's first needle exchange program, and an activist politics compelled his artistic practice and the immersive bonds he forged to insular and marginal environments. After moving to New York in 1976 from Chicago, his hometown, he began to photograph peripheral scenes and identities, starting with his sex pictures in 1979. For this two-year series he placed advertisements in S-M newsletters looking for practitioners to engage in bondage scenes and simulate sex with animals. In those years he also photographed gay rodeos, amateur boxers, and wrestlers, but he was dissatisfied by the mere play and pretend or seemingly contrived nature of these performed identities. Weil's method of total immersion allowed him to gain access to difficult-to-reach, private communities traditionally closed to outsiders; his commitment to infiltration—and the fact that several years of undercover-like work yielded arguably little photographic product—would seem to suggest that he relished the act and labor of entrée itself and the attendant feelings generated by proximity. Between 1982 and 1985 he shadowed homicide detectives in Miami, traveling there for two weeks out of every month to ride on all-night excursions and record forensic crime scenes and prisoner processing. The project ended when the police department offered Weil official employment as a county crime photographer, in part based on his diligent work ethic and quiet, deferential demeanor.

Weil continued to make pictures about insular scenes by infiltrating social spaces that he should not, by all accounts, have been able to access. Between 1985 and 1987 he photographed the Satmar Hasidic Jews (a notoriously private and ultraorthodox sect) in Williamsburg, Brooklyn, and at summer bungalow colonies in the Catskills. Weil himself was a secular Jew and got into what he called "Hasidic drag" to take pictures of bar mitzvahs, weddings, and other celebrations. He was adept at navigating social cues and rigid environments, and, again, his biggest artistic expenditure was time and a commitment to process. In 1985 Weil began volunteering at the Gay Men's Health Crisis as a mentor and "buddy" to assist HIV-positive people in navigating medical treatment. There, and initially at the request of his mentee, he began to make images about the disease. He also started a volunteer program in the pediatric AIDS unit at Metropolitan Hospital and later founded the city's first needle exchange program, Bronx-Harlem Needle Exchange (later incorporated as CitiWide Harm Reduction), before harm reduction methods were legal.[3] Weil's relationship to the AIDS crisis was foremost as an activist, and photography became increasingly irrelevant to Weil's sense of social and political engagement; as Ric Curtis, his collaborator at the needle exchange, recalls: "I worked with Brian for a year before I knew he was an artist. We were more focused on building the movement."[4] An overwhelming frustration toward photography as a means of response to the AIDS crisis, along with an anxiety about reception and desire to control images, led Weil to stop documenting the disease and to denounce photography altogether, that is, until he began his video documentation of Susan.

In total, Weil had twenty-one solo exhibitions and showed work at spaces including the New Museum, Wexner Center for the Arts, St. Louis Art Museum, Queens Museum, and Moderna Museet in Stockholm. He was often associated with other participant-observer photographers like Nan Goldin and Larry Clark and the Pictures Generation artists including Cindy Sherman (who curated Weil's first solo show at Artists Space in 1980). Importantly, Weil was not "a maker of evidentiary images."[5] For him, photography represented a method, process, and practice, rather than a product for commerce or display. As Amy Sadao, director of ICA, observes of Weil's place in an art historical archive, "As we reconsider the Pictures Generation, and its enormous influence on art today, it is significant to note Weil's pointed insistence that works remain politically reflective and socially immersed."[6] For Weil, photography was an integral yet imperfect archive, and yet it operated alongside or even to the side of friendship, access, proximity, activism, and education. The image in his artistic practice and archive is not a bounded object. Instead, it is seeping with the excess of the encounter—his labor-time, or the hours, weeks, and years of forging contact, followed by the artistic and technical development and the manipulation of film. Gregory notes, "Weil's aggressive embrace of the participant-observer position, far from apolitical, posited instead what he saw as the uselessness of disengaged practices of looking *or* making."[7] He was not particularly interested in reception, exhibit, and display, but preferred to focus instead on building access, connections, and *connectivity*: "My method of being involved is through photography."[8] It was, Gregory continues, "a justification for forging relationships where they would otherwise not exist" and something of an "excuse" or an alibi that Weil "deployed as a deferral, to gain otherwise illicit time, and to open up unaccounted, unquantifiable space for indulgent experience."[9]

The vexing relation of Weil to participant-observer photography is illuminating in art historical debates about photography's role in representation, politics, and authenticity and especially relevant to his documentation of transgender life. His notion of "being in the world" served as a motivation, inspiration, and guide, and the complexity of the encounters with his subjects led Weil to assert: "I think a problem with photography is that, too often, it has the presumption of being real."[10] In place of representational evidence, Weil sutured visuality to the haptic, to process and labor-time, and to artistic techniques of manipulation and alteration. He staged, simulated, baked, and burned his film, and the labored aesthetic of his photography is aligned with what I call the *handmade labor of transgender identity*: an affective theorization of the ordinary feelings and textures of transgender embodiment. In the spaces between camera, object, and art maker, proximity is disoriented as the visual does the work of something in excess of evidencing difference.

"My Other Half Was a Great Man"

"I am personally interested in the secret lives people lead," Weil tells Susan in a direct-to-camera interview, and he wants to know "how this all began." She speaks at first in a clunky nervous voice, describing the material constraints of binary gender in her childhood and how she struggled with self-doubt, anxiety, fear, and rejection: "I always grew up knowing something was different." In the eighth grade Susan recognized a version of herself on a talk show about transsexuality, figuring, "So this is what the problem is." Still, to be "identified with transsexualism" didn't alleviate the pressure she felt to conform to her assigned gender.[11] At seventeen Susan joined the military's special forces in a special training outfit for counterterrorism, eventually working as an antinarcotics officer in Kuwait during the Gulf War. As a soldier she obviously needed to conceal her transsexuality and defer any kind of physical or legal transition. It is difficult to bear witness to Susan's discomfort, vulnerability, and exposure. Her slow wrestle of feeling strange and her intense desire to remedy pain generates an opportunity for those of us watching Susan to meditate on the uncertainty of gender, how we all fail, in different ways, to cohere to its demands and how those failures are emotional and material and always conscripted.

Because the videos of Susan are an incomplete and unedited body of work, we can't know how Weil intended to intervene on and shape them; we can, however, consider the multiple ways Susan edited her voice, image, and experience to perform for Weil and his camera. Other questions remain, too: What were Susan's feelings about the work, and how did she want to control, edit, or circulate her story? In the interviews with Weil, Susan sometimes leans on the diagnostic language of "wrong" embodiment to do the work of translating her identity, perhaps as a gesture of explanation for Weil's benefit. In those moments the camera functions as gatekeeper, eliciting her identity as a performance of difference and containing her experience in the singular event of medical transition. We can't know if Susan strategically deploys the language and emotionality of diagnosis or if the camera and/or Weil incite her speech, as all of our speech is incited in different ways. In the knotty connections between self-determination, coercion, and how we know (or are capable of knowing) ourselves it is always more complicated than any one thing might suggest. Watching the tapes, I hear leaks in the formula as Susan explains herself in different dimensions; while she sometimes defers to the diagnosis to do the work of translating her identity, it doesn't contain the totality of her experience. Surgery is the "final stage," and yet transition is also a process. In one scene her penis is a "birth deformity," and, in another, "just because you have a vagina and breasts doesn't mean all your problems go away."

Although Weil wasn't explicit with Susan about his motivation to document transgender identities, we can hazard that his investment in invisible and marginalized spaces compelled his artistic practice, and as an activist in ACT UP Weil might have known something about the burgeoning transgender movement and conflicts with mainstream gay and lesbian politics.[12] His questions to Susan gesture to a curiosity about the erasure of transgender and the differences between sexuality and gender; he asks, for example, if Susan would have identified as a gay man if her geographic and life circumstances—if she had lived in New York City or San Francisco, for instance—were different. His interest is always in the boundaries of tight-knit communities or experiences and in the movements of entrance and access. He asks Susan how she managed her multiple identities as a closeted soldier in the military, her public and private selves as a man and a woman. "What's the difference between being a man and woman, since you've been both?" he asks, and Susan warns, "You're not gonna like this, Brian." Their back-and-forth illustrates the potential of participant-observer methods to create a dimensional exchange and reframe how action and passivity function in documentary.

On June 30, 1993, Susan and her friends preside at a campy Irish wake for her male identity. As military retirement provides an opportunity for her physical transition, the ceremony—part funeral, wedding, and birth—honors the totality of her life experience. In a melodramatic performance, Susan wears a black dress and veil and wails out, "My other half was a

Susan at an Irish wake; her home in St. Louis, Missouri, on June 30, 1993. Stills selected by Stamatina Gregory. VHS tapes transferred to DVD. Center for Creative Photography, University of Arizona, Brian Weil Archive

great man, and now it's time to put him down—I mean—put him to rest." She can't help but burst into laughter. After all, this is a party, too. The basement of her St. Louis home is carpeted and has wood-paneled walls and a bar, reminiscent of a vintage suburbia. Propped onto metal folding chairs, a rectangular cardboard box is draped in white fabric, the shine of packaging tape visible at its edges—"He was buried in a wardrobe," someone jokes—and decorated with candles, flowers, and a photograph of the "deceased" posed with his arms folded, dressed in a black suit and red tie, aviator sunglasses, and a gun in his hand. Friends encircle the makeshift casket with commemorative objects of army browns and greens and an insignia of the Criminal Investigation Command. Weil cuts the video, and in his next scene Susan is born again in a white dress as "Oh, Pretty Woman" plays on the stereo. She is commemorated for her military service, "having faithfully carried out her duties to the United States of America," and as at her official retirement ceremony, she receives a plaque, but this time it recognizes her accomplishments in her chosen name. Susan is the grief-stricken widow *and* the deceased, a different way and at a different time, and so she mourns for something lost. The memorial honors "the circular nature of this passing" and all the ways it means to pass. As her friend wishes "Have a glorious reincarnation of your next life," the wake is a performative archive of a gender self-determination too often contained by the disciplinary forces that demand erasure.

On May 6, 1994, Weil traveled with Susan and her mother to the Theda Clark Medical Center in Wisconsin, to document her breast augmentation and vaginoplasty. A few days into her recovery she is stoned on morphine but alert enough for lipstick and blush and to worry that the beep-beep-beep of hospital noise will interfere with her interview. Susan is the object of the camera's eye; conscious of its needs, she shares in the process of her documentation. Weil interviews Susan's mother as she looks on with a mix of anxiety and pride. He wants to know what she thinks about transsexuality. "I can still see the headlines in the paper," she exclaims, recalling Christine Jorgensen and the news of 1952. The transformation of the American soldier, beautiful and the embodiment of a heteronormative, racialized femininity, is forty-two years in the past but is the most accessible way for her mother to make sense of Susan's difference. "She wore my clothes," she blurts out next, as if to offer Weil some evidence and reconcile Susan's capacity for militarism and masculinity with the daughter she's become. For her mother, the camera is an object of extraction; it seeks truth and she wants to provide it, in spite of how Susan or Weil interprets the exchange.

Reflecting on Susan in her hospital bed, physically passive and temporarily immobile, what are the ethics of staging her body, and how does the camera enact, perpetuate, and archive a diagnostic and medical gaze? As the public health scholar T. Benjamin Singer asserts, "The medical gaze creates the illusion of anonymous bodies, suspended in time and placed outside of any habitable social world, and thus disallows the very possibility of subjectivity," and yet Weil's method of image capture does not deny the hierarchies of looking.[13] The video camera is an instrument of extraction, shaping gender transformation as a diagnosis of a "wrong" body, but it is also a teletechnologic vehicle of self-determination. Insofar as photography is method for Weil, a way to gain access and forge an encounter, his long-standing use of

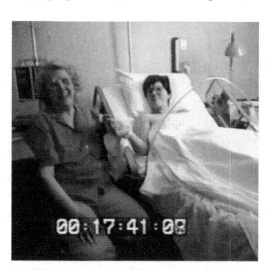

Susan and her mother at Theda Clark Medical Center, Neenah, Wisconsin, on May 11, 1994

motion cameras and eventual turn to video is critical to his practice of photography as collaboration. In this way, the camera performs, as Singer notes of the transgender sublime in image making, to "enact the *ambivalence* of living in a nonstandard body that is constantly bombarded by prurient medical, talk show, or pornographic gazes."[14] If the camera is an obstacle, a blockade, a blockage, forming a triangle and triangulating between shapes—let's say one is "object" and one is "subject"—Weil and Susan consciously manipulate the camera to form a different kind of triangulated archive. Between their performances of evasion and staging is recognition and reworking of the angles, akin to what Judith Halberstam has theorized as the "transgender look," or "a mode of seeing and being seen that is not simply at odds with binary gender but that is part of a reorientation of the body in space and time."[15] Although the camera is always a staging apparatus, Weil in his video work with Susan is able to access emotional and interpersonal formations, moments that we can observe in the footage as both Weil and Susan tinker with what it means to look and be looked at.

The video documentation Weil made of Susan between 1993 and 1996 is a quasi-complete body of his work, but it is also a record of a life in excess of an archive. The myth of the coherence of gender unravels between the language of Susan's diagnosis and self-narration, making any kind of evidentiary analysis of her impossible and unwanted, pointing us again to the representational limits of the archive. In rereading and rewriting history, and in encountering Susan as a historical object, we discover a dimensional record and a dense triangulation between Weil, Susan, and the camera—which is both an object extracting and shaping her narrative in a diagnostic frame and a vehicle for her self-determination. Of all the moments Weil documented, one of Susan lying in the hospital in postsurgical recovery is especially instructive. He asks, "How does it feel now that you're finished?" and her single-word answer is a question: "Finished?" Susan's response demonstrates the always unfinished and incomplete nature of the queer and transgender archive.

Notes

1. Susan Stryker, "(De)Subjugated Knowledges: An Introduction to Transgender Studies," in *The Transgender Studies Reader*, ed. Susan Stryker and Stephen Whittle (New York: Routledge, 2006), 4. The infamous invocation of the "posttranssexual" made by Sandy Stone in her manifesto for transgender studies marks a discursive shift from transsexual to transgender. Sandy Stone, "The *Empire* Strikes Back: A Posttranssexual Manifesto," in ibid., 221–35.

2. Gregory notes that "Weil repeated this phrase often in reference to a socially engaged practice of living." Stamatina Gregory, "Anatomy of an Excuse," in *Brian Weil, 1979–95: Being in the World*, ed. Stamatina Gregory (Los Angeles: Semiotext(e), 2013), 111.

3. Between 1987 and 1991 in a project partly funded by the World Health Organization, Weil traveled to Thailand, the Dominican Republic, and South Africa, and in 1991 the International Center of Photography organized an exhibition of his photographs of AIDS and transgender sex workers and printed the catalog *Every Seventeen Seconds: A Global Perspective on the AIDS Crisis* (New York: Aperture, 1992).

4. Quoted from *Brian Weil* exhibition talk with Ric Curtis, Stamatina Gregory, and Patrick Moore, ICA, Philadelphia, February 24, 2013.

5. Gregory, "Anatomy of an Excuse," 110.

6. Amy Sadao, "Brian Weil at ICA," in Weil, *Being in the World*, 107.

7. Gregory, "Anatomy of an Excuse," 113.

8. Quoted in Jennifer Burris, "The Four Acts: Brian Weil's Inscription of the World," in Weil, *Being in the World*, 139.

9. Gregory, "Anatomy of an Excuse," 111.

10. "Interview with Brian Weil," by Claudia Gould, in Weil, *Being in the World*, 146.

11. Given the way performances of gender nonconformity circulate as abject on television and in the media, it isn't surprising that the talk show is a touchstone for Susan's articulation of her transsexual identity. For a pedagogical critique of the talk show confessional and the way it authorizes a singular and digestible narrative of trans identity for the public to consume, see Shana Agid and Erica Rand, "Introduction: Beyond the Special Guest—Teaching 'Trans' Now," *Radical Teacher*, no. 92 (2011): 5–9.

12. In 1993, the year Weil began his documentation of Susan, the organizers of the gay and lesbian march on Washington voted to exclude transgender.

13. T. Benjamin Singer, "From the Medical Gaze to *Sublime Mutations*: The Ethics of (Re) Viewing Non-normative Body Images," in Stryker and Whittle, *Transgender Studies Reader*, 611.

14. Ibid., 609.

15. Judith Halberstam, *In a Queer Time and Place: Transgender Bodies, Subcultural Lives* (New York: New York University Press, 2005), 107.

Queer Archives, Queer Movements

The Visual and Bodily Archives of Vaginal Davis

Robert Summers

It is the summer of 2004, I am walking down Wilshire Boulevard to the Wilshire Westlake Building, which was the location of Vaginal Davis's newest studio, a stone's throw from her previous one in Koreatown, and the last one she would have in Los Angeles (LA). In 2005 she would be leaving for Berlin. Davis, who grew up in LA and remains connected there, proclaimed during a 2012 performance, "My pussy is still in Los Angeles (I only live in Berlin)": "My pussy resides permanently in Los Angeles, where it first emerged a millennium ago from the primordial ooze of the La Brea Tar Pits."[1] Throughout this performance Davis drew on marginal histories in LA, including feminist art movements from LA to Fresno, California. Her performance was no doubt an archival one, in the form of a nonlinear, fragmented, oral history-telling.[2] At the performance, all attendees received an eight-by-ten-inch box containing the performative text of her act, "visualities," and letters.[3] These boxes-cum-archives, wrapped in hand-dyed fabrics, are simultaneously singularities and multiples. Her "body/self" meshes with her archives, and vice versa; in no small way she embodies aspects of Diana Taylor's theory of the body, the archive, the repertoire.[4] As I show here, there is a queer archival impulse to Davis's studios, performative arts, and body/self—all the while revealing that queer art and archives produce counterknowledges and histories, which are nonenlightenment based over what was the "true," "real," and linear event/s; a strand of queer performativity refuses traditional systems of knowledge-production binary operations, and chronology.

Radical History Review
Issue 122 (May 2015)   DOI 10.1215/01636545-2849522
© 2015 by MARHO: The Radical Historians' Organization, Inc.

Davis self-identifies as an African-Mexican-American transgendered visual and performing artist whose primary artistic tactic is, in her words, "the indefinite nature of my own whimsy."[5] Her performances often deploy her body as archive, and her queer aesthetic practices create other types of archives as well. For example, Davis's infamous (and renowned) "art rock concept bands"—such as ¡Cholita! and Pedro, Muriel and Esther, or PME—document places, bodies, and music with lyrics drawn from minoritarian historical events and people, lived experiences, and oral histories of queers of color. These bands have created the various stages for Davis's body/self that "disidentifies," which, following José Esteban Muñoz, is understood as "a performative mode of tactical recognition that various minoritarian subjects employ . . . to resist the oppressive and normalizing discourse of dominant ideology."[6] She (sometimes as a he) performatively creates queer scenes and characters that unhinge identity as something fixed and natural. For example, she often describes herself as an "alcoholic, tranny whore," whether she is in "female" or "male" clothes—all the while crisscrossing masculinity/male and femininity/female. Describing herself as "a poor, tragic mulatto," Davis deconstructs race by hyperbolically and humorously exposing its fabricatedness.[7] In her brilliant video-zine "The Fertile La Toya Video-Zine" and her performance of "The White to Be Angry," Davis twists "black culture" and "Latin culture."[8] In both, she troubles the very idea of a unified subject, as well as the naturalness of race, sex, and gender by hyperbolically playing out stereotypes that expose the political and historical constructedness of the subject. Davis's performances demonstrate "a reformatting of self within the social."[9] These politico-aesthetic structures of Davis's queer performances have been the focus of academic attention with regard to her art.[10] However, Davis's crafting of queer archives, as well as her performative use of her body/self as an archive, has been underresearched and undertheorized, even though archiving is a large part of her art practice. That Davis's queer archives are antisystematic, I argue, accentuates ways that we can begin to rethink and reorganize all archives—*oddly, queerly*. My brief reflections here provide a glimpse of Davis through the frame of the archival. Reflecting on Davis's own archives inspires questions about the "queering" of the body/self, the archive, and the process of auto-archivalization.

At Wilshire Boulevard I reach the Wilshire Westlake Building; I enter, go up eight floors, and walk down the hall into Davis's studio. Once inside I have a curious feeling, which I have had before. It is a feeling of disorientation—of being slanted or sideways. I am confronted by an "open mesh of possibilities, gaps, over-laps, dissonances and resonances, lapses and excesses of meaning."[11] These are the same feelings and experiences I had when entering Davis's Koreatown studio a few years before. Eight floors up: I am caught in a field of intensities and virtualities; I experience the erratic and immense chaos of thousands of cutouts from fashion, celebrity, and gay porn magazines; photos of performances and groupies; posters of art announcements; and photos of friends—so many LA queer denizens, in and out of costume, and all of them enacting their queer bodies/selves in front of the camera (fig. 1). As Davis states, "My art and life always draws in people with fluid genders, sexualities, and identities."[12]

I was first immersed in Davis's artwork and world making when I visited her Koreatown studio. The walls were covered with photos—some cut out haphazardly, others with a razor's precision—amounting to a barrage of visualities. I was disoriented from the intensity of these walls—which seemed to converge and separate.

All the while, I was in the middle of white string that crisscrossed the rooms with photos and cutouts taped to the string and the walls (fig. 2): a literal line of flight gliding across space and the visual plane. Her closets were filled with gowns, various wigs, and dozens of shoes, and in a single wooden dresser all the drawers were packed with photographs, flyers, and other ephemera from her various concerts, performative lectures, and performance art. Later it would seem that much of the contents of this dresser (itself an archive inside of a studio-archive) would end up being displayed across the walls of her Wilshire Westlake studio-archive. Indeed, taking in the entire archive-studio-home, it was difficult to tell what

Figure 1. Vaginal Davis's archive at the Wilshire Westlake Building. Photograph by author, 2004

Figure 2. Vaginal Davis's Koreatown home-studio-archive. Photograph by Larry-Bob Roberts, 1998. Photographer has granted permission to use.

room was what; all the rooms functioned as any other room: the bedroom was also the dining room, the kitchen was also the office, the office was also the storage and studio area, and the places in between were archives—indeed, *everything bled into everything else.* There were seemingly few discrete locations, few proper places: everything was deterritorialized—a queering of place for a queer figure.

At her Wilshire space, the visualities cover all the walls, and most of the ceiling—constituting a veritable art installation. Davis, in her own words, "is a walking installation piece" and "an art director: directing my life as art and other's lives as art."[13] The studio-archive contains performance art props, shelves of books, small paintings by Davis, stacks of LPs and CDs as well as queer and punk zines, and towers of her art videos—all of which serve to generate queer history. Observing them, I am reminded of questions posed by queer theorist William Haver: "What if queer research were to be something other than the hermeneutic recuperation of a history . . . or a philosophy of homosexual subjectivity? What if . . . queer research were to be *something more essentially disturbing* than the stories we tell ourselves of our oppressions in order precisely to confirm, yet once more, our abjection, our victimized subjectivity, our wounded identity?"[14] Davis's walls, her visualities-cum-archives, are filled with life, optimism, and friendship. In her whimsical way of crafting and staging archives, Davis shows an instantiation of a multifaceted queer art praxis that confronts fixed hierarchies and proper forms of knowledge, which Davis states are "patriarchal forms of governance."[15] Davis's aesthetic practice of whimsy encourages us to see differently.

Queer-Knowledge Movements

In Davis's massive visual archive at the Wilshire Westlake studio-archive (fig. 1), a poster served as a dynamic axis, if not exactly a formal center. The viewer can make out the top of it: VAGINAL DAVIS—the camera's flash blows out the bottom half. In an unsteady and uneven centrifugal fashion, disparate imagery, which has been taped to the wall or to other images, seems to swirl out from this poster, with some particles congealing into little image fields, while other matter extends into densely layered conglomerations, but all seem in movement—this is one mode of Davis's archiving through which other ways of looking and thinking begin to emerge. As Georges Didi-Huberman observed, describing the radical art historian Aby Warburg's archive of the early twentieth century, what such collages and montages generate is "a *knowledge-movement* of images," which cultivate "a knowledge in extensions, in associative relationships, in ever renewed montages, and no longer knowledge in straight lines, in a confined corpus, in typologies."[16] Warburg was anachronistic and drew on visual culture in his art-historical practice; he continuously changed the arrangement of his archives, his visualities-in-movement.[17] Davis, too, offers a knowledge-movement. Her practice is Warburgian, though Davis was unaware of his work; like Warburg, her practice refuses unidirectional progression and systematic orders that are demanded by the archons to validate a particular history that becomes naturalized through a legitimate archive, which then is used to validate the history that is desired. Instead, Davis's archive becomes art through her artistic embodiment of the archival—as her body/self is a walking installation and archival piece. Davis crafts and enacts her body/self in order to queerly perform an intricate and vibrant tapestry of not only countermemories, counterhistories, and nonce taxonomies, but she also moves queer embodiment, performance, and art to far more dangerous places—places William Haver asked we go to as quoted above—far more toward "something more essentially disturbing"—which I discuss below.

In a photograph taken by Manuel Vason in 2010, we see Davis in her studio-archive in Berlin. We see her performing herself in front of her visual archives (fig. 3). She stands in the center of the photo, her head in three-quarter profile; she dons black, elbow-length leather gloves by Rick Owens, a fox stole, and mink earrings. She grabs her crotch, her lips are parted, and her chest is pushed out. In the flash of this moment (and let us remember, per Eve Kosofsky Sedgwick, that queer may only be a moment), Davis is becoming undone (read: queer): she denies the camera her face, thus refusing proper representation.[18] But the "proper" archive seeks to demand clear evidence

Figure 3. Vaginal Davis Performing herself in her Berlin studio. Photograph by Manuel Vason, 2010. Photographer has granted permission to use.

and the proper placement of identifiable people, objects, and texts in a systematic fashion. This is the proper archive's aesthetics.[19] Indeed, Davis resists the proper archive, and even if she becomes archived properly, her art's work will remain a site of impropriety and queer archival engagements.

An interesting aspect of the "Berlin photo" is that the flash of the camera creates white reflections on Davis's brown body—flattening out the entire mise-en-scène. There is no differentiation between foreground, middle ground, and background. It appears to depict Davis's incorporation of herself within her walls as archive. The binaries subject/object, life/art, archive/archivist are unhinged. A mode of queer archiving emerges and spotlights what it can do in its *doing*—giving bodies, selves, space, and thought to an "open mesh of possibilities," which refuses and resists fixity.[20] Indeed, what one may ultimately deduce from this photo is that the simple putative veracity of *any* archive is that it stands as mere cover for more complex archival fabrications.

Notes

I would like to thank Amelia Jones for having me meet Vaginal Davis so many years ago and Donald Preziosi for having me work on her and/as her work.

1. "My Pussy Is Still in Los Angeles (I Only Live in Berlin)," performed at Southwestern Law School, Tea Room, 3050 Wilshire Boulevard, fifth floor, LA, on Sunday, January 29, 2012. Davis is working within a larger art-historical genre, here, performance art, but she surfaces the queerness in it. She uses the title of her zine in her performance.

2. Another example of this historical, oral storytelling is Davis's "lesbian separatists' tea party" (*anyone could go!*) during which she showed an art/archival installation. Another is her "Present Penicative" installation, which was part of the feminist group show *The Way That We Rhyme: Women, Art, and Politics* at the Yerba Buena Center for the Arts, San Francisco, March 29–June 29, 2008. See Robert Summers, "Vaginal Davis's 'Present Penicative,'" *ArtUS*, January 2007.

3. I take the term *visualities* to mean a regime of images that continually circulate within certain (sub)cultures.

4. I borrow the term *body/self* from Amelia Jones's theorization of the subject always being finite, material, and phenomenological, thus anti-Cartesian and nontranscendental. See Amelia Jones, *Body Art / Performing the Subject* (Minneapolis: University of Minnesota Press, 1998). See also Diana Taylor, *The Archive and the Repertoire* (Durham, NC: Duke University Press, 2003), chap. 3.

5. Vaginal Davis, e-mail correspondence with the author, January 24, 2010; hard copy in the author's possession.

6. José Esteban Muñoz, *Disidentifications: Queers of Color and the Performance of Politics* (Minneapolis: University of Minnesota Press, 1999), 97.

7. It should be noted that Davis was performing this deconstructive crossing of sex/gender long before Judith Butler theorized the instability of the sex/gender binary.

8. Davis uses *video-zine*, a term she invented, to refer to a homemade video. For an account of "The White to Be Angry" performance, see Muñoz, *Disidentifications*; see also Jennifer Doyle, *Sex Objects: Art and the Dialectics of Desire* (Minneapolis: University of Minnesota Press, 2006). Neither Muñoz nor Doyle focuses per se on the archival aspects of Davis's performance. See Davis's "VD as VB" performance, as well as the reading of it in Doyle, *Sex Objects*, 143.

9. Muñoz, *Disidentifications*, 97.

10. Ibid. See also Michael du Plessis and Kathleen Chapman, "Queercore: The Distinct Identities of Subculture," *College Literature* 24, no. 1 (1997): 45–58; Doyle, *Sex Objects*; and Robert Summers, "Vaginal Davis *Does* Art History," in *Dead History, Live Art? Spectacle, Subjectivity, and Subversion in Visual Culture since the 1960s*, ed. Jonathan Harris (Liverpool: Liverpool University Press and Tate Liverpool, 2007), 71–78.

11. Eve Kosofsky Sedgwick, *Tendencies* (Durham, NC: Duke University Press, 1993), 8.

12. See: *My Pussy Is Still in Los Angeles (I only live in Berlin)*, handmade zine, 2012.

13. See her biography: www.vaginaldavis.com/bio.shtml. Last visited October 19, 2013; see also "My Pussy Is Still in Los Angeles."

14. William Haver, "Queer Research; or, How to Practise Invention to the Brink of Intelligibility," in *The Eight Technologies of Otherness*, ed. Sue Goldin (London: Routledge, 1997), 278; italics mine.

15. See "My Pussy Is Still in Los Angeles."

16. Georges Didi-Huberman, "Knowledge: Movement (The Man Who Spoke to Butterflies)," in

Aby Warburg and the Image in Motion, by Philippe-Alain Michaud, trans. Sophie Hawkes (New York: Zone Books 2004), 10.

17. See Christopher D. Johnson, *Memory, Metaphor, and Aby Warburg's Atlas of Images* (Ithaca, NY: Cornell University Press, 2012).

18. Sedgwick, *Tendencies*, 9. For a sustained and brilliant discussion of becoming undone and queerness, see John Paul Ricco, *The Logic of the Lure* (Chicago: University of Chicago Press, 2002), chap. 1.

19. Donald Preziosi, *Brain of the Earth's Body: Art, Museums, and the Phantasms of Modernity* (Minneapolis: University of Minnesota Press, 2003).

20. Sedgwick, *Tendencies*, 8.

What's the Tea

Gossip and the Production
of Black Gay Social History

Kwame Holmes

During a research trip to Washington, DC, to conduct archival on the intertwined history of black, gay, black gay identity and urban development politics in the nation's capital since desegregation, at the Library of Congress, I went to dinner with a black gay man and native Washingtonian who shared a rather scandalous piece of gossip with me concerning the family life of a DC politico who plays a prominent role in my larger project. I instantly became excited at the prospect that this individual would agree to an interview, contributing a bit of salacious intrigue to his explication of local politics. However, when I asked him to go on record with his story, he refused, citing that he had always preferred to work for gay rights "behind the scenes," rather than in public and did not wish to embarrass the family. Pleasure soon soured into disappointment. His disinterest in transforming his story into a reproducible and verifiable document foreclosed its potential inclusion within a social history project.

Though I will not reveal the details of his story here, this issue's mandate to queer archives invites a closer look at the methodological and historiographical problems that sit at the heart of our interaction. While queer historians are familiar with reluctant witnesses to the history of sexuality, at the gap between these two research experiences—the systematic perusal of the archival collections and

Radical History Review

Issue 122 (May 2015) DOI 10.1215/01636545-2849531

© 2015 by MARHO: The Radical Historians' Organization, Inc.

the messier transmission of gossip between two black men in a Dupont Circle gay bar—lies an opportunity to ask if gossip could function as an archive of experience even as it resists recognition and institutionalization. Moreover, how might gossip authorize black queer subjects to speak back to modern identity politics?

In addition to the immediate mandate of this issue, the preceding questions invite a timely reevaluation of the primary assumptions of social history given the sea change in the structure and logic of oppression produced by the ascendency of neoliberalism within US political culture in recent decades. Founded at the height of the student movements of the 1960s and 1970s, social history initially confronted a world where power reproduced itself by systematically silencing and excluding nonelite, white, male, and heteronormative voices from participation within institutional power.[1] Because historical narratives produce and police the borders of full citizenship, social historians aligned themselves with labor, ethnic, black, women's, and LGBT studies movements to expand archival territory devoted to minoritarian experience in hopes of cementing marginalized communities' sense of communal and national belonging amid structural vulnerabilities and exclusions.

Yet given the significant black feminist and black queer studies literature that illustrates the West's transhistoric inability to recognize black gender and sexual formation outside of the context of theft and captivity, historians cannot presume that black sexual minorities encountered the politicization of gay visibility after Stonewall in a parallel or analogous relationship to sexual marginality as with their white counterparts.[2] As C. Riley Snorton notes, because the queer threat of black sexuality emerges from its seemingly boundless capacity for duplicity, a range of governmental and cultural regulatory bodies have emerged in the United States that ritualistically surveil and expose that for black people which is censured to the private sphere for whites.[3]

In what follows then, I trace histories that condition the entry of black articulations of same-sex desire into the archives, engage the structural vulnerabilities that limited the preservation of a black LGBT past in postwar decades—pivotal years for the formation of modern sexual politics—and, finally, read *Blacklight*, one of the earliest newsletters produced by and for black gay, lesbian, and bisexual readers as an archive of black queer gossip discourse that actively pushes back on the efficacy of identitarian politics from 1979 to 1985.

For most of the twentieth century, evidence of black same-sex desire entered historical archives through multiple layers of translation structured by the omnipresent nature of the West's surveillance of black sexuality. It is not coincidental, for example, that one of the most important recent works on black lesbian experience at the turn of the century is Cheryl Hicks's history of incarcerated women in New York City.[4] While Hicks notes incarcerated black women who, prison officials and case workers at least believed, were unapologetic about their desire for women, it is impossible to separate their evaluations from broader rhetorics that framed black women in prison as sexual predators. As both the historical and literary work on black cultural production during the Harlem Renaissance indicates, black people, queer or not, who wanted to publicly display their genius were forced to rely on racialized networks of exchange and patronage, be they performative, sexual, or both.[5] As Chad Heap indicates, many of the sociological studies documenting various modes of queer black sexuality in the urban North and before World War II did so amid the uneven playing field of slumming culture, where observers' access to the security of whiteness necessarily shaped the behavior of their sources.[6] Nor should we forget that even evidence of same-sex longing among the black elite often comes to us under duress. Take, for example, the letters and diaries of DC socialite Angelina Grimké, who, according to Genny Beemyn, hid explicit identification with homosexuality because of a perennial fear that her father spied on her.[7]

With few exceptions, histories of white gay, lesbian, or transsexual experience prior to World War II had to rely on similarly compromised sources given the criminalization of homosexuality in the pre-Stonewall era. However, as the post–World War II decades ushered in a massive upheaval in the rhetorical, performative, and psychological dimensions of sexual identification in the United States, so too did proximity to white, middle-class masculinity structure how same-sex desire was experienced and documented. While white gay and lesbian experience could continue to be found in the arrest records of police departments bent on "cleaning up" urban vice districts, or in the reports filed on antihomosexual employment purges from the Lavender Scare to the Save Our Children campaign, predominately white homophile organizations provided gay men and lesbians wrestling against the pressures of heteronormativity with access to correspondence and meeting space designed to lessen social isolation. For white lesbians unable to resist the inexorable inertia of marriage, opportunities for same-sex desire occasionally opened within the private domestic sphere of postwar suburbia. As Nicholas Syrett's work indicates, white male business travelers took advantage of their greater access to the invisibility provided by short-term mobility to indulge in same-sex activity away from home.[8]

By contrast, because the vast majority of black sexual minorities were as likely to be caught up in the daily struggle of surviving the postwar urban crisis, documented evidence of black homosexuality became, as Kevin Mumford argues, evidence of the "pathology" of the ghetto.[9] While sociology told policy makers that "damaged masculinity" explained black participation in antisocial behavior, urban anthropology produced the most widely distributed documentation of black homosexuality as an index of inner-city poverty. Studies like Ulf Hannerz's *Soulside: Inquiries into Ghetto Culture and Community* and Elliot Liebow's *Tally's Corner: A Study of Negro Streetcorner Men*—both based in "the Washington ghetto"—not only helped establish the ethnographic method; they were international best sellers, with *Tally's Corner* selling over a million copies worldwide since its 1967 publication.

While urban sociology in the Moynihan era was concerned with quantifying the rate of "dysfunctional" family structure in the inner city, anthropologists worked out of their discipline's imperialist penchant for translating the foreign other into understandable terms. As Mitchell Duneier notes of *Tally's Corner*, "Liebow took his readers into the social world of a group of black men in their twenties and thirties to explain why they seemed so different from white middle-class Americans in the priority they placed on holding down a job and in their commitment to their children, wives, lovers, and friends."[10] Indeed, as Charles Lemert's 2003 foreword to *Tally's Corner* indicates, black inner-city sexuality offered anthropologists the starkest illustrations of the necessity of the project of cultural translation between "the ghetto" and the middle class. In chapter 5, "Lovers and Exploiters," Liebow recalls the experience of witnessing "Sea Cat," one of his anonymous informants, getting ready for a night on the town. "I flopped on his bed to wait for him and a package of prophylactics fell out from under the mattress. In replacing it, I discovered a dozen or more similar packages. I asked Sea Cat if he always used them. . . . 'It depends on the girl. If she's nice, . . . the kind I wouldn't mind helping out, then I don't use them. But if she's not nice, I don't take any chances.' "[11] While lauding Liebow for achieving so "intimate" a relationship with his informants such that he took liberty to "flop" on Sea Cat's bed, Lemert also characterizes Sea Cat's "weird reply" as establishing the rationale for the study itself by establishing "a distance, bridged by the talk of sex, between the apparently opposite sexual ethics of the middle classes and the street-corner man."[12]

Equally concerned with disrupting Patrick Moynihan's pathology thesis through anonymous translation of black experience, urban anthropologists deployed black homosexuality as an index of how inner-city poverty demanded survival strategies that disintegrated social and material borders that kept sexual deviance behind closed doors in the suburbs. In Hannerz's work, black homosexuality functions as a metric of the inability of "ghetto" families to protect precocious children from awareness of deviant sexuality. "Very casual observations in the ghetto also lead one to believe that male homosexuality is not particularly infrequent in the community. Small ghetto boys are well aware of what a 'faggot' is (but also what a 'bulldagger'— lesbian—is; there are obviously sociopsychological forces propelling toward female homosexuality as well)."[13]

Liebow offers a more specific example of this phenomenon by way of "Calvin," whom Liebow describes as "a frail and ailing forty-year-old alcoholic and homosexual." Calvin shared an apartment with "Charlene," who was the on-again, off-again paramour of one of Liebow's street-corner men protagonists, "Leroy." Liebow describes Charlene as regularly placing the couple's children in Calvin's care, despite his reputation as a homosexual, sex worker, and petty thief. "Even more than to Leroy," Liebow writes, "the children were attached to Calvin. When he could summon the courage, Calvin often interceded on their behalf when their mother was dealing out punishment. There was little Calvin did not do for the children. He played with them during the day when they were well and stayed up with them at night when they were sick." Liebow also transforms "Calvin's" sexual subjectivity into evidence that poverty generates desperate sexual behavior among the black urban poor. "During one period, when [Calvin] had resolved to stop his homosexual practices (he had been married and a father), he resumed them only on those occasions when there was no food or money in the house and only long enough to 'turn a trick' and get food for the children."[14] Writing amid the simultaneous pathologization of homosexuality and black poverty, Liebow's Calvin serves the dual purpose of revealing the extent to which inner-city poverty robbed black parents of their ability to properly protect their children from potentially damaging sexual practices and of advancing the notion that black homosexuality, like other forms of antisocial behavior, was itself a constituent of the urban crisis.

In neither Hannerz's nor Liebow's work do black queer protagonists take center stage. Calvin is not one of the "streetcorner men"; he only appears in the margins of Leroy and Charlene's story. Had he been, given Liebow's expansive interviews with his main characters, it might be possible to view Calvin as an agential participant in the construction of Liebow's archive. As is, Liebow conditions our engagement with Calvin's homosexuality on its utility within his primary claim that, rather than "damaged masculinity" at the hands of a black matriarch, the deviances of the ghetto are desperate responses to poverty. Liebow's and Hannerz's methods, which included offering subjects cash and anonymity in exchange for their stories, only heighten the exploitation at the root of their public excavations of black sexuality. Indeed, both studies were conducted in 1960s Washington, DC—a city with fewer and fewer economic opportunities for black residents without college degrees—where Liebow relied on the economic vulnerability that he argued produced Calvin's homosexuality to gain access to the interior lives and sexual practices of "the ghetto" as a whole. Given the proliferation of federal and academic studies on black poverty in DC, might it be possible that resistance to positivist political and archival projects speaks to an acknowledgment of the exploitative component of these relationships?

White and black queers' differing relationship to the urban crisis also shaped their access to the storage space necessary to preserve textual evidence of their experiences. For example, black Protestant congregations played a vital role organizing the distribution of federal antipoverty dollars to neighborhoods within John F. Kennedy's and Lyndon B. Johnson's Great Society initiatives. In crafting the Great Society's Model Cities program, a new strategy for urban renewal meant to encourage African American's sense of full citizenship by allowing them to contribute to urban renewal planning in their neighborhoods, policy makers relied on black churches to legitimize their programs. While few funds actually made their way to black congregations in Washington before the rebellions that erupted in the wake of the April 1968 slaying of Martin Luther King Jr., the Johnson and then the Richard M.

Nixon administration's fear that another "riot" was imminent pushed the federal government into action. Between 1968 and 1978, 523 housing units in DC were constructed or rehabilitated under the auspices of black churches.[15] While the paltry number speaks to the failure of the federal government to provide housing for the territory's poorest residents, it also suggests that the stakes of access to subsidized housing were significant for black sexual minorities. How might the combination of residential instability endemic to publicly subsidized housing and the sexual regulation of congregations interact to discourage the accumulation of black gay archives? Considering the limited access to storage space, the need to move at a moment's notice, and the institutional support that came from church members, queer black Washingtonians may have needed to make quick-dash decisions surrounding what to keep and what to discard.

By the late 1980s, the stakes of articulating an LGBT identity were profoundly different for inner-city African American and white queers. The HIV/AIDS epidemic sparked new "radical" gay political formations, which increasingly, and understandably, understood the cost of invisibility as death. As the epidemic launched a nationwide backlash against visible homosexuality, predominately white organizations like ACT UP ignored gay liberalism's concerns with upsetting the sensibilities of the broader public and testified to their grief, trauma, and injury in as many public forums as possible. The HIV/AIDS epidemic also encouraged greater numbers of black queer people to identify with gay liberalism, believing it to be their duty to direct funding for HIV/AIDS resources to underserved black communities.

Simultaneously though, if publicly testifying to their vulnerability to injury amid the AIDS epidemic expanded the influence of white gay politics and, as Christina B. Hanhardt argues, secured their access to discrete gay territory in the city, black queer voices could still be manipulated for projects outside of their control.[16] Indeed, in late 1980s DC, real estate developers wielded black testimony to claim control over valued urban land that played host to black queer leisure. In 1987, a newly formed investment group called the Franklin Square Association opposed the liquor license renewal of the Brass Rail, one of DC's oldest black gay clubs, on the grounds that it was a "public menace." While by no means one of the most well-respected, or even well-liked, clubs in town, the Brass Rail had faithfully served its clientele in the New York Avenue red-light district since the mid-1960s.[17] Yet in their brief before the Alcohol Control Board, the Franklin Square Association used black queer experience and testimony against the bar's owners. Franklin Square Association lawyers called metropolitan police sergeant John Hickey to testify about "five reported cases of drug arrests inside the Brass Rail" and complaints from patrons "who claimed they had been victims of beatings and a throat slashing." While it is unclear whether the police responded to the reports filed by patrons, in the public transcript of the liquor license hearing, those complaints were remade into an argument for the elimination of not only the Brass Rail but all establishments that catered to black sexually marginalized communities.[18] Only a year later, the Franklin Square Association succeeded in blocking a proposed downtown "nightclub zone" that would concentrate "sexually oriented businesses" into the downtown area after recent reforms to the District liquor law made it more difficult for bars in commercial areas to remain open. While black queer people were not part of either process, their experience and their vulnerability to street crime became a rationale for eliminating their own access to leisure space in the city, rather than an argument that the public recognize their humanity.

By contrast, evidence of white gay and lesbians' greater access to urban land served as a buffer between the documentation of gay history and the economic instability of post–civil rights DC. The most expansive collection of postwar gay experience in the nation's capital is the Frank Kameny papers, currently housed in the manuscripts division of the Library of Congress. Kameny's longtime position as the most important gay civil rights activist in the District, and arguably the nation, before the AIDS epidemic makes his records the ideal choice for integration into the nation's narration of itself. The collection is voluminous, including his constant correspondence with DC newspapers, local politicians, federal lawmakers, and officials as well as activist colleagues around the nation. Kameny kept every member directory, group charter, newsletter, and pamphlet produced by those organizations he was a part of or corresponded with. However, while Kameny consistently pushed white gay and lesbian groups to diversify, his collection contains scant records of black gay and lesbian experience.

Simultaneously though, the *Washington Blade*'s coverage of the news that Kameny's records would be institutionalized reveals the way differing scales of urban precarity structure access to archives during a period of profound urban transformation. Here is how *Blade* reporter Charles Francis recalled his trip to Kameny's home in Mount Pleasant before Kameny's death: "Well into his 80s, he climbed into the attic to join me in a dusty netherworld of political papers. Boxes by the score overflow with single-spaced, multi-page typewritten letters and carbons, newsletters, transcripts, umpteen boxes of Washington Blades, every gay publication from 'Drum' to 'One' and two black typewriters that looked like anvils. . . . The man saved everything. He never moved. He never discarded. He never denied gay history."[19]

Kameny's residential stability (he never moved) and his allegiance to gay visibility (he never denied gay history) speak to a certain kind of urban privilege in the neoliberal city. Even though Kameny's annual income never fully recovered after he was fired during the Lavender Scare, he was able to maintain a residence in Mount Pleasant large enough for him to hold on to an enormous number of documents for decades. The immaculate quality of the material, its lack of stains or wrinkles or deterioration all speak to Kameny's geographic fixedness within a neighborhood that, like so many interracial communities in northwestern DC, experienced a profound decline and then gentrification between the 1960s and the turn of the century. In covering Kameny's residential stability as a political virtue, rather than a metric of economic privilege, the *Blade* reifies the naturalization of whiteness in gay politics by positioning it exclusively as the result of hard work and personal responsibility.

The emergence of a black gay political and cultural movement, centered in mid-Atlantic and West Coast cities from the late 1970s to the emergence of the black HIV-AIDS epidemic, ushered in a new era in black sexual minorities' relationship to the politics of political and historical visibility. Indeed, the Washington Metropolitan Area was a capital region for the movement as Billy Jones and Louis Hughes founded the DC and Baltimore chapters of what would become the National Coalition of Black Lesbians and Gay Men (CBLG) in 1978.[20] Colevia Carter and Valerie "Papaya" Mann helped establish the Sapphire Sapphos in 1981 and, in that same year, Howard University Professor James S. Tinney attempted to create a "Black Lesbian/Gay" archive collection within Moorland Spingarn Library.[21] In 1979, the Washington Chapter of the Gay Activist Alliance elected Mel Boozer that organization's first black president. A year later, Boozer became the first openly gay black person to be nominated for vice president at the 1980 Democratic convention.[22]

Yet despite the achievements of these individuals, they represent only a small microcosm of nonheterosexual black people in the nation's capital. Particularly for Boozer, their participation in white gay politics at times produced resentment among black gay Washingtonians who were utterly disinterested in alliance, be it political or romantic, with white gay men or formal politics in general. As Sidney Brinkley, publisher and editor of the Washington-based black gay and lesbian publication *Blacklight* wrote of DC's black gay political groups in 1983, "neither DCCBG [DC Coalition of Black Gays] nor Sapphire Sapphos can claim much influence beyond its membership."[23] Elaborating on "Black gay" ambivalence toward these groups, Brinkley writes, "It is an insular community and much of the activity occurs behind closed doors."[24]

Evidence of these tensions can most readily be found in the pages of *Blacklight*, which ran from 1979 to 1985. Founded by Brinkley, an early member of the CBLG, *Blacklight* offers textual evidence of black Washingtonians' ambivalence toward the politics of visibility and their interest in "spilling tea" (gossiping) as a mode of political analysis. In one of *Blacklight*'s earliest issues, Bill Stevens answers readers' questions about what participation in "gay rights" actually looks like for black gays and lesbians. His report proved less than encouraging. Stevens articulated the frustration of having to represent the entirety of the black gay experience for white gay organizers. "Because you will be one of few Black Gay activists, you will be expected to address every issue, attend every meeting and be involved in every project. Expected by whom? By Whites. If you miss a meeting, they will use that to reinforce previously held attitudes that Blacks don't care."[25] Stevens's pro-

Under GRACE'S Hat

by GRACE

Welcome to this little corner, "Under GRACE'S Hat." Believe me, it's one place to be!!! This corner in future issues will attempt to keep you abreast of some happenings and events going on in the metropolitan area as well as provide a place for the exchange of some ideas. It's going to be hot, saucy, sexy, bare, square, in, out, on top, up under, ---do I have to go on?

If there are any questions, complaints, items, or events that

then, the new group, SPIRIT OF LIFE, gave one a few weeks after THE CONSTITUENTS were supposed to. It was kinky but had no spirit or life...

meets at 7pm every Monday in B21, Douglass Hall on Howard's campus...

On the subject of the Gay murders, GRACE is very happy to hear that a task force between the LAMBDAS and the COALITION OF BLACK GAYS is assist-

Under Grace's Hat, *Blacklight* 3, no. 4 (1982): 14. Illustration by Ossippio

posed solution was to avoid "living up [to] their expectations. Set your priorities and your own pace."[26] Despite his criticisms of representational politics, Stevens had little that was positive to say about the potential for intraracial cooperation by black gay men and lesbians in predominately white groups. "As for the Blacks you will come into contact with, the Lesbians will lean toward feminism but will not be as radical as their White counterparts. . . . As for the Black Gay men overall very little political awareness exists, but there will be individuals who will do what they can. However, don't expect too much."[27] Rather than white racism within gay politics, Stevens's column suggests that a profound, yet playful, disinterest in the efficacy of political mobilization might animate black gay disinterest in activism.

Blacklight readers played significantly closer attention to Under Grace's Hat, a semiregular, and utterly hilarious, gossip column pseudonymously penned by "Grace." While Grace spent her time "serving tea" and getting the denizens of black gay Washington together on a regular basis, her column spoke to some black queer subjects' understanding of their position in Snorton's "glass closet." In two stories in the October 1982 issue, Grace indicated her belief that her readers did not understand that "the closet" did not function in similar ways for black gays as it did for other sexual minorities. Grace used the two stories to illustrate this notion. First, in typically audacious fashion, after asking readers if they had "heard about that party that was given in N.E. not too long ago," Grace writes: "Well it seems that one of the guests he was into . . . (Dare Grace say it?) *fist-fucking*. Well, another guest was very interested and decided he would like to do it while the other guest watched."[28] After taking the blame for such a display—"After all, in one of Grace's recent columns she did say that live entertainment does add a touch of class to an affair; however, she was not referring to *that* type of entertainment"—Grace chided the party's organizer for ever expecting their activities to avoid the light of day. "Yes dear, we understand that it *was* a private party. Yes dear, we understand that it *is* none of our business. But, face it honey, this is Washington, D.C. and, with the crowd you've been running with, there is no such thing as privacy!"[29] Later on, Grace addressed concerns that her columns had recently gone too far, revealing hints as to the identity of a reader who was currently seeking security clearance with the federal government. She responded with the following:

Now dears, let's be realistic. We are living in America. America runs nothing so efficiently as she does her FBI [Federal Bureau of Investigation] and CIA [Central Intelligence Agency]. The person in question has been gay since day two (he somehow missed day one). If indeed they are investigating him they must already have a folder full of information. Anyway, Grace did not say he was gay; she just said he lived with his lover. But, if he is so concerned, he should give up his lover. Better yet, give him to Grace 'cause Lord knows, the man is *fine*.[30]

In both instances, Grace's reading of the impossibility of privacy for those "running" in Washington's black gay circles offers insight into a potential source of queer black ambivalence toward political mobilization. In the face of the federal government's massive accumulation of the authority to investigate and expose, in light of queer black Washingtonians' historically compromised access to sexual privacy, the liberatory power of "coming out" may have emerged as anticlimactic, a continuation of the sexual order rather than an intervention against it.

Indeed, as members of DC's black gay social clubs consistently attest, the ultimate goal was to work "behind the scenes" to advance gay rights, rather than out in public. As Aundré Scott, co-owner of DC's most popular black gay disco, the Clubhouse, told the *Washington Post* before the 1978 DC mayoral and city council elections: "Every candidate I know of has some member of my club on their campaign committee. They may not know that these people are gay, but they don't need to know right? No matter who wins, black gays are going to have some influence in this city. If you want to call gay kids spies, then we have spies in every camp."[31] Lacking confirmation from any of the campaign committees in question, Scott's statement is unquestionably gossip. Yet in shining a light on black gays' comprehensive infiltration of local politics Scott also articulates a notion of gay political power that is not beholden to visibility and instead takes recourse within private spaces available to "spies." Scott's decision to spread gossip about black gay presence within local politics with the *Washington Post* also represents an oddly public gesture toward discretion, one that disrupts any effort to characterize modern black gay experience or politics as operating within a public/private binary.

While features like Under Grace's Hat reflected the sensibilities of DC's black gay elite, *Blacklight* also functioned as a critical bridge between those black Washingtonians committed to being out and those who chose to remain unidentified, while also playing fast and loose with the very notion of ever-present risk that encircled some black gay Washingtonians' lives. Gossip emerged as a strategy to bring media and police attention to a series of murders committed against black gay men in the District. In a 1981 column, titled "Rough Trade," Brinkley brought attention to a rash of murders committed against gay men in the city in the previous twelve months. Brinkley introduced the story by referencing a wave of attacks on black children in Atlanta, perhaps as a means of figuring a closer relationship between the shared vulnerability of black children and black gay men, rather than positioning the story within the context of DC's "crime problem." He writes: "We are all familiar with the murders that have taken place in Atlanta. But closer to home, right here in Washington, D.C., there have been a number of murders of another type. Gay murders. The straight media often times do not report it as such, but *we* know. We know because many of the victims have been friends and family."[32]

By September, there were eleven such murders, with eight of the victims African American. In emphasizing a general "we" who was aware of the actual nature of the crimes, Brinkley speaks to a broader, if unnamed, community who not only knew the sexual identity of the victims but also knew of the economies of desire that attract black gay men to their victimizers. Brinkley writes that future murders are inevitable because "too many Gay men are into hustlers or rough trade. You've seen the type—they're usually dirty, foul mouthed, under educated, sexually repressed, emotionally immature and angry. Unfortunately, too many Gay men equate those 'qualities' with being a 'real man' and eagerly pay for a few minutes of one-sided sex. Sometimes they pay with their lives." On the one hand, Brinkley reproduces rhetoric popular within urban antiviolence activisms that linked the maladjustments of racialized poverty to urban violence.[33] On the other hand, at the end of his column Brinkley chooses not to call on protection from the police, or even any formal political organization. Instead, he writes: "How do we as family, friends or concerned citizens bring an end to these attacks? The answer is *we* can't. The solution lies solely within the future victims. Until they decide to re-evaluate their self-concept and their concept of manhood . . . there is very little we can do. If you know someone who likes his trade rough, have him think about this: The next one he picks up . . . may kill *him*." In repeating the emphasis of "we," Brinkley actively embraces the impossibility of black gay engagement with formal politics, offering instead solutions that stress internal transformation or private, interpersonal conversation. While *Blacklight* consistently showcased positive coverage of public forums on black gay issues, the magazine regularly suggested that visibility could not ameliorate the community's challenges.

The AIDS epidemic brought *Blacklight* to a rather abrupt end in 1985. A 1983 feature issue on the spread of the disease in black communities illuminates the way rumor, as well as gossip, produced a unique queer black political subjectivity. Titled "The File on Aids," the issue included an interview with Vinod Modi, chief of infectious diseases at Howard University Hospital, who answered questions about how AIDS was spread and whether blacks were more or less susceptible to the disease. In the same issue though, Brinkley offered space to Ron Simmons, a radical black gay nationalist who in 1989 went on to found Us Helping Us, a black gay AIDS community organization.[34] Drawing connections between the CIA's alleged distribution of germs into the New York subway, the United States' complicity with Japan's Devil's Brigade, and the Tuskegee experiment, Simmons points out that AIDS is "a government experiment on a grand scale" and that "the intended target of this experiment is not gay people; it's black people."[35]

Simmons's assessment of AIDS speaks to his connection to indigenous black political culture in DC, a city where conspiracy theory has historically informed the disfranchised population's relationship to structural inequality in the federal territory. For example, as early as the Nixon administration, the District's black radio DJs, street-corner preachers, and beauty salon technicians began to spread rumors of "the Plan," which predicted that African Americans would be expelled from Washington, DC, by the year 2000 and, as one unnamed woman told the *Washington Afro-American*, put "on a reservation like the Indians soon unless we get ourselves together."[36] So too do conspiracy theories concerning the planned nature of HIV/AIDS proliferate in black communities in Washington and around the nation. Then-senator Barack Obama's otherwise smooth post-Iowa caucus run for the 2008 Democratic primary was partially derailed when his former pastor, Jeremiah Wright, accused the federal government of manufacturing AIDS to kill the black community. Similar notions circulate within a range of black community spaces from barbershops to radical blogs. As Simmons argued in his 1983 essay, public discourse on AIDS only seemed to confirm that the disease was designed to eliminate unwanted populations at home and abroad: "The type of people most likely to contract AIDS were identified as 'drug addicts, Haitians and gays.' Note that these are segments of the population that white America is least concerned about."[37] Simmons connects the inevitable failure of a black gay response to AIDS as the result of political apathy, but for him that apathy emerges in black gays' ambivalent relationship to the black community. "Some Black gays have become defensive adults who rigidly hold to Eurocentric definitions of 'gay rights' while remaining ambiguous about their relationship to the overall Black community. Thus, most Black gays will probably accept the official explanation of AIDS, rather than acknowledge the historic Black struggle and the possibility that AIDS is a government conspiracy."[38] Here, then, Simmons positions rumor and innuendo about the origins of AIDS as an example of rational historicism and engagement in "gay rights" as the form of false consciousness.

Conclusion

This essay's persistent gesture towards "gossip" is in part structured by the way the HIV-AIDS epidemic has narrowed the documentary record for black LGBT experience in the postwar decades. Washington, DC is relatively fortunate in this regard. In addition to *Blacklight*, the Moorland-Spingarn Research Center's James Tinney papers, the Schomburg's Essex Hemphill/Wayne Moreland collection, offer critical glimpses into black gay life before the crisis. Under Mark Meinke, the Rainbow History Project has conducted dozens of interviews with black gay Washingtonians, many of them native to the city, and makes audio files and transcripts available to researchers. Yet, even in Washington, the HIV-AIDS epidemic utterly reworked both the archival landscape for black gay history and the black gay community's relationship to a politics of visibility.

It is in response to the epidemic that DC's black gay social clubs banded together to organize an education forum on HIV-AIDS in the black community, even as they began to lose members at an alarming rate. *Blacklight*'s promotion of the forum was published in one of the magazine's final issues, before Brinkley escaped Washington for the Bay Area. While the CBLG held a fundraiser for Marion Barry's 1982 re-election campaign, it was the astronomical HIV-AIDS infection rates in the city's prison system that brought Billy Jones to the floors of Congress in 1987, articulating the unique needs of black gay men both within and outside of the prison system. Black gay and lesbian Washingtonians begin to appear as political agitators in the personal papers of DC city councilmembers in the late 1980s and early 1990s, demanding state funds to construct clinics and provide services outside of Washington's now gentrified gay-friendly neighborhoods. Tragically then, as the HIV-AIDS epidemic robbed black gay communities of invaluable intergenerational cultural memory, it produced a critical mass of politically and historically legible black gay subjects in Washington, and around the country, for the first time.

The persistence of high HIV-AIDS infection rates among black gay or same-gender loving men in the present day has produced projects designed to excavate a usable black gay history from within the overwhelming loss suffered by those who survived the epidemic. In addition to the Queer Newark Oral History Project, Charles Stephens's Counter Narrative Project and Dan Royles's African American HIV-AIDS Activism Oral History Project are working to stitch together black gay activist histories designed to ameliorate the trauma of survivors and inspire black lesbian, gay, bisexual, transgender, queer, and same-gender-loving people who continue to struggle against an intersecting matrix of structural and quotidian oppression. Still, the history illustrated above instructs us to think how we can also narrate the experience of black gay subjects who resisted power by sidestepping or rethinking the very category of the political representation.

Notes

This essay would not have been possible without the keen insight and advice of Daniel Marshall, Kevin P. Murphy, and Zeb Tortorici, as well as two anonymous reviewers. Thank you to Mark Meinke for supplying PDF copies of *Blacklight* many years ago and to the Rainbow History Project for providing transcripts of essential oral interviews.

1. Peter N. Stearns, "Social History Present and Future," *Journal of Social History* 37, no. 1 (2003): 9–19.
2. Hortense J. Spillers, "Mama's Baby, Papa's Maybe: An American Grammar Book," *Diacritics* 17, no. 2 (1987): 65–81; Zakkiyah Iman Jackson, Waking Nightmares" in *Gay and Lesbian Quarterly (GLQ)* 17, no.2 (2011):357–63.
3. C. Riley Snorton, *Nobody Is Supposed to Know: Black Sexuality on the Down Low* (Minneapolis: University of Minnesota Press, 2014). In addition to Snorton's work, I draw upon a genealogy of black feminist and black queer explorations into black subjects' deployment of evasion or excess in response to the presumption of their queerness. On evasion, see Darlene Clark Hine, "Rape and the Inner Lives of Black Women in the Middle West, Preliminary Thoughts on the Culture of Dissemblance," *Signs* 14, no. 4 (1989): 919–20; Charles Nero, "Towards a Black Gay Aesthetic: Signifying in Contemporary Black Gay Literature," in Joseph Beam and Essex Hemphill, eds., *Brother to Brother: New Writings by Black Gay Men* (Boston: Alyson, 1991), 229–52; Evelyn Brooks Higginbotham, *Righteous Discontent: The Women's Movement in the Black Baptist Church, 1880–1920* (Cambridge, MA: Harvard University Press, 1993); E. Patrick Johnson, *Sweet Tea: Black Gay Men of the South* (Chapel Hill: University of North Carolina Press, 2008); Carlos Decena, *Tacit Subjects: Belonging and Same-Sex Desire among Dominican Immigrant Men* (Durham, NC: Duke University Press, 2011); Jeffrey McCune Jr., *Sexual Discretion: Black Masculinity and the Politics of Passing* (Chicago: University of Chicago Press, 2014). On excess, see Roderick A. Ferguson, *Aberrations in Black: Toward a Queer of Color Critique* (Minneapolis: University of Minnesota Press, 2004); Cathy J. Cohen, "Deviance as Resistance: A New Research Agenda for the Study of Black Politics," *Du Bois Review: Social Science Research on Race* 1 (2004): 27–45. On the governmental and cultural regulation of black sexuality, see Cheryl Hicks, *Talk with You like a Woman: African American Women, Justice, and Reform in New York, 1890–1935* (Chapel Hill: University of North Carolina Press, 2010); Dorothy E Roberts, *Killing the Black Body: Race, Reproduction, and the Meaning of Liberty* (New York: Pantheon, 1997); Alison Lefkovitz, "Men in the House: Race, Welfare, and the Regulation of Men's Sexuality in the United States, 1961–1972," *Journal of the History of Sexuality* 20, no. 3 (2011): 594–614.
4. Hicks, *Talk with You like a Woman.*
5. Marlon B. Ross, *Manning the Race: Reforming Black Men in the Jim Crow Era*, Sexual Cultures (New York: New York University Press, 2004); Shane Vogel, *The Scene of Harlem Cabaret: Race, Sexuality, Performance* (Chicago: University of Chicago Press, 2009).
6. Chad Heap, *Slumming: Sexual and Racial Encounters in American Nightlife, 1885–1940* (Chicago: University of Chicago Press, 2009).
7. Genny Beemyn, *A Queer Capital: A History of Gay Life in Washington, D.C.* (New York: Routledge, 2014).
8. Nicholas Syrett, "A Busman's Holiday in the Not-So-Lonely Crowd: Business Culture, Epistolary Networks, and Itinerant Homosexuality in Mid-Twentieth-Century America," *Journal of the History of Sexuality* 21, no. 1 (2012): 121–40.
9. Kevin Mumford, "Untangling Pathology: The Moynihan Report and Homosexual Damage, 1965–1975," *Journal of Policy History* 24, no. 1 (2012): 53–73.

10. Mitchell Duneier, "On the Legacy of Elliot Liebow and Carol Stack: Context-Driven Fieldwork and the Need for Continuous Ethnography," *Focus* 25, no. 1 (2007): 33.

11. Elliot Liebow, *Tally's Corner: A Study of Negro Streetcorner Men* (Lanham, MD: Rowman and Littlefield, 2003), 99.

12. Charles Lemert, "Foreword to the 2003 Edition: *Tally's Corner* and the Black Man of the City," in ibid., xii.

13. Ulf Hannerz, *Soulside: Inquiries into Ghetto Culture and Community* (New York: Columbia University Press, 1969), 118–19.

14. Liebow, *Tally's Corner*, 55.

15. Walter E. Washington and Washington, DC, City Council, *Ten Years since April 4, 1968: A Decade of Progress for the District of Columbia; A Report to the People* (Washington, DC: District of Columbia, 1978), 7–9.

16. Christina B. Hanhardt, *Safe Space: Gay Neighborhood History and the Politics of Violence* (Durham, NC: Duke University Press, 2013).

17. Anne Simpson, "Battle Rages Over Downtown Bar: Club Catering to Black Gays Is a Menace, Developers Claim; Developers Try to Close Downtown Bar," *Washington Post*, February 5, 1987.

18. Ibid.

19. Charles Francis, "Kameny's Storybook Ending," *Washington Blade*, October 20, 2011, www.washingtonblade.com/2011/10/20/kamenys-storybook-ending.

20. A. Billy S. Jones, "Coming Out and Staying Alive—D.C. Blacks," *Washington Blade*, July 1978, 2.

21. "Black Lesbian/Gay Archives Begins to Take Shape" *Habari, Habari, The Newsletter of the Coalition of Black Gays*, 1981, 1.

22. Thomas Morgan, "A Black Gay Leader Speaks Out: Scholar Wants to Erase 'Negative Images,'" *Washington Post*, October 13, 1979.

23. Sidney Brinkley, "Who's Who in Gay Politics, Part 2" *Black Light*, vol. 4, no. 4, n.d., 15.

24. Ibid.

25. Bill Stevens, "Gay Politics: Notes for an Emerging Black Gay Activist," *Blacklight*, April 1980, 1.

26. Ibid., 7.

27. Ibid.

28. Grace, Under Grace's Hat, *Blacklight*, October 1982, 23.

29. Ibid., 24.

30. Ibid.

31. Thomas Morgan, "Gays Hope to Cast the Deciding Votes for Barry," *Washington Post*, September 4, 1978.

32. Sidney Brinkley, "Rough Trade," *Blacklight*, June 1981, 2.

33. Ibid.

34. It must be noted that Simmons now disavows his accusations against the government as evidence of his "more radical" youth. Still, concerning the persistence of the epidemic among African Americans, he points out: "I was right." Ron Simmons, phone conversation with the author, September 8, 2014.

35. Brother Ron [Simmons], "AIDS: A Government Conspiracy," *Blacklight*, n.d, 24.

36. Hodari Ali, "Shaw Residents Critical of City Hosing Policy," *Washington Afro-American*, August 7, 1976.

37. [Simmons], "AIDS," 21.

38. Ibid.

Drawn from the Scraps

The Finding AIDS of Mundo Meza

Robb Hernández

Born on July 19, 1955, in Tijuana, Mexico, and raised in Huntington Park, California, Edmundo "Mundo" Meza was one of the most provocative young talents to emerge out of Southern California in the late 1960s, a period characterized by the Chicano civil rights struggle, organized boycotts, and culturally affirming arts and literary movements. Regarded for his conceptual performance art collaborations with artists Robert "Cyclona" Legorreta and Gronk in 1969–72, Meza took to the streets of East Los Angeles (LA) rupturing the mundane with glittering spectacle, billowing fabrics, and optical trickery. A young painter regarded for his natural skill, he quickly garnered a reputation for large-scale photo-realist acrylic painting, surrealist drawing, and metamorphic self-permutations. He was the youngest member of an influential cohort of Chicano cultural workers that came to define avant-garde practice. Harry Gamboa Jr., Gronk, Willie Herrón, and Patssi Valdez were among the esteemed alumni from Garfield High School developing an experimental vocabulary grounded in experiences of the "urban exile": racial violence, police brutality, warmongering, and oppressive gerontocracies.[1] Whereas these aforementioned artists came together as the lauded art collective Asco (Spanish for "nausea") in 1972–87, Meza remained in the margins, embarking on a promising commercial career in LA's art and fashion industry.[2] That was all about to change, however. On February 11, 1985, Meza lost his battle with AIDS. He was twenty-nine years old.[3]

After a brief posthumous show at Otis-Parsons Exhibition Center in down-

Radical History Review
Issue 122 (May 2015)   DOI 10.1215/01636545-2849540
© 2015 by MARHO: The Radical Historians' Organization, Inc.

town LA on September 17, 1985, nearly all traces of his work went missing. The absence wrought by the AIDS crisis had profound implications for Meza's place in Chicano avant-gardism. Arguably, this prevailing void has consequence for our present moment, shaping the archive from which cultural criticism is written. Chicano cultural history, art history, ethnic studies, and literature perpetuate skewed narratives, permeating curatorial treatments and historical interpretations.

His obscurity was visible throughout the Getty Museum's "Pacific Standard Time: Art in L.A., 1945–1980," which presented a remarkable 170 exhibitions from 130 partnering museums and galleries in Southern California, marking the "birth" of LA as an art capital.[4] Though the festival engendered a historic number of Chicano-themed exhibitions, art publications, and catalogs showing their undeniable influence in the city's visual culture, AIDS cultural discourse was minimally cited. Meza, whose major body of cubist-inspired monochromatic abstract paintings was produced as a metaphorical reflection of his terminal diagnosis, was all but omitted in an amnesiac maneuver that appeared to forget AIDS. Instead, his presence was reduced to a few Polaroid snapshots. His paintings were unidentified sightings in photo-documents of another time, partially glimpsed in backdrops of domestic interiors. Looking for Mundo was an exercise in futility.

I argue that Meza's elision is symptomatic of the inadequacies of empiricist archive methodologies predicated on authorial objects, salient chains of custody, and authenticated whole documents arranged in self-evident record bodies. His absence intensifies a related disciplinary anxiety to privilege "lost art." This refusal to legitimate the nonextant undercuts "the kind of relation to an extant work that a ghost has to a person."[5] Such tendencies even permeate finding aids as systems of document representation encoding and registering their locations in ways that "support the continued existence of records after their migration from one system into another."[6] For racialized queer subjects, these inventories prescribe restrictive taxonomies and categorizations for otherwise complex identities across collection descriptions, perpetuating what Mathias Danbolt sees as the "institutional ideology of 'hard facts' that dominates the humanities—an ideology that excludes the temporary and performative knowledges of queerness."[7] As such, the "evidentiary logic of heteronormativity" falters under the mélange of loss, ruin, and dispersed debris that lies in the wake of AIDS devastation.[8]

Meza's imprint at the borders and corners of photocompositions demands a queer archive methodology that can contend with *near* absence and the unknown conditions of provenance. In this essay, I propose what I term "queer detrital analysis," arguing for the ways that residues, margins, and parts lend queer meaning to the collection and document form itself. By this I mean that the queerness of paper scraps, fragments, and remnants allows for a complex understanding of the artist archive by foregrounding its "failure" and incompletion. Material instability, decay, and destruction are never quite satisfactory as means of documentation, and thus evidentiary paradigms founded on record "families," wholeness, and presence perpetuate a heteronormative logic deeming these traces insufficient.[9]

This is not to falsely presume that all institutional archive collections are inherently "complete" bodies of record. Redactions, omissions, editorial revision, and rediscovered "lost" manuscripts abound. However, it is to posit that the traditional understanding of provenance as "the origins of an information-bearing entity or artifact" is based on "proof of a continuous chain of custody and therefore authenticity of the work."[10] Therefore, reading Meza's archive through a queer detrital analytic eschews the custodial chains and permits new meaning in the multidirectional loci of finding *AIDS*. That is, I want to think about the double meaning of finding aids as both a technology for (re)search, retrieval, and description and a navigational system of AIDS cultural memory tracing different archival body configurations in a queer vision for debris.

This essay proceeds with a queer detrital analysis of Legorreta's "Cyclona Art Collection: The Gay, 'Chicanismo in el Arte'" at ONE National Gay and Lesbian Archives in LA. Acquisitioned in 2001, partially processed, and released for public use ten years later, Legorreta's collection holds the only assortment of "Mundo art" in the nation. However, rather than consist of fine art paintings, prints, and photography, the series contains detrital remains. Legorreta inventoried these works, writing an adjoining vernacular finding aid. In it, he presents a curious registry and descriptive network of textual annotations bordering on performative, rhetorical, and diaristic appeals. His assembly and bibliographic inventory not only radically rethinks what states of record are required to document the artist's life but also exemplifies how loss and ruin elicit other archival formations where Meza's body is found.

Drawing on "body of evidence" as metaphor, queer detrital analysis expands archival body discourse by considering it as an exteriorization of the individual, social, and cultural self in a type of ontological surrogacy constituted by the material record and, in particular, paper. Owing much to performance, contemporary art, and material culture theorists' redress of the presumed divisions between subject and object, I am interested in the types of agency that emerge from the cohabitation and interdependence of the artifactual, humanist, and private record-keeping assembly. My interest is in keeping with what art historian Hal Foster calls "archival art[, which] is as much preproduction as it is postproduction: concerned less with absolute origins than with obscure traces . . . these artists are often drawn to unfulfilled beginnings or incomplete projects—in art and in history alike—that might offer points of departure again."[11] Much of the "archival impulse" Foster describes takes its cue from the "artist-as-curator," where institutional and informal archives are arranged "according to a quasi-archival logic, a matrix of citation and juxtaposition, and present[ed] . . . in a quasi-archival architecture, a complex of texts and objects."[12] I want to position archival art in Foster's terms more broadly as material processes, detrital ruins, and, in particular, agents themselves performing an "accumulated being," rather than take aim at administrative systems of information management in site-specific installations.[13]

Doing so, my thinking about the archival body is indebted to Jennifer González's thoughts on autotopographic memory landscapes and material iconologies of Mexican American women's *altares* (home alters) as well as Amelia Jones's ruminations over the intersection of body and archive as both the "repertoire" of experience and "bits of things touched, manipulated, or otherwise used by performance artists, [in] a kind of material embodiment, especially as it is mobilized in historical narratives and exhibitions."[14] I hang my questions on this body's rearticulation through impressions, residues, and imprints with paper in its divergent textual, visual, and physical material conditions. Archival body in this sense is a dispersed constellation of record exposing a different experience and subjugation for the alternative record-keeping "self," especially for queers beseeched by vandalism, confiscation, omission, and erasure. A body whose very survival is exemplary of racial, sexual, and gender cultural neglect, it thus intensifies the significance of the detrital as it estranges the relationship between the historical and evidential. This conjunction is epitomized in Legorreta's surrogacy of Meza across the scattered debris that followed after his death.

Archival Heteronormativity, Queer Evidence, and Other Material States

From the outset, it is critical that we question the heteronormative power of the document. Imported from the golden age of archive theory is Sir Hilary Jenkinson's espousal of "unbiased" and "objective" records administration as defined by unbroken chains of custody.[15] His formative approach largely privileged document generation from "official" state-sanctioned and corporate bodies. The document constituted an "untainted" collection unspoiled by threat of mismanagement, inauthenticity, incompletion, or processual error. In the context of nineteenth-century England, provenance was a clear chain of original order and ownership resulting in the mere transference of organizational papers through the unbiased stewarding of the administrator.[16] Termed *respect des fonds*, it is based on a French archival idea that, according to the Ministry of the Interior on April 24, 1841, "all documents which come from a body, an establishment, a family, or an individual form a fonds, and must be kept together."[17] Drawing on varied record categories including those organized by family, original order was carefully defended, ensuring that the collection remained completely deposited into a singular institutional repository. This practice guaranteed that the "archival bond" between records sealed the "organic linkage generated between agency and record group."[18] In this sense, the body of record was stabilized and authenticated from evidentiary "wholes." Historical truth was controlled in the material possession, preservation, and promise of administrative custody.

Following the polemical work of Jacques Derrida in *Archive Fever*, post-modern archive theorists' suspicions and redefinitions of archive led with an eye on "form" and "power."[19] They sought ways to expose the sociocultural politics of archives, demonstrating that the bond or "organic linkage" was built on Eurocentric, colonialist, and, I might add, heteropatriarchal ideologies that favor progressive teleology and what Lee Edelman calls "reproductive futurism."[20] This conflation twisting archival practice with the metaphor of family was furthered when critical archive scholars like Joy Atherton, Frank Upward, and Sue McKemmish steered away from life-cycle approaches in record management by better accounting for those interstitial evidentiary acts and multilateral transactions in a "records continuum model," where "the underlying unifying or linking factor in the continuum was the service function to the records' creators and all users."[21] Jay Kennedy and Cherryl Schauder expanded on these ideas, organizing record groupings into "families."[22] Doing so, they "link" archive functions into natural biological norms in information management and archive administration.

Though advocates for this model radically challenged the terms of record keeping from a passive and fixed autonomous body to an active one, advancing through the vision of the regenerative "family" perpetuated a heteronormative pre-occupation with progeny—an archival episteme traced to early French conceptions of the *respect des fonds*. This was something unrealized in the lives of queer people and, in particular, gay men, where the consequence of AIDS-related death often resulted in the dissolution, deaccessioning, and looting of private archival collections by biological families. These men's "queer kinships" were routinely denied ownership, property rights, or joint claims to estates; at times they served as floating signifiers for infection, contamination, and disease.[23] Under the "records continuum model," it is difficult to understand what is to become of those orphaned parcels of paper with no recognizable record "family" to belong to. More to this point, the compulsory heterosexuality of this archival thinking pervaded discourses of the document itself.

Such heteronormative "house arrest" is indicative of what Richard J. Cox calls "the romance of the document."[24] By this, he argues that "the pull of the document can be an all absorbing one. . . . Rather than feeling guilty about such emotions, records professionals need to realize that the romance of the document is a powerful means of understanding why our records are important in society."[25] Cox speaks to shifting modes of documentation capturing the "general fascination" of the public vis-à-vis journals, letters, diaries, oral storytelling, and websites (1). Each record type requires different approaches to document storage of cultural knowledge—documents that "[convey] something about this romantic attraction" (12). And yet what this "something" *is* is never quite explicated in Cox's assessment. Just what desire drives this "romantic attraction" for the document? Moreover, if a "romantic appeal" was engendered not by documentary evidence but rather by the debris that "fails" to meet the barometer of authenticity, then how do we account for other "romantic attraction[s]" that deviate from the document's normative and appropriate allure (1)? How do we rectify those strange, odd, or queer appeals for evidence consisting not of "untainted" romantic papers but rather of the "taint" of the detrital?

Strange attractions for other states of evidence are a critical lynchpin in Meza's archival body, a body whose dissolution and displacement can hardly satisfy Cox's romantic desires for the "all absorbing" pull of the document (12). Meza's is a collection of residues that belongs to no "natural" family of record. In fact, efforts to certify and authenticate provenance is hard to delineate with little information about the origin of scraps. Meza's "queer detritus" requires a remove from these heteronormative archival logics and a move toward other methodologies and evidential possibilities. Queer performance theorists' understanding of archives through the ephemerality, vanishing, and eclipses of movement, speech, and live presence is quite beneficial. I am reminded of what José Esteban Muñoz argues is "the key to queering evidence . . . by suturing it to the concept of ephemera. Think of ephemera as trace, the remains, the things that are left, hanging in the air like a rumor."[26] Muñoz's position is laudable, sharing an important critique of queers' "vexed relationship to evidence," a relationship that can no longer rely on the stable document but rather must rely on queer acts of reembodied cultural transmission.[27]

In light of growing attention to queer feeling as archive, it is perhaps surprising that I want to reconsider other material states of documentation by seeking meaning not through the sutures of ephemerality alone but also through the anachronistic ware of AIDS devastation.[28] I find that fleeting queer performance gestures and Meza's archival debris are not mutually exclusive but coterminous at the shared vanishing point of disappearance. Neither an ephemeral act nor a concretized object entirely, Meza's queer detritus lies somewhere in between, expanding the terms of document and evidence showing other materialities—an archival body degrades, dematerializes, and wastes to the point of near absence. These gradients pose ways to read queer lives through a reenvisioning of the debris and the disarticulation of the wreckage. Like Muñoz, I, too, suggest that "the ephemeral does not equal unmateriality," and so my thinking about Meza's remains shares much with the fluctuating state of the material record itself as it ruins, wastes, and deteriorates.[29]

As cultural geographer Caitlin DeSilvey argues in her excellent assessment "Observed Decay: Telling Stories with Mutable Things": "An approach that understands the artifact as a process, rather than a stable entity with a durable physical form, is perhaps able to address some of the more ambiguous aspects of material presence (and disappearance)."[30] DeSilvey's position seems to circumvent systemic or "traditional" preservationist practices that leave Muñoz suspect, practices that strive for permanence and concretization in a way that evokes Cox's normalizing "romantic attraction" for documents that "pull" and "absorb." By drawing on the mutable states of evidence as processes, it is possible to challenge the reductive terms of document preservation relayed by historian David Lowenthal when he argues that "however venerated a relic, its decay is seldom admired."[31] Under his premise, decay is something to be abhorred by archivists and historians because it "also symbolizes failure."[32] Conflating a decaying relic with failure, Lowenthal's thinking perpetuates heteronormative archival epistemologies predicated on "success" of the new.

As queer theorist Judith (Jack) Halberstam notes, "Failing is something queers do and have always done exceptionally well."[33] Using this as my cue, we can use degradation as an episteme to rethink archive as failure. I want to embrace archival bodies ruined by decay as "ways of being and knowing that stand outside of conventional understandings of success."[34] After all, DeSilvey claims, "the disarticulation of the object may lead to the articulation of other histories, and other geographies."[35] Investigating Meza's discard in its strewn aftermath demands a queer detrital analysis that resists privileging particular modes of heteronormative document authority and rearticulates Chicano AIDS narratives, queer art histories, and material cultures across dissembled margins and detrital parts.

Told through the efforts of Legorreta, I discuss below his collection's finding aid, looking for Mundo in an unusual arrangement of discard and scrap. Critical ways of thinking about Meza's other materialities emerge with significant implications for the pair's life narrative, artistic production, and collaborative performance expression in East LA.

Mutating Materials: A Dance of Discard and Scavenge

In 2001 ONE National Gay and Lesbian Archives, one of the largest grassroots lesbian, gay, bisexual, and transgender (LGBT) repositories in the United States, secured an important acquisition from Legorreta, a formative figure in Chicano experimental performance art. A muse and cultural gadfly renowned for his conceptual street interventions festooned in barrio found materials, paints, and thrift store couture, Legorreta's alter ego "Cyclona" is part urban legend and part scandal. His visual and verbal assaults on unwitting Chicano publics in East LA were the stuff of rumor. Legorreta's autobiographical discourses about his own artistic becoming are quite fascinating because they closely intertwine with Meza.

First meeting in 1967, Legorreta and Meza were inseparable, finding a mutual affection, feeling of sexual alienation, and shared philosophical belief in "open[ing] people's minds."[36] Though Meza was three years younger, he and Legorreta stormed East LA, contesting heteromasculinist social norms and disciplining stares through convincing *chola* female impersonations, confrontational spectacles, and androgynous appearances. Their collaborations in the late 1960s demonstrate the ways that Chicano queers responded to the growing visibility of the gay liberation movement in LA coupled with the burgeoning political ideologies and artistic practices occurring in Southern California's barrios. Legorreta recollects: "We became a team, me and Mundo, running up and down Whittier Boulevard in this semidrag. . . . Of course, there was an element of our society at that time that couldn't dig it."[37]

Adding Legorreta's Garfield High School classmate Gronk to their gender-bending trinity in 1969, they collaborated in a variety of performance pieces, literally drawing on Legorreta's garish embodiments as a self-proclaimed "live art artist" and producing performance art interventions, same-sex wedding actions, and guerrilla liberation activities in LA's schizophrenic urban dystopia, freeway labyrinths, and sublime coastal landscapes.[38] The most iconic and frequently cited example of their brief union was *Caca-Roaches Have No Friends* performed in 1969 in East LA's Belvedere Park, where a simulated orgy and staged castration onstage incited the audience, fueling public outcry and explosive rioting.[39]

Legorreta's bodily excess produced an equal level of paper excess in terms of both performance documentation and, more importantly, "live art" figure studies. Taking Cyclona as subject, Gronk and Meza generated several life drawings in pen and ink, graphite, and color pastels, centering his androgynous form and introducing an iconoclastic language privileging the queer, strange, and bizarre in Chicano art. The Cyclona image traveled in paper illustrations, photographic snapshot, mail-art collage, and newspaper and literary journal publications, including *Gay Sunshine: A Newspaper of Gay Liberation* in 1973 and *Regeneración* in 1974.[40] In particular, Meza's work proved memorable because his propensity for surrealist fantasy, optical illusion, and photo-realism was sophisticated for his age.

While Gronk gradually departed from the triad, preferring to collaborate with Asco in 1972, their artistic activity continued through informal artist networks and social circuits in the "gay funky dances" organized through the Gay Community Services Center at Trouper's Hall.[41] The old auditorium on South La Brea served as the setting where photographer Anthony Friedkin developed a focus on East LA Chicano queers in his 1972 series *Gay: A Photographic Essay.*[42] Meza, Legorreta, and transgender artist-collaborator Jaime Aguilar were compelling subjects for the budding nineteen-year-old social documentarian. Just as Friedkin had discovered, Trouper's Hall was an undeniable cultural nexus for Chicano avant-gardists, urban fashionistas, and *cholo* bon vivants "living [their] art."[43] He recalls: "Suddenly, I'm in Trouper's Hall and all these young Chicano kids are coming into this gay dance. And they're coming into these restrooms, and they are so expressive [that] not only did . . . the women and the men have fantastic fashion and wardrobe and makeup, but they were open about who and what they were."[44] Gay liberation dance spaces catalyzed collaborative possibilities and social formations for East LA's youth acting out experimental ways of being in outrageous adornment and glamorous facades, a queer cultural infusion largely unacknowledged in Chicano cultural history and the story of the Chicano art movement, overall.

Though Meza and Legorreta's artistic collaborations waned later in the

Figure 1. This untitled pen-and-ink illustration by Mundo Meza is found in the "Silverlake Terrace Drawings" sketchbook (1979), one of the last compendiums of the young artist's works-on-paper from the Cyclona Collection. Ink on paper, 8 × 6 in. Cyclona Collection, ONE National Gay and Lesbian Archives, USC Libraries. Courtesy of Pat Meza, Elizabeth Signorelli, and Robert "Cyclona" Legorreta

1970s, their friendship persisted. Even when Meza ended a difficult relationship with his then boyfriend, Carlos, in 1979, he retreated to Legorreta's Silver Lake Terrace apartment, where he produced a small sketchbook of intricately lined figurative drawings, quoting German expressionism, pre-Columbian iconography, and postpunk style motifs derived from New Romanticism, a flamboyant fashion import personified by Leigh Bowery, Boy George, Steve Strange, and other Blitz Kids from the UK underground club scene in the late 1970s (see fig. 1).[45] In the collection, Meza's fragile spiral-bound notepad titled "Silverlake Terrace Drawings" remains one of the last compendiums of his works-on-paper.[46] Influenced by his extensive work in window display installation, mannequin aesthetics, and fashion merchandising at Maxfield Bleu's and Melon's on Melrose Avenue, Meza collaborated with Legorreta on a performance art series titled *Frozen Art* in June 1981.[47] These exercises signal Meza's burgeoning attention to duration, stillness, and the tableau vivant form, gesticulations forwarded in his collaborations with photographer Steven Arnold, who shared a mutual interest in suspended animation and the artist's "freeze frame eye."[48] When Meza died, Legorreta was deeply bereaved. So immobilized by grief, he refused to go to the funeral: "[I] could never see him dead, it really affected me very, very badly. He was like my best friend of twenty-five years. . . . That [affect] was a very, very weird thing, and a very, very psychic thing."[49]

From this loss, the Cyclona collection developed, appearing several decades later. Stewarded under the auspices of gay historian Stuart Timmons, it arrived at ONE in an assortment of black garbage bags, plastic shopping sacks, and battered cardboard boxes. The unruly excess of this amorphous archival form mimed the disordering chaos of garbage. Professional techniques founded on "original order," "evidentiary value," or "authenticity" were meaningless in Legorreta's conceptual repudiation of linearity, chronological arrangement, or document allure. Efforts to process and organize the collection also proved haphazard.[50] The enormity of his assembly, which included scraps, costumes, photographs, pornography, and props, remained only partially processed and made available to the public in 2011.[51]

Accompanying the gift was an equally curious finding aid written by Legorreta, titled "Cyclona Art Collection: The Gay, 'Chicanismo in el Arte.'" Reappropriating *Chicanismo en el Arte*, a historic exhibition cojuried by the Vincent and Mary Price Gallery at East Los Angeles College and the Los Angeles County Museum of Art in 1975, Legorreta's counterdiscourse denies these institutions' curatorial authority and historical representation of Chicano art.[52] In a conceptualist gesture, he authors a truer iteration of the past, archiving "The Gay" and affixing it to the original title. His intervention stages a reencounter with the show, uprooting its grip on Chicano art history and actualizing our complacent acceptance of the museum as an apparatus of cultural propaganda. Such political liberation could happen only through Cyclona's "mind-bending" mediation in this postmodernist archival form.

Unbound and handwritten on nearly sixty pages of text on loose-leaf notebook paper, Legorreta's vernacular finding aid presents a series of four Chicana/o artists: Gronk, Roberto Gutierrez, Meza, and Valdez. They are joined not by their aesthetic unity but by their mutual points of encounter with the Cyclona figure, a discourse omitted from the original *Chicanismo en el Arte* exhibition in 1975. The registry writes Legorreta's narrative, relaying personal memories, career highlights, anachronistic citations, and social documentation in accordance to his artist subjects. Legorreta's descriptive verse navigates the discards. His inventoried set of annotations inscribes an interpretative schema onto the collection, displacing more traditional practices founded on the unseen hand of the archive administrator.

Empirical proof is inconsequential to Legorreta's fact telling in a maneuver that similarly echoes Muñoz's thoughts on queer evidence "hanging in the air like a rumor."[53] For example, regarding a scant illustration drawn by Meza, Legorreta writes: "Self-Portrait of Mundo in his First week at Garfield High School. He looks somewhat puzzled. Didn't we all [?], Circa 1971 East, L.A."[54] Whether this drawing is Meza's self-portrait from high school is a minor consideration when compared to Legorreta's affirming appraisal. His historical citation pivots from third-person to second-person narrative writing with a style that merges performance oration with library science. "Didn't we all [?]" is a clever rhetorical shift taking the reader from visual interpretation to corroborating informant, appealing to the inventory user directly. The reader becomes an incidental collaborator.

Legorreta marks each discard with a number in purple ink, generating a corresponding code retrieval system. In the series "Mundo Art," which forms the bulk

Figure 2. Mundo Meza's *Laughing Fish* (ca. 1970) was found on the inverse side of a school bell schedule from Garfield High School in East LA. Ink on paper, 4 ½ × 6 ¾ in. Cyclona Collection, ONE National Gay and Lesbian Archives, USC Libraries. Courtesy of Pat Meza, Elizabeth Signorelli, and Robert "Cyclona" Legorreta

of the collection, careful classification and lengthy diatribes follow detrital castoffs, interlinking extratextual layers to the seeming frivolity of the material itself, material that appears more scrap than document romance. For instance, item 7 refers to a surrealist illustration titled *Laughing Fish*, circa 1970. The diminutive drawing discovered on the back of a Garfield High School class bell schedule was presumably produced during an ordinary school day (see fig. 2). Between 1970 and 1971 Meza was briefly enrolled there, attending alongside Asco members Gamboa, Gronk, Herrón, and Valdez. The illustration contains no title or date, hinting at its happenstance production. With no formal evidence of transfer, we might deduce that the drawing was orphaned, discarded, or gifted.

If record appraisal must defer to the "source in the order designated by the originating agency," then Legorreta's "thick description" provides sufficient support from which authenticity and validation are satisfied.[55] His annotation attributes a name, but the lack of title in Meza's penned hand suggests the scrap's ambiguity, hanging onto the inventory itself for meaning. The entry continues: "The piece depicts Mundo's coming of age with his sexuality. The piece shows androgynous characters and has in most of Mundo's early art. He uses his body within the characters drawn. Mundo was in harmony with both parts of his sexuality. Also depicted in the piece is Cyclona on the upper right corner of drawing."[56] Legorreta's interpretation allows for more explicitly personal, relational, and biographical details to appear anchored in Meza's pen and ink work. His observations elevate the ordinary paper scrap as an interface, a picture window where Meza is seen. His body is drawn into the interlocking nude figures compositing the androgynous arrangement. Quoting the Cyclona figure in the far right perimeter of the image allows Legorreta to unify his alter ego with Meza's body in a harmonious transgender and trans-species ecology. The autobiographical testimony he enlists through the registry furthers this permeability by showing how the paper fragment is a critical means of finding Mundo and traces of his bodily imprint.

Laughing Fish elucidates the mutability of the paper's material form. The reversibility of the visual picture plane bends the textual surface back, revealing Meza's body inscribed beneath. Legorreta's finding aid consists of these ephem-era shape-shifters expanding the utility of remnants and scraps. Abandoned pencil studies, frayed paperboard, and torn drawing paper demonstrate Meza's human impressions in word, mark, and image. A pink phone message slip doubles as a homoerotic sketch of male nudes in graphite. A temporary parking pass from Barnsdall Art Park in Hollywood reverses to show an offhand pen-and-ink illustration of abstract lines and amorphous shapes. A trivial wrapper for Zig-Zag tobacco paper popularly used to roll marijuana cigarettes mutates, becoming the stage from which the "Zig-Zag Drag Queen" appears. Arguably, Meza's multiple reuse of refuse was not uncommon, particularly among Latina/o artists with limited means. In Chicano cultural studies, Tomas Ybarra-Frausto refers to it as a *rasquache* sensibility, a vernacular expression finding "resilience and resourcefulness . . . from making do with what is at hand," drawing "its essence within the world of the

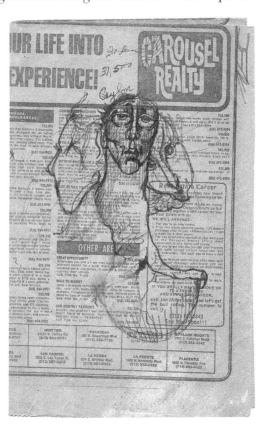

Figure 3. According to Legorreta's finding aid, Meza frequently used newsprint in the absence of sketch paper. This illustration, ca. 1974, is one example later recovered in the Cyclona collection. Ink on newspaper, 7 ¼ × 11 ½ in. Cyclona Collection, ONE National Gay and Lesbian Archives, USC Libraries. Courtesy of Pat Meza, Elizabeth Signorelli, and Robert "Cyclona" Legorreta

tattered, shattered, and broken."[57] A similar practice might be observed in Meza's artistic expressions on paper.

This aesthetic is indicative in item 48, where a piece of newsprint is "one of the many newspaper drawings done by Mundo on a spare moment while there was no paper around" (see fig. 3).[58] Meza's multiple uses of newsprint indicate that his art practice "with what is at hand" was common in the absence of sketch paper.[59] The versatility of the printed surface was not only a matter of limited means in Ybarra-Frausto's sense but also a method of visual messaging and artist communication. Meza and Legorreta's personal transactions took place on commercial paper materials. Phone messages, birthday greetings, and playfully coded referents to drug paraphernalia were conveyed in mimetic illustrations of the occasion. Art and life blur in a way that recalls Gronk's comparable approach, about which he says: "I think if you look at the drawings in my journals, it is me biographically. It's just like automatic writing in a way, but with drawings."[60] Together, these artists demonstrate analogous modes of experimental writing and social documentation in Chicano avant-gardism, especially if we consider Gronk's related artistic expressions on paper napkins.[61] However, Meza and Legorreta's practice is explicitly relational, withstanding Gronk's more monologist visual psychography. Reliance on formal written communication was less characteristic of their correspondence. Bits of paper, text, and picture trail their interactions.

In addition to identifying Meza's imprint in *Laughing Fish*, Legorreta makes similar claims elsewhere in the finding aid, observing the artist's body residues in fashion design illustrations, androgynous subjects, and surreal fantasy landscapes. For instance, in item 21 he regards a water-stained pen-and-ink sketch of mannequin sculptural heads as a self-portrait exercise: "Mundo was still working on his image. [He] drew several face shapes and personality shapes on each face, circa 1978, Hollywood."[62] Legorreta finds Meza plotting himself through unstable bodily surfaces, artistic allusions, and oscillating personas. His apparent rescue of these drawings in varied stages of physical distress says as much about Meza's image production as it does the causal relationship he held for his work. If these drawings could be produced at a "spare moment" on widely available paper materials mined from the barrio, how does this explain Legorreta's collecting of them mutating the borders between art, record, and waste?

The multiple detrital discards that proliferate in Legorreta's finding aid not only provide critical insights into Meza's nearly careless relationship with his works-on-paper but also expand the definition of provenance. For instance, the lengthiest annotations in the inventory are items 3 and 3b, a set of four "spiritual and cosmic" pen-and-ink illustrations on poster-board pieces, remnants perhaps from a completed art project. In a three-page entry, Legorreta claims that the *Orange Sunshine* series, a reference to the popular psychotropic drug, was produced by a twelve-year-old Meza in late 1967 at Doc's People, an alternative art space named after

H. G. Wells's 1896 science fiction novel *The Island of Dr. Moreau*.[63] In January 1968, Legorreta joined this cadre of mostly Chicano teen artists unified in their literary fantasy of mutant rebellion and interspecies splicing, an apt metaphor given the violence and nihilism engulfing East LA at this time. As he describes: "[I] found these pieces scattered all over [the garage] floor. So I said to myself, 'Who would throw these fabulous pieces of art away?' So I picked them up, took them home, [and] put them away. Several years later I mentioned these to Mundo. . . . I showed them to him and he said, 'Yes! That's me!' "[64]

Legorreta's finding aid establishes that these orphaned discards appear with minor consideration of self-preservation, record keeping, or the art marketplace (something unimaginable for most young, self-taught Chicano artists at this time). They are evanescent creative expressions, and much like the trailing newsprint drawings, they can happen "on a spare moment." In the finding aid, the *Orange Sunshine* series gains legibility and, in turn, evidentiary value only when Meza confirms artist attribution in declaring, "Yes! That's me!" However, his initial self-citation in the *Orange Sunshine* series does not end here, suggesting Legorreta's resistance to more conventional definitions of provenance. Through the inventory, he contends that the paper scraps do more than authenticate the record creator; they literalize Meza's "power," "energy," and rebirth "cleansed by the flames of life and now reach[ing] beyond himself."[65] While it is not clear if Meza supplied this metaphysical assessment after the lost drawings' rediscovery in 1968, Legorreta inscribes this view in his weighty annotation.

Observing that Meza's self-picturing reaches beyond human mortality toward higher ways of being, Legorreta's found scraps are anything but ordinary, providing clairvoyant portals into Meza's lifespan. The found drawings speculate AIDS-related loss, a loss that can be seen and prophesied through the discarded picture planes. Legorreta continues: "Mundo was a very old wise spirit. . . . . [He] would be on Earth for only 29 years and left a body of incredible artwork."[66] Writing his finding aid retrospectively in 2001, several years after Meza's death, Legorreta in his annotation discursively bonds anachronistic moments of creation, death, and rebirth, "finding AIDS" in the queer detritus recovered from an East LA garage in 1968.

Legorreta assumes the role of the scavenger recovering the residues, protecting the detrital, and safeguarding the waste. He finds meaning in Meza's bodily discards strewn along the floor like trash. Meza, however, functions as the discarder, orphaning drawings, scattering materials, and dropping personal affects in his path. Together, they choreograph a dance of presence and absence, lost and found, a contentious duet that relieves itself in the "live art" embodiments and found object personas that defined their experimental performance art practice.[67] Meza's momentary acts of artistic creation and Legorreta's propensity to acquire enabled closer correlations between the material record and body surface, engendering other ways of being Chicano in this tumultuous period of social unrest, a queer racialized subjectivity drawn from the scraps.[68] It comes as no surprise that Legorreta's later archiving work continued this formative conceptualist practice, looking for Mundo against the dissolution of AIDS in the remnants, surrogacies, and castoffs structuring his transgressive archival body.

Between Lost and Found: Toward Queer Detrital Analysis
Finding AIDS at the ends of material culture, the search for Meza intensifies what constitutes "document" and "evidence," particularly considering the neglect of queer racialized cultural histories in both mainstream and gay and lesbian repositories. Though Legorreta initially gifted his materials to ONE National Gay and Lesbian Archives (now an affiliate of the University of Southern California [USC] Libraries), his queer vision for debris proved overwhelming, prompting the formation of an equally eclectic collection titled The Fire of Life / El Fuego de la Vida, acquisitioned by the University of California, Los Angeles (UCLA), Chicano Studies Research Center in 2004. His occupation of both institutions is a strategic intervention, showing queer Chicano cultural remains irreconcilability in a singular repository, especially in sprawling LA. In identitarian terms, the incompleteness of these organizations, one gay and the other Chicano, necessitated acts of archive promiscuity, resulting in Legorreta's simultaneous depositing across public record administrations and institutional thresholds.

Throughout this essay, I have questioned the heteronormative bias undergirding conventional archive methods and practices predicated on families of record, document desire, and untarnished chains of custody and ownership. The perspective I posit gleamed from a queer detrital analysis expands the terms of bodily remaining, the mutability of remnants, and the navigational possibility of finding aids in wading discards, imperceptible debris, and textual incompletion. Thus the fragments that compose Meza's archival body lead one to ask: What state of documentation must be mined to sufficiently articulate an artist's life? What tests of evidentiary meaning must be met to satisfy document authority and authenticity? How do detrital states of things challenge the uneven assignment of historical and literary "significance"? More specifically, how does a direct confrontation with the queerness of record "failure" allow for other archival methodologies founded on *near* absence?

For those of us working on the fallout occurring in the early years of the AIDS crisis, queer detritus is a familiar experience. The castoff is often all that is left, and so the restoration of missing artworks in conventional archival, historical, or curatorial discipline is hardly satisfactory. Returning archival bodies to some heteronormative evidentiary logic or measure of document validity is equally discomforting.[69] I echo what art historian Bethan Stevens poses, that "artworks whose whereabouts is unknown . . . make rewarding objects of study in their own right. . . . Like memory, lost works can turn disciplinary definitions on their heads."[70] As I continue to explore the wreckage of Meza's discards, some reports have surfaced offering the whereabouts of his vanished art collection, but as Muñoz eloquently reminds us, "it hang[s] in the air like a rumor."[71] Not yet publicly accessible in its entirety, it looms in what Diana Taylor calls "repertoire," existing as bits of speculation or gossip.[72] According to Gavin Butt, gossip has a crucial role keeping sexual knowledge in "discursive play" due to the "paucity of sexual evidence."[73] Like Butt, I parlay "art rumor" as another evidentiary facet shaping an extratextual layer of the Meza archive. A direct path to these vanished works beyond the talk is unclear and, in queer detrital terms, even necessary. Instead, we must embrace other states of things and interpret the residues, allowing for a queer vision of debris in the fragments of paper and picture to come through. Thus the archival bodies emerging from this plague ask that we expand the terms and methods where queer evidence is used, finding *AIDS* at the brink of ruin and human loss.

Notes

1. *Urban exile* is a term famously coined by Gamboa. See Harry Gamboa Jr., "Urban Exile," in *Urban Exile: Collected Writings of Harry Gamboa Jr.*, ed. Chon A. Noriega (Minneapolis: University of Minnesota Press, 1998), 51–55.

2. Several new art-historical texts have been invaluable to unfettering the relationships between Chicano avant-gardists. See, e.g., C. Ondine Chavoya and Rita Gonzalez, eds., *Asco: Elite of the Obscure; A Retrospective, 1972–1987* (Los Angeles: Los Angeles County Museum of Art; Ostfildern, Germany: Hatje Cantz), 2011.

3. Meza's last years are touchingly retold in elegiac and witty prose by his former lover, roommate, and fellow window dresser, Simon Doonan. See Simon Doonan, *Beautiful People: My Family and Other Glamorous Varmints* (New York: Simon and Schuster Paperbacks), 2005.

4. Adam Nagourney, "Los Angeles Stakes Its Claim as a World Art Center," *New York Times*, October 13, 2011.

5. Bethan Stevens, "Remembering Lost Paintings: Vanessa Bell's *The Nursery*," *Memory Studies* 3, no. 3 (2010): 250.

6. Chris Hurley, "The Making and the Keeping of Records: (1) What Are Finding Aids For?" *Archives and Manuscripts* 26, no. 1 (1998): 60.

7. Mathias Danbolt, "Touching History: Archival Relations in Queer Art and Theory," in *Lost and Found: Queerying the Archive*, ed. Mathias Danbolt, Jane Rowley, and Louise Wolthers (Copenhagen: Nikolaj, Copenhagen Contemporary Art Center, 2009), 36.

8. Ibid., 37.

9. James M. O'Toole, "On the Idea of Permanence," in *American Archival Studies: Readings in Theory and Practice*, ed. Randall C. Jimerson (Chicago: Society of American Archivists, 2000), 490.

10. Shelley Sweeney, "The Ambiguous Origins of the Archival Principle of 'Provenance,'" *Libraries and the Cultural Record* 43, no. 2 (2008): 193.

11. Hal Foster, "An Archival Impulse," *October*, no. 110 (2004): 5.

12. Ibid.

13. Greg Noble, "Accumulating Being," *International Journal of Cultural Studies* 7, no. 2 (2004): 233–56.

14. Jennifer González, "Autotopographies," in *Prosthetic Territories: Politics and Hypertechnologies*, ed. Gabriel Brahm Jr. and Mark Driscoll (Boulder, CO: Westview, 1995). "Repertoire" references the key text by Diana Taylor, *The Archive and the Repertoire: Performing Cultural Memory in the Americas* (Durham, NC: Duke University Press, 2003). Amelia Jones, "Lost Bodies: Early 1970s Los Angeles Performance Art in Art History," in *Live Art in LA: Performance in Southern California*, ed. Peggy Phelan (New York: Routledge, 2012), 117.

15. On the development of the "golden age" of archive theory, see Terry Cook, "What Is Past Is Prologue: A History of Archival Ideas since 1898, and the Future Paradigm Shift," *Archivaria*, no. 43 (1997): 17–63. Also, the intersections of archivist and historian are debated with attention to Jenkinson's early theorizations of archive record administration. See Francis X. Blouin Jr. and William G. Rosenberg, *Processing the Past: Contesting Authority in History and the Archives* (Oxford: Oxford University Press, 2011).

16. See, e.g., Sweeney, "Ambiguous Origins."

17. Ibid., 197.

18. Blouin and Rosenberg, *Processing the Past*, 30–31.

19. See Jacques Derrida, *Archive Fever: A Freudian Impression*, trans. Eric Prenowitz (Chicago: University of Chicago Press, 1998); and also Joan Schwartz and Terry Cook, "Archives, Records, and Power: The Making of Modern Memory," *Archival Science* 2, nos. 1–2 (2002): 1–19.

20. Lee Edelman, *No Future: Queer Theory and the Death Drive* (Durham, NC: Duke University Press, 2004), 2.

21. Xiaomi An, "An Integrated Approach to Records Management," *Information Management Journal* 37, no. 4 (2003): 25. Also consider Sue McKemmish, "Placing Records Continuum Theory and Practice," *Archival Science* 1, no. 4 (2001): 333–59.

22. An, "An Integrated Approach to Records Management," 25. See also Jay Kennedy and Cherryl Schauder, *Records Management: A Guide to Corporate Recordkeeping*, 2nd ed. (South Melbourne: Longman, 1998).

23. I draw on the term *queer kinship* with specific allegiances to key works on the matter. See, e.g., Elizabeth Freeman, "Queer Belongings: Kinship Theory and Queer Theory," in *A Companion to Lesbian, Gay, Bisexual, Transgender, and Queer Studies*, ed. George Haggerty and Molly McGarry (Malden, MA: Blackwell, 2008), 293–314.

24. Derrida, *Archive Fever*, 4; Richard J. Cox, "The Romance of the Document," *Records and Information Management Report* 22, no. 1 (2006): 1–13.

25. Cox, "Romance of the Document," 12.

26. José Esteban Muñoz, *Cruising Utopia: The Then and There of Queer Futurity* (New York: New York University Press, 2009), 65.

27. Ibid.

28. See Ann Cvetkovich, *An Archive of Feelings: Trauma, Sexuality, and Lesbian Public Cultures* (Durham, NC: Duke University Press, 2003).

29. Muñoz, *Cruising Utopia*, 81.

30. Caitlin DeSilvey, "Observed Decay: Telling Stories with Mutable Things," *Journal of Material Culture* 11, no. 3 (2006): 324.

31. David Lowenthal, *The Past Is a Foreign Country* (Cambridge: Cambridge University Press, 1985), 143.

32. Ibid., 147.

33. Judith Halberstam, *The Queer Art of Failure* (Durham, NC: Duke University Press, 2011), 3.

34. Ibid., 2.

35. DeSilvey, "Observed Decay," 324.
36. "Cyclona and Early Chicano Performance Art: An Interview with Robert Legorreta," by Jennifer Flores Sternad, *GLQ: A Journal of Lesbian and Gay Studies* 12, no. 3 (2006): 481.
37. Ibid.
38. Robb Hernández, *The Fire of Life: The Robert Legorreta–Cyclona Collection* (Los Angeles: University of California, Los Angeles [UCLA], Chicano Studies Research Center, 2009), ix.
39. Ibid., 6–8.
40. Selections of Anthony Friedkin's photo shoots with Mundo Meza, Jaime Aguilar, and Cyclona were featured in *Gay Sunshine: A Newspaper of Gay Liberation*, September–October 1973. An illustration of Cyclona and Meza by Popcorn, one of Gronk's alter egos, appeared in *Regeneración*, 2, no. 4 (1974–75): 16.
41. Joey Terrill, interview by the author, August 23, 2007, Los Angeles, CA.
42. See Anthony Friedkin, *The Gay Essay*, ed. Julian Cox with Nayland Blake and Eileen Myles (San Francisco: Fine Arts Museums of San Francisco; New Haven, CT: Yale University Press, 2014), 66–71.
43. Terrill, interview.
44. Anthony Friedkin, interview by the author, September 4, 2010, Santa Monica, CA.
45. Van Dyk Lewis, "Music and Fashion," in *The Berg Companion to Fashion*, ed. Valerie Steele (New York: Berg, 2010), 525.
46. For more, see "Silverlake Terrace Drawings," 1979, item 22, Mundo Art, "Cyclona Art Collection: The Gay, 'Chicanismo in el Arte,'" finding aid, ONE National Gay and Lesbian Archives, University of Southern California (USC) Libraries, Los Angeles.
47. Hernández, *Fire of Life*, 18.
48. Peter Weiermair, ed., *Steven Arnold: "Exotic Tableaux"* (Kilchberg/Zurich, Switzerland: Edition Stemmle, 1996), 9.
49. Quoted in Hernández, *Fire of Life*, 20.
50. On the alleged deaccessioning of Legorreta's collection at ONE, see ibid., 29–31.
51. Legorreta developed The Fire of Life for the UCLA Chicano Studies Research Center under librarian Yolanda Retter, a former archivist of ONE. See Frank Morales, "Liberating Unleashed Latino/Gay-Themed Artifacts," *Orange County and Long Beach Blade*, July 2004, 60–61. For insights into Legorreta's relationship with Retter, see Herndon Davis, "A Home for L.A.'s Gay Latin Performers, Dr. Yolanda Retter's Quest to Preserve the Past," *Frontiers* 25, no. 3 (2006): 179.
52. Jeanne D'Andrea, *Chicanismo en el Arte*, exhibition catalog (Los Angeles: Los Angeles County Museum of Art and East Los Angeles College, 1975).
53. Muñoz, *Cruising Utopia*, 65.
54. *Self-Portrait of Mundo*, early 1970s, item 54, Mundo Art, "Cyclona Art Collection Finding Aid." Note: Legorreta has publicly addressed his personal learning difficulties due to dyslexia. I transcribed all entries and take full responsibility for any error of word or meaning.
55. Sweeney, "Ambiguous Origins," 199. Also, "thick description" refers to Clifford Geertz's regarded ethnographic approach in cultural anthropology. See Clifford Geertz, *The Interpretation of Cultures* (New York: Basic Books, 1973).
56. *Laughing Fish*, ca. 1970, item 7, Mundo Art, "Cyclona Art Collection."
57. Tomas Ybarra-Frausto, "Rasquachismo: A Chicano Sensibility," in *Chicano Art: Resistance and Affirmation, 1965–1985*, ed. Shifra Goldman et al. (Los Angeles: Wight Art Gallery, 1991), 156.
58. Newsprint drawing, ca. 1974, item 48, Mundo Art, "Cyclona Art Collection."

59. Ibid.

60. Quoted in Jennifer Flores Sternad, "Painting Stages / Performing Life: Gronk," *Contemporary Theatre Review* 15, no. 3 (2005): 341.

61. For example, consider Max Benavidez, *Gronk* (Minneapolis: University of Minnesota Press, 2007), 7, 63.

62. Pen-and-ink self-portrait of Mundo's face, ca. 1978, item 21, Mundo Art, "Cyclona Art Collection."

63. H. G. Wells, *The Island of Dr. Moreau* (London: W. Heinemann, 1896).

64. *Orange Sunshine* (series of four drawings), ca. 1967, items 3 and 3b, Mundo Art, "Cyclona Art Collection."

65. Ibid.

66. Ibid. Similar sentiments are relayed by Legorreta in Hernández, *Fire of Life*, 20.

67. Hernández, *Fire of Life*, ix.

68. Ibid., 14.

69. See Danbolt, "Touching History," 36.

70. Stevens, "Remembering Lost Paintings," 250.

71. Muñoz, *Cruising Utopia*, 65.

72. See Taylor, *Archive and the Repertoire*.

73. Gavin Butt, *Between You and Me: Queer Disclosures in the New York Art World, 1948–1963* (Durham, NC: Duke University Press, 2005), 5.

The Queer Archivist as Political Dissident

Rereading the Ottoman Empire
in the Works of Reşad Ekrem Koçu

Rüstem Ertuğ Altınay

In 1971, Istanbul, Muzaffer Gökman was working on a biography of the historian Ahmed Refik Altınay. When he contacted Altınay's former assistant Reşad Ekrem Koçu, who had also written a biography of the historian, Koçu asked Gökman to visit him in his apartment. Koçu was a prolific popular historian who had produced an important canon on the Ottoman Empire. At the time, he was sixty-six years old, and he seldom left his apartment. Having retired from his teaching career, he had devoted his life to his archival practice and *İstanbul ansiklopedisi* (*The Encyclopedia of Istanbul*), a massive project he started in 1944 and continued until his death in 1975. Gökman's narration of their encounter is an intense story of melancholic relations with the past, sustained through archival practice and disordered "book packages":

The whole apartment, all corridors and all rooms, were full of book packages. Without disturbing the heaps of packages on the floor, we jumped over them to enter the living room. . . . He explicated the paintings adorning the walls of the room and the corridor. Every painting suddenly turned into a piece of history. . . . He ran to the other room. He didn't come back for a while. Then he brought a His Master's Voice brand windup gramophone, which he said he had taken out from among the packages, and very carefully placed it on the table

Radical History Review
Issue 122 (May 2015)   DOI 10.1215/01636545-2849549

that was chock full of books and notes. Again with great care, he cleaned a
dusty record. With his weak arm, he wound the gramophone with difficulty; he
didn't let me help. Then we sat at the opposite sides of the table and listened to
Münir Nureddin sing. . . . A teardrop emerged in the corner of late Koçu's eye
and ran down his cheek that had not been shaved for a few days.

    Reşad Ekrem Koçu was living a history.

    The record stopped spinning and silence filled the room. A home full of
history, a room full of history, and a historian who was in love with Ottoman
history, a species that has gone extinct.[1]

The melancholia described by Gökman was characteristic of Koçu's life and works.[2]
Defined by a queer subjectivity bearing the mark of national and personal traumas, Koçu's melancholia was also the guiding force behind his archival practice that
evolved into a physical and affective communion. Koçu believed that "those who
thought, knew, loved, and wrote never died," and he used the archive as a medium
to communicate with the ghosts of the past.[3] With the aid of paintings, records, and
a plethora of objects and documents, he unearthed what Michel Foucault terms
"subjugated knowledges": the forms of knowledge or experience that "have been
disqualified as inadequate to their task or insufficiently elaborated: naive knowledges, located low down in the hierarchy, beneath the required level of cognition
or scientificity."[4] As he explored the marginal and submerged voices, Koçu not only
reinscribed these subjects into the history of the nation but also resisted the hegemonic modes of historical knowledge production and challenged the legitimacy of
the social norms that regulate the present.

    In this essay, I present an overview of Koçu's life and works in relation to
the dynamics of modernization, archiving, and nation building in Turkey. As I analyze the ramifications of these processes on the politics of historiography, I discuss
how Koçu's archival practice, guided by his melancholia for the empire, operated as
both a form of political resistance and a strategy for queer self-making. Focusing on
the conservative politics of neo-Ottomanism in contemporary Turkey, I investigate
the reconfiguration of the political potentials of Koçu's works at the intersection of
conflicting political projects. A case study of Koçu also facilitates a discussion on
the ambiguities of the queer archive as a political project as well as the study of
queer resistance in the humanities. *Queer* here refers to an analytical tool to study
the embodied practices, structures of feeling, and modes of identification that are
"at odds with the normal, the legitimate, the dominant" in ways that are intrinsi-
cally related to gender and sexuality.[5] Not all the people, practices, and spaces Koçu
wrote about involved such strong tensions with the norms of gender and sexuality in their time. Nevertheless, as a consequence of the sociohistorical contexts in
which Koçu produced his texts and his occasional use of the mid-twentieth-century
Western paradigms of sexuality in his accounts of Ottoman history as well as the

genealogies he constructed across centuries, many of them also produce this effect anachronistically.

Nation Building and the Politics of Historiography in Early Republican Turkey

The formative years of the Republic of Turkey, following the country's inception in 1923, were characterized by a series of legal, political, cultural, social, and economic reforms that aimed to construct a modern, Western, secular (albeit implicitly Sunni Muslim) nation-state. Ernst Renan argues that forgetting is central to the creation of any nation, and Turkey was no exception.[6] The regime required the citizens in the making to forsake their memory of and affective investment in the elements of Ottoman political, cultural, and social life so that they could invest in the nation-state project. In 1930, under the directive of the president, Mustafa Kemal Atatürk, prominent historians of the time embarked on researching Turkish history to produce a new past for the young nation-state. These efforts culminated in the "Turkish History Thesis," which was first presented in the volume *Türk tarihinin ana hatları (Outlines of Turkish History)* in 1930 and later developed in other works.[7] The thesis argued that long before the Ottoman Empire, the ancestors of Turks had established higher civilizations in Central Asia, but they were forced by environmental circumstances to migrate, and it was these people who established many of the world's major civilizations. With the invention of this foundational myth, the Ottoman Empire was framed as a relatively short and rather unsuccessful phase in Turkish history. The shift in historiography operated hand in hand with the language policies. With the Law on the Adoption and Implementation of the Turkish Alphabet, passed in 1928, the Turkish form of the Arabic script that was used in the Ottoman Empire was replaced by a modified version of the Latin script. This policy was designed to sever the country's ties with its Ottoman past and its Middle Eastern neighbors. In 1932 the script reform was supplemented with a language reform that aimed to eliminate the words borrowed from foreign languages, particularly Arabic and Persian. Thus Ottoman Turkish soon became a "foreign language," and the archives were rendered illegible to the vast majority of the population. As people depended on the mediation of a second language to access Ottoman history, they became alienated from this past.

While many historians joined the official historiography movement, there were also some, including Koçu, who chose not to be involved. Koçu was born in Istanbul in 1905. His father, Ekrem Reşad, was a school administrator and journalist, who also worked for history magazines.[8] After early childhood in Istanbul, Koçu completed his elementary and high school education in Konya and Bursa. Spending the formative years of his life in three of the Ottoman Empire's major cities exposed him to both the country's rich cultural heritage and the destitution of the war-torn empire during its final years. After graduating from high school in 1927, Koçu returned to Istanbul to study in Istanbul Darülfünun's Department of History, where he worked closely with the department's chair, Altınay, a prominent historian of the Ottoman Empire.[9] Altınay's canon, comprising more than 120 books and countless newspaper articles, prioritized accessibility, literary pleasure, and gripping subjects— strategies that helped him reach readers across generations. This popular historian whom Koçu loved dearly would be very influential to him. Following his mentor's footsteps, Koçu would frequent public archives and secondhand booksellers, trace and collect unusual documents, and publicize these archives at the intersection of literature and historiography.[10] After completing his studies in 1931, he became a teaching and research assistant for Altınay, a position that in the Turkish academic system was expected to operate on a tenure track.[11] In Koçu's case, however, this would not be an option due to his mentor's resistance to complying with the official trends in historiography. Unlike many historians of the period, Altınay insisted on working on his passion, the Ottoman Empire. In the sociopolitical context of early republican Turkey, Altınay's work was interpreted as irrelevant if not dangerous, and his political activities in the late Ottoman era also cast doubt on his loyalty to the regime.[12] Despite being a productive and well-known scholar, he lost his post after the university reform of 1933. Altınay spent the remaining years of his life as a lonely author in poverty and died of pneumonia in 1937.[13] Koçu shared his mentor's curiosity and passion for the history of the Ottoman Empire. Hence when Altınay lost his university post, so did he.[14] Never returning to academia, he continued his life as a high school history teacher and writer. Koçu's early works, such as his graduation thesis on the Ottoman conquest of Crete and the book *Osmanlı muahedeleri ve kapitülasyonlar 1300–1920 ve Lozan Muahedesi 24 Temmuz 1923 (Treaties and Capitulations of the Ottoman Empire, 1300–1920, and the Treaty of Lausanne, July 24, 1923)* adhered to the conventions of academic writing.[15] Nevertheless, his rise to fame would come with his popular history books and historical fiction.

At a time when the republican elite rejected the country's Ottoman heritage, Koçu and Altınay's archival and historiographical practices operated as a mode of melancholic resistance to the politics of the nation-state. José Esteban Muñoz, in his study of the disidentificatory survival practices available to minoritarian subjects, presents a reading of melancholia that defines this structure of feeling not as pathology but, for certain subjects, as a part of the everyday processes of dealing with catastrophes. For Muñoz, melancholia "is a mechanism that helps us (re) construct identity and take our dead with us to the various battles we must wage in their names—and in our names."[16] As the subjects of an empire defeated first by the European powers and then by the republic, as disoriented citizens in the making who were forced to forsake the affective and political investments they previously had in order to invest in a new governmental order, as historians who were punished for not forgetting the history that they lived and loved, Koçu and Altınay resisted the politics of the nation-state with their melancholic attachment to the empire.

Koçu and Altinay's historiography work challenges the way we tend to conceptualize queer resistance today. In the 1980s, a preoccupation with "resistance" increasingly gained power in the humanities and social sciences literature. These works reflect a concern with "unlikely forms of resistance, subversions rather than large-scale collective insurrections, small or local resistances not tied to the overthrow of systems or even to ideologies of emancipation."[17] Another important aspect of this literature, which is still powerful in the liberal Western academy, is the assumption that there is a necessary relationship between resistance and the goals of progressive politics. The case of Koçu and Altınay complicates this logic because the subject of their melancholic attachment is the empire. I would not propose an ethico-political hierarchy between the empire and the nation-state—the complex nature of the two systems, the heterogeneity inherent in their long histories, and the diversity of the subjects' experiences within and around their borders would render a comparison infeasible. Nevertheless, the various forms of violence that define imperial politics as well as the inequalities that characterize the empire's social structure make it an unconventional object for a study on queer resistance. Still, this melancholic attachment does operate as a mode of resistance because it entails imagining and investing in a world that is different from the one that is presently available—in this case an investment that defies the logic of capitalism and even survival as demonstrated by the fact that both authors lost their academic careers and wealth as well as social support networks.

The sexual desires of Koçu that conflicted with the norms allow him to be classified as a queer subject. The authors' queerness, however, is also grounded in their political imaginations and the functioning of the nation-state as a political project. The concept of the nation-state as a site where a nation formed by individuals sharing a history and cultural and ethnic heritage coincides with a sovereign territorial unit with clearly defined borders is by definition a utopian one. Since all nation-state projects rely on an imaginary history to legitimize their existence and the physical and affective investment of individuals living in the present toward a desired future, the production of national subjects is of central importance for their sustenance. And because gender and sexuality play a key role in subject-formation processes, the failure to become a national subject is, in a sense, a queer experience independent from the subject's sexual desires and practices of pleasure.[18] In that sense, the historians' investment in the Ottoman Empire in early republican Turkey is productive of queer subjectivity because of the fundamental conflict between the hegemonic imaginations about "the Turkish man" at the time and their objects of political attachment and desires for belonging.

A Queer Archivist and His Narrative Strategies

An important element that defined Koçu's melancholic attachment to the Ottoman Empire and his archival practice was his sexual subjectivity. Koçu's desires became a topic of public debate primarily after Orhan Pamuk wrote about the subject first in an essay published in the Turkish edition of *National Geographic* magazine in 2002 and later in the book *Istanbul: Memories and the City*, where he identified Koçu as "homosexual."[19] In a response to Pamuk in 2002, historian Murat Bardakçı, who has also published on the queer history of the Ottoman Empire, acknowledged that Koçu was "homosexual" yet argued that he belonged to a specific category of male sexual subjectivity, known as *cemal aşığı*, "a lover of facial beauty."[20] This sexual category was characterized by the pleasure derived from watching beautiful young men, and it is mentioned in a number of biographies in *The Encyclopedia of Istanbul*. The article "Galib (Çımacı) [the Dockhand]" written by Vasıf Hiç suggests that being "a lover of facial beauty" was considered to be morally higher than engaging in sexual intercourse: "He performed abstinence. He was only a lover of facial beauty; he would revel, but he would never lose his manners or act immorally."[21] However, this epistemic/ontological category of male sexuality as well as the social and cultural contexts in which same-sex desires and relationships were regarded as permissible had largely disappeared from mainstream culture before Koçu's time.

Dror Ze'evi demonstrates in his study of sexual discourse in the Ottoman Middle East how, in the seventeenth century, same-sex relations were legally frowned on yet were accepted as a fact of life and often ignored.[22] Nevertheless, according to Ze'evi, as the strict orthodox dogma that saw same-sex practices as abominable gained power, the earlier sexual discourse disintegrated in the late nineteenth century. This process coincided with "the two-pronged criticism of sexual morality by European travelers to the Middle East and by Middle Eastern travelers to the West" between the mid-eighteenth and the mid-nineteenth centuries (168). The literature produced by these travelers to the Ottoman Middle East not only rendered this sexual culture more visible but also framed it as a source of shame. Moreover, Middle Eastern travelers who visited Europe countered these narratives and criticized Europeans for a perceived loss of sexual morals (169). These Occidentalist authors reproduced conservative discourses and heterosexist norms in the empire. In this context, Ottoman written and expressive culture was purged of its overt homoerotic content. The heterosexualization of Ottoman print culture intensified after the printing press was introduced, and only the books that were deemed fit to be read by the masses could be legally printed (170). Consequent to these processes, the texts on the abandoned categories of sexuality, such as the lovers of facial beauty, were confined to the realm of the archive—a realm that was later rendered inaccessible to the majority of the population by the linguistic and archival policies of the nation-state.

The article "Galib Efendi (Çivicizade from Kayseri)" in the encyclopedia demonstrates Koçu's concerns about the heterosexualization of history and society and the implications of these processes for people he identified with. Born in 1876, Galib Efendi, like Koçu, was a teacher, poet, and "lover of facial beauty." After losing Halet, the object of his platonic love, he spent two years in a mental asylum. After his release, Koçu writes, "he was given a nasty nickname by some of his boorish townsmen, and he became a subject of gossip because he would walk in the streets wearing his turban and his robe and watch every beauty with admiring eyes."[23] In 1906, at the governor's estate, a child mocked Galib Efendi for "loving beautiful boys."[24] This insult, according to Koçu, led him to suicide at the age of thirty. After narrating this short life, Koçu mourns Galib Efendi with a song he wrote for Halet and poetry written by others after Galib Efendi's death. At a time when even his grave had disappeared, Koçu used these archival documents in an attempt to give voice to Galib Efendi's ghost, to let him speak about the pleasures of the gaze, the queer time and place that had been lost, and what these processes implied for the modern queer subjects.

As a historian who had been exiled from the privileged systems of knowledge production and as a subject whose homoerotic desires had been marginalized in the recent past, queerness informed Koçu's archival practice in complicated ways. Ann Cvetkovich argues that the queer archivist resembles "the fan or collector whose attachment to objects is often fetishistic, idiosyncratic, or obsessional," because the queer archive operates as "an archive of feelings" and the connections between feelings, memories, and objects is arbitrary and ephemeral.[25] For Koçu the stories, texts, images, and objects associated with the imperial past—his archive—gained such a fetishistic quality both because of the queer structure of feeling they reproduced and because they sustained the archivist's present-day melancholic existence and eroticized attachment to the empire. Koçu did collect materials that are easier to classify as "queer" even if, to an extent, anachronistically—such as love poems and songs written by men for men, stories of same-sex love, rape, and murder, and drawings depicting beautiful shop boys. However, other popular themes in his archive and publications can also be interpreted in terms of a queer archival practice: medical curiosities, scenes of torture, grotesqueries, murders, myths, and the details of various local, ethnic, religious, and professional subcultures. Depicting the ways these subjects and practices challenged the norms in their time and often in the present, the documents about them and the feelings they invoked fostered the queerness of Koçu's archive. Moreover, with the aid of images and descriptions, subjects like military history or architectural structures were also presented in eroticized ways, again serving the queer erotics of imperial melancholia.

Cvetkovich emphasizes the role of "the passionate desire to claim the fact of history" in queer archival work.[26] Koçu had a desire to claim the fact of history not only as a queer subject but also as a loyal subject of the Ottoman Empire and be acknowledged as an expert and a legitimate source of historical knowledge. To this end, he used the material in his private archive that documented the subjugated knowledges about the empire to create a public repository. Even though he was capable of interpreting the documents in a more "scholarly" style, Koçu chose to be a storyteller and presented them in a language that was entertaining and accessible, often without much interpretation. With the aid of Koçu's books, even people who were born as citizens of the republic could gain a memory of the empire and develop an affective investment in it. In the author's accounts of everyday life, the mundane was replaced by thrilling stories, and the Ottoman Empire emerged as an exciting land of adventure and curiosities. His narratives of the Ottoman dynasty operated as a reminder of not only the recently abandoned structure of Ottoman governmentality but also a multicultural and cosmopolitan life that was rejected by the nation-state. Most importantly, with the aid of the ghosts of the "other" subjects of the Ottoman Empire, Koçu challenged the legitimacy of the social norms governing the present. Still, he wrote not only historical novels, poetry, and children's books but also encyclopedias, dictionaries, history books, and essays. These modern, Western genres associated with "scholarly knowledge" added a certain degree of legitimacy to his works, earning him the respect of historians in academia and eventually enabling collaborations with them.

Koçu reached maturity as a writer during the period Levent Cantek terms "the adolescence of the Republic."[27] In the aftermath of World War II, as the United States became the cornerstone of Turkish foreign policy and the country reoriented itself within the Cold War political order, the single-party regime was abandoned for a multiparty democracy. The government also took measures to facilitate a shift from the strictly controlled and autarkic economy to a liberal free-market economy. As a consequence, between 1945 and 1950, debates over public culture and national identity were particularly heated, and popular mass culture products diversified and flourished in Turkey. In this context, the often violent and erotic content of Koçu's works worked their way into mainstream culture. Such elements are particularly strong in his books about the history of everyday life in the Ottoman Empire, such as *Tarihte İstanbul esnafı* (*Artisans of Istanbul in History*), *Tarihimizde garip vakalar* (*Curious Incidents in Our History*), *Yeniçeriler* (*Janissaries*), and *The Encyclopedia of Istanbul*.[28] Koçu's encyclopedia also includes numerous references to the famous actors, beauty queens, singers, popular movies and songs, and thrilling murder stories of its time. Publishing these articles side-by-side with those on the Ottoman Empire helped Koçu render the imperial history familiar for his readers and imply a sense of historical continuity as well as erotic and affective ties with the imperial past, which was also an important aspect of his queer politics.

Koçu and His Queer Subjects

The Encyclopedia of Istanbul is of central importance to understanding the author's queer politics as well as the tensions inherent in this project. Combining historiography and memoir, the encyclopedia was a project that allowed Koçu, the queerly anachronistic subject of modern Turkey, to locate himself in history and legitimize his existence with reference to a largely forgotten past while also making a personalized claim over the fact of history. Throughout the articles on queer subjects, spaces, and practices, Koçu built a genealogy for those citizens of Turkey whose subjectivities bore the mark of nonnormative sexual desires, constructing a historical grounding for their existence. In the article "Gece sokak fuhuşu" ("Street Prostitution at Night"), for instance, Koçu writes: "Since the conquest of Istanbul to our day, despite some strict prohibitions on prostitution and night curfews from time to time, plebeian misfit men have engaged in prostitution with the cheapest of prostitutes and particularly corrupt young men like themselves in the streets, ruins, holes in the city walls, graveyards, and remains of burned down buildings."[29] The article provides a historical background for male same-sex prostitution, acknowledging that it was still a widespread phenomenon. Moreover, by marking the city's conquest as his start date, Koçu frames these practices as particularly Ottoman/Turkish. Similarly, in the entry "Galata Hotels," Koçu narrates how the hotels in the Galata district of Istanbul, in the nineteenth century, hosted same-sex couples, including sex workers. He ends the article by saying that "dirty hotels still exist in Galata" and mentions a newspaper article, again implying erotic, archival continuity.[30]

The illustrations in Koçu's works also serve his genealogy project. Even when visual materials were available in his archive, Koçu preferred to commission illustrations. Working with popular newspaper illustrators enabled Koçu to present persons, objects, and locations that belong to different periods in a coherent style that reflected the popular aesthetic conventions of his period. This strategy rendered the Ottoman history familiar for his readers. By eliminating the technological and stylistic differences inherent in different genres of images and building a coherent visual world, Koçu also established a visual genealogy that spanned the history of the empire and the republic. In the encyclopedia, not only the entries such as "Civan" ("Handsome Young Man"), where these images are of immediate relevance to the text, but also many others feature illustrations depicting handsome young men.[31] The lengthy entry "Çeşme" ("Fountain") for instance, where the author presents a list of Istanbul's fountains and discusses the city's fountain culture, is accompanied by illustrations depicting young men standing by famous fountains.[32] Through these images as well as the passionate narrative descriptions of young men and boys, Koçu invites his readers to partake in his eroticized melancholic desire and his visual practice of pleasure as a "lover of facial beauty"—a practice of pleasure grounded in a different type of archive. Koçu's own powerful authorial voice as well as the contemporary stories that entered his personal archive through chance encounters, newspaper articles, or conversations with friends also allowed the readers to imagine a contemporary queer community to which they may not have otherwise had access—a community of individuals who fail to conform to the hegemonic norms that regulate gender and sexuality. Among many others, such stories included the German artist Hans Fischer, whose Turkish boyfriend wanted to have him circumcised; the transgender tavern owner Male Aynur, who blinded a woman in a fight; and Mehmed Gökçınar, who wrote poetry for the androgynous beauty of his male hippie friends.[33] By publicizing his private archive, Koçu helped his queer readers cultivate a sense of belonging in the context of the nation-state, where their past had been largely erased and their present-day existence was ignored, if not punished.

As the article "Çilergül (Kız oğlan [The Girl Boy])" demonstrates, Koçu's genealogy project was marked by strong conflict. Çilergül was the stage name of Erdoğan Özeltaş, a young male belly dancer who would dress in women's clothes and perform in the nightclubs of Istanbul in 1958. Koçu knew Çilergül from newspaper articles, where their troubles with the police seem to have been narrated without much sympathy. In this article, Koçu defended Çilergül with reference to the history of cross-dressing in Ottoman performance genres, such as the improvised comedy *orta oyunu*. He also quotes an eighteenth-century poem by Nedim, where the poet praises the beauty of a *köçek*, a male dancer performing in women's clothes. Thus, ignoring the historical paradigm shifts in the norms of gender and sexuality, Koçu suggests some continuity between Çilergül's performances and the Ottoman performance genres that had, to a large extent, already disappeared or gained new meanings. What makes Çilergül's case particularly interesting is the later reference to their story in the article "Gipsy," where Koçu describes an Italian transgender performer who visited Istanbul. His article ends with the sentence "Now we see such young male sexual perverts in our country as well, and we believe that Erdoğan Özeltaş has been a pioneer."[34] Was Çilergül a performer coming from the once highly popular *orta oyunu* and *köçek* traditions or the pioneer of a new, Western category of "perversion" in Turkey? The answer to this question depended on the frame of reference, and Koçu had multiple. As Gökman narrates in his account of the visit to Koçu's apartment, his archival practice that evolved into a physical and affective communion enabled him, to an extent, to reconfigure time and space and to "live a history" that he constructed with the aid of the many archival ghosts he communicated with. Perhaps the dust of those who resided in Koçu's archive—the Ottoman *köçek*s Feryal, Samurkaş, İsrail, Todori, Kaspar, Fulya, and many others—led Koçu to interpret and depict Çilergül as one of them. The archive provided Koçu with an alternative paradigm, which he carefully constructed from the vestiges of a dead empire, to understanding the world. Nevertheless, his subjectivity still bore the marks of the norms and social structures of his lifetime. Hence Çilergül was also "a pervert"; the same-sex relationships of female dancers were classified as "homosexuality, an infirmity of the soul as diagnosed by medicine"; and the Vampire of Eyyüb, who kidnapped four young boys between the ages ten and fourteen and sucked their necks until he bruised them, was "a sexual pervert . . . worthy of analysis by social scientists and criminologists."[35] Still, in all these stories that Koçu loved to read, collect, and retell, there was an element of pleasure that informed (and was informed by) the history he constructed through his archival practice.

(Not) Reading *The Encyclopedia of Istanbul* in Contemporary Turkey

Koçu's melancholic attachment to the Ottoman Empire reveals that the relationship established in the liberal Western academia between queerness and the goals of progressive politics is at best a contingent one. It is not only that those whose sexual subjectivities may be interpreted as "queer" may invest in political fantasies that are ambivalent to the ideals of progressive politics but that these political fantasies and feelings of belonging (that often conflict with the hegemonic power relations in the present) may also create a queer subjectivity defined not by sexual desires and practices of pleasure but rather by the failure to become good political subjects. These complex political dynamics that define queerness also have ramifications for archival praxis. The case of Koçu demonstrates that the epistemic and affective politics of queer archiving can be defined by ambiguities, allowing these projects to be employed for various (and conflicting) nationalist, amnesiac, historiographical, archival, and queer ends.

The tensions that characterize Koçu's archival project are particularly visible in the context of neo-Ottomanism in contemporary Turkey. As the inception of the republic was framed as a sudden breach with the empire by the proponents and critics of this shift alike, the Ottoman Empire emerged as a nostalgic object of desire not only for a melancholic archivist like Koçu but also for generations of conservative Muslim Turks. Largely thanks to the city's imperial glory and Islamic architectural heritage as well as the central role of its conquest in Islamic and nationalist mythmaking, the geographic locus of this desire has been the empire's last capital, Istanbul. The conservative investment in the Ottoman Empire found its expression in mainstream politics with the rise of neo-Ottomanism, which was first articulated by liberal and secular intellectuals under the presidency of Turgut Özal. In the early 1990s, this initial formulation of neo-Ottomanism emphasized the multiethnic composition of the empire and the relative tolerance of Ottoman Islam as sources of pluralism and openness in social and political life.[36]

Consequent to the rise of political Islam toward the end of the 1990s and the successive Justice and Development Party (Adalet ve Kalkınma Partisi), or JDP, governments since 2002, a more conservative and Islamist reformulation of the neo-Ottomanist discourse increasingly gained power. The JDP's policies are characterized by a combination of neoliberalism and social conservatism. In this context, the neo-Ottomanist discourse and imperial fantasies have been employed to legitimize the authoritarian policies and the oppressive political atmosphere in the country. As the government has embarked on major projects of urban renewal and gentrification in Istanbul, neo-Ottomanism has also become the aesthetic framework redefining the cityscape. As neo-Ottomanism thus has gained power as a political discourse and aesthetic strategy, popular history books and history-themed television shows have proliferated, though they remain under close scrutiny. While Mustafa Altıoklar's 1996 film *İstanbul kanatlarımın altında (Istanbul Beneath My Wings)* could depict Sultan Murad IV's (1612–1640) same-sex relationships and still be broadcast on television, in 2012 Prime Minister Recep Tayyip Erdoğan publicly condemned and tried to ban the Ottoman-themed soap opera *Muhteşem yüzyıl* (*Magnificent Century*) for depicting Sultan Süleyman I (1494–1566) as too interested in (heterosexualized) romance.

In the context of the resurgence of neo-Ottomanism, many people were excited to learn a few years ago that *The Encyclopedia of Istanbul*, commonly believed to be Koçu's "unfinished masterpiece," had actually been completed. Although the final article in the last published volume was "Gökçınar, Mehmed," the biography of his poet friend, Koçu had written most of the articles, taken notes for others, and commissioned and collected the illustrations. Nevertheless, the lack of financial resources prevented him from publishing the remaining volumes.[37] After the author's death, his adopted son sold these documents to a wealthy family. Because of the new copyright laws, it would cost approximately $1.5 million to publish the encyclopedia. In 2010, when Istanbul was named a "European Capital of Culture" by the European Union for the year and the government invested in various cultural projects in and around the city, the municipality, also governed by the JDP, declared that it would publish the encyclopedia in complete form if it could find a sponsor.[38] Soon after the news came out, Bardakçı, a historian and an admirer of Koçu's work, expressed his concerns about the project and worried that the editors would modify the content.[39] Given the conflicts between the Ottoman Empire imagined by Koçu and the twenty-first-century governing elite as well as the politics of censorship in the country, Bardakçı's concerns were not ungrounded. Koçu occupies a liminal and rather dangerous space in relation to neo-Ottomanism. On the one hand, thanks to his commanding prose and engaging subjects, his canon can potentially satisfy the demand for popular history books. In fact, many of his books that were reprinted in the early 2000s are now out of print, and the average price for a complete eleven-volume set of the encyclopedia is approximately $2,000. On the other hand, the underworld seething with excitement and forbidden pleasures depicted in Koçu's works deviates from the strict Sunni Muslim autocracy imagined by the governing elite to support their violent neoliberalism as well as conservative Islamist policies. *Reşad Ekrem Koçu: "İstanbul konuşmaları"* (*Reşad Ekrem Koçu: "Istanbul Talks"*), a volume published by the municipality in 2005 to celebrate the centennial of Koçu's birth, supports Bardakçı's concerns.[40] The book is based on the interviews folklorist Sadi Yaver Ataman conducted with Koçu, but neither the interviews nor the introduction reflect the sexual content of Koçu's works. In the hands of the municipality, the encyclopedia could also be purged of its controversial content and put in the service of the conservative Islamist formulation of neo-Ottomanism. Hence it might be fortunate for his readers that the municipality's promise is yet to be fulfilled and that the labor of Koçu's life—his invaluable archive—is still in boxes, waiting to reveal its many secrets and queer pleasures to future readers.

Notes

This research was made possible with the support of the Turkish Cultural Foundation and the Remarque Institute at New York University. I am grateful to Karen Shimakawa, Melis Süloş Akyelli, Danyel Ferrari, Olivia Gagnon, Jale Karabekir, James Sawyer, Carrie Shanafelt, and the reviewers and editors of this issue, particularly Zeb Tortorici, for their generous comments and suggestions. This essay is dedicated to the memory of my late advisor, José Esteban Muñoz.

1. Muzaffer Gökman, *Tarihi sevdiren adam Ahmet Refik Altınay: Hayatı ve eserleri* (*Ahmet Refik Altınay, the Man Who Made People Love History: His Life and Works*) (Istanbul: Türkiye İş Bankası Kültür Yayınları, 1978), 119. All translations from Turkish are mine unless otherwise noted.

2. For a discussion on melancholia in Koçu's works, see Orhan Pamuk, *Istanbul: Memories and the City*, trans. Maureen Freely (New York: Knopf, 2005).

3. Reşad Ekrem Koçu, *Acı su* (*The Salty Water*) (Istanbul: Koçu Yayınları, 1965), 42.

4. Michel Foucault, *Power/Knowledge: Selected Interviews and Other Writings, 1972–1977*, ed. Colin Gordon (New York: Pantheon, 1980), 82.

5. David Halperin, *Saint Foucault: Towards a Gay Hagiography* (New York: Oxford University Press, 1997), 62.

6. Ernst Renan, "What Is a Nation?," trans. Martin Thom, in *Nation and Narration*, ed. Homi K. Bhabha (New York: Routledge, 1990), 8–22.

7. Afet [İnan] et al., *Türk tarihinin ana hatları* (*Outlines of Turkish History*) (Istanbul: Devlet Matbaası, 1930).

8. Jale Gülgen, "Reşad Ekrem Koçu'nun hayatı ve eserleri" ("The Life and Works of Reşad Ekrem Koçu") (master's thesis, Afyon Kocatepe University, 2003), 16.

9. The institution would be renamed Istanbul University after the university reform in 1933.

10. Gülgen, "Reşad," 16.

11. In fact, Gökman describes Koçu's position as "a kind of associate professor." See Gökman, *Tarihi*, 119.

12. Pamuk, *Istanbul*, 157.

13. Reşad Ekrem Koçu, *Ahmed Refik: Hayatı, seçme şiir ve yazıları* (*Ahmed Refik: His Life, Selected Poems, and Essays*) (Istanbul: Sühulet Kitabevi, 1938), 9.

14. Pamuk, *Istanbul*, 157.

15. Murat Bardakçı, "Reşad Ekrem 'cemal aşığı' idi ama ıntihalci değildi" ("Reşad Ekrem Was 'a Lover of Facial Beauty' but He Was Not a Plagiarist"), *Hürriyet* (*Freedom*), May 26, 2002, hurarsiv.hurriyet.com.tr/goster/haber.aspx?id=74394. For the volume, see Reşad Ekrem Koçu, *Osmanlı muahedeleri ve kapitülasyonlar 1300–1920 ve Lozan Muahedesi 24 Temmuz 1923* (Istanbul: Muallim Ahmet Halit Kütüphanesi, 1934).

16. José Esteban Muñoz, *Disidentifications: Queers of Color and the Performance of Politics* (Minneapolis: University of Minnesota Press, 1999), 74.

17. Lila Abu-Lughod, "The Romance of Resistance: Tracing Transformations of Power through Bedouin Women," *American Ethnologist* 17, no. 1 (1990): 41–55.

18. For a similar discussion on the operation of queer failure in Lale Belkıs's paintings in relation to the politics of the nation-state, see Rüstem Ertuğ Altınay, "From a Daughter of the Republic to a Femme Fatale: The Life and Times of Turkey's First Professional Fashion Model, Lale Belkıs," *Women's Studies Quarterly* 41, nos. 1–2 (2013): 113–30.

19. Pamuk, *Istanbul*, 158.

20. Bardakçı, "Reşad Ekrem 'cemal aşığı' ıdi."

21. Vasıf Hiç, "Galib (Çımacı)," in *İstanbul ansiklopedisi* (*The Encyclopedia of Istanbul*), ed. Reşad Ekrem Koçu (Istanbul: Koçu Yayınları, 1972), 11:5956.

22. Dror Ze'evi, *Producing Desire: Changing Sexual Discourse in the Ottoman Middle East, 1500–1900* (Berkeley: University of California Press, 2006), 168.

23. Koçu, "Galib Efendi (Kayserili Çivicizade)," in *İstanbul ansiklopedisi* (1972), 11:5970.

24. Ibid.

25. Ann Cvetkovich, *An Archive of Feelings: Trauma, Sexuality, and Lesbian Public Cultures* (Durham, NC: Duke University Press, 2003), 253–54.

26. Ibid., 242.

27. See Levent Cantek, *Cumhuriyetin büluğ çağı: Gündelik yaşama dair tartışmalar 1945–1950* (*The Adolescence of the Republic: Debates on Everyday Life, 1945–1950*) (Istanbul: İletişim, 2008).

28. Reşad Ekrem Koçu, *Tarihte İstanbul esnafı* (Istanbul: Doğan Kitap Yayınları, 2002); Koçu, *Tarihimizde garip vakalar* (Istanbul: Varlık Yayınevi, 1972); Koçu, *Yeniçeriler* (Istanbul: Koçu Yayınları, 1964).

29. Koçu, "Gece sokak fuhuşu" ("Street Prostitution at Night"), in *İstanbul ansiklopedisi* (1973), 11:6058.

30. Koçu, "Galata otelleri" ("Galata Hotels"), in ibid., 11:5920.

31. Koçu, "Civan" ("Handsome Young Man"), in *İstanbul ansiklopedisi* (Istanbul: İstanbul Ansiklopedisi ve Neşriyat Kollektif Şirketi, 1965), 7:3586–88.

32. Koçu, "Çeşme" ("Fountain"), in ibid., 7:3852–60.

33. Koçu, "Fischer (Hans)," in *İstanbul ansiklopedisi* (1971), 11:5768; Koçu, "Erkek Aynur" ("Male Aynur"), in *İstanbul ansiklopedisi* (1971), 10:5192; Koçu, "Göbek çalkalamak, göbek dansı" ("Belly Shaking, Belly Dance"), in *İstanbul ansiklopedisi* (1974), 11:7059.

34. Koçu, "Gipsy," in *İstanbul ansiklopedisi* (1973), 11:7030.

35. Koçu, *Tarihimizde*, 44; Koçu, "Eyyüb Vampiri" ("The Vampire of Eyyüb"), in *İstanbul ansiklopedisi* (1971), 10:5469.

36. Nora Fisher Onar, "Neo-Ottomanism, Historical Legacies, and Turkish Foreign Policy" (Istanbul: EDAM Centre for Economics and Policy Studies, 2009), 10, trends.gmfus.org /doc/Discussion%20Paper%20Series_Fisher.pdf.

37. Murat Bardakçı, "Reşad Ekrem'in ansiklopedi macerası" ("Reşad Ekrem's Encyclopedia Adventure"), *Habertürk* (*Newsturk*), August 20, 2010, www.haberturk.com/yazarlar/murat -Bardakçı/544064-resad-ekremin-ansiklopedi-macerasi-1.

38. Sefa Kaplan, "İstanbul Ansiklopedisi eksiksiz basılıyor" ("*The Encyclopedia of Istanbul* Will Be Published in Complete Form"), *Hürriyet*, August 18, 2010, www.hurriyet.com.tr /gundem/15577561.asp.

39. Murat Bardakçı, "Reşad Ekrem'in ansiklopedi macerası: 2" ("Reşad Ekrem's Encyclopedia Adventure: 2"), *Habertürk*, August 23, 2010, www.haberturk.com/yazarlar/murat -Bardakçı/544891-resad-ekremin-ansiklopedi-macerasi-2.

40. Süleyman Şenel, ed., *Reşad Ekrem Koçu: "İstanbul konuşmaları"* (*Reşad Ekrem Koçu: "Istanbul Talks"*) (Istanbul: İstanbul Belediyesi Kültür A.Ş. Yayınları, 2005).

Sex in the Archives

David Louis Bowie's New York Diaries, 1978–1993

Barry Reay

There are some very queer diaries in the not always queer archives of the Manuscripts and Archives Division in the Humanities and Social Sciences Library of the New York Public Library. They are embargoed until 2068, but I was granted special permission to consult them. I have trouble recalling what initially piqued my interest, but it must have been the catalog entry: "David Louis Bowie Diaries, 1978–1993 . . . Illustrated diaries of the daily activities and sexual encounters of a Queens resident who died of AIDS-related causes. (Restrictions apply.)" This brief description by no means prepares the reader for the contents of these remarkable documents.[1]

Bowie—not to be confused with his more famous namesake—worked in the transport service industry, first as a passenger service supervisor for Pan American Airways and then for a firm that specialized in shipping expensive artworks. The diaries cover the years from 1978 until 1993 when Bowie died of AIDS. But they are the remnants of a larger archive, for we learn from the entries themselves that Bowie was burgled in 1986 and that the vanishing safe contained his diaries from 1964 to 1977 as well as the one for 1983. "Every day of my entire life during those years is in those diaries. The most passionate, emotional, erotic, jet-set crazy years . . . On top of that, I had done the most exotic and erotic graphic art I ever created in those books along with photographs."[2] So what we have is only a little over a half of the diaries that might have been. The 1960s and early 1970s, clearly of interest in US sexual history, are lost. There are also tantalizing references to photograph albums

Radical History Review
Issue 122 (May 2015)   DOI 10.1215/01636545-2849558
© 2015 by MARHO: The Radical Historians' Organization, Inc.

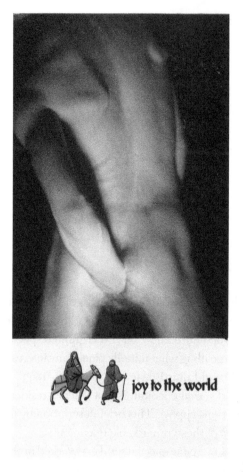

joy to the world

Figure 1.

and slides and Polaroids of trysts, but this separate visual archive seems not to have survived.[3] He was an amateur artist, and the Leslie-Lohman Museum of Gay and Lesbian Art in New York has one of his paintings and a file of slides of his art, including *A Green Nocturnal Dream* (1966), a Salvador Dali–like painting of a tree of penises.[4]

The diary format appears relatively uncomplicated. Volumes start with color photographs of "My Boy of the Year" (in 1978, of a young Hispanic male, "Miguel"), tabulation of sexual contacts, month by month and for the year (the totals include multiple contacts)—273 in 1978—and then the diary text. They usually conclude in the same manner, with comments on the previous twelve months—"This era of gay liberation had allowed me to enjoy the excesses of permissiveness like I never experienced before," he noted of 1978—and copies of his handmade Christmas cards in two versions for "straight" and nonstraight friends, respectively. The alternatives for Christmas 1982 were photographs of a flying seagull and an ejaculating penis (in flight, too, in a sense). His "erotic" card for 1981 was an image of a man fisting himself, above the festive ("fistive") caption "joy to the world" (fig. 1).[5]

The diaries contain references to day-to-day living (watering the houseplants, mowing the lawn) and work-related activities, but they are principally chronicles of sexual encounters:

Raul, Mario and I fisted each other into the night. Then Raul made Demitasse while I took a shower . . . later I dropped Mario off at his place in "The Village" and I continued on to "The Ramrod." . . . Then Dewey and I went on to "The Mine Shaft" where I carried on with two humpy guys in two different sex sessions. Dewey and I got home . . . at 0640. After a hot, spermy sex-session on the living room floor, Dewey and I settled down for some much needed sleep at 0725.[6]

Then, interspersed with the text, are the drawings: mainly of the penises of Bowie's sexual partners. An illustrated example is the combined text and drawing for the pages of January 2 and 3, 1978, where it is as if the penis is draped over the open diary—a potentially embarrassing archival moment for the reader if observed by fellow researchers (fig. 2.) These texts are graphic in both senses of the term.

They are not philosophical or romantic reminiscences but sex diaries. They contain sexual accounts, sexual histories, yet they are also sexual exhibits. This article deals with both a described sexual world and the source that represents it.

The diaries provide details of New York sex in the periods before and after AIDS, what their author called a "Daily Diary of a American Gay Experience."[7] They

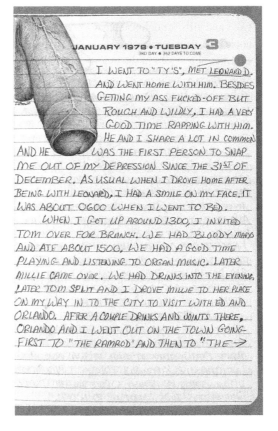

Figure 2.

provide an extended glimpse of a sexual milieu that, as Andrew Holleran once observed, can now seem "as exotic as ancient Egypt."[8] As well as casual sex and organized fisting, more of which later, Bowie engaged in solitary masturbation using dildos and other sex aids, all dutifully recorded. He took drugs to enhance his sexual experiences: cannabis (marijuana, hash, THC, and Purple Haze), LSD (acid), the amphetamine Eskatrol, angel dust (PCP), cocaine (nasally and anally), mescaline, crystal meth (nasally and anally), the psychedelic MDA, and amyl nitrite. He frequented New York's numerous clubs: the Mineshaft, the Ramrod, Badlands, the Cockring, Kellers, the Candlelight, Chaps, the Strap, Billy the Kid, the Spike (where he met the famous photographer Robert Mapplethorpe in 1982), J's, Ass Trick, the Eagle, Alex in Wonderland, Rawhide, and the Anvil. The evocatively named Alex in Wonderland "has something for everyone . . . three levels of decadence from the fist-fuck bar on the cellar level to the pumping disco on the main level to the pool room, coat check and orgy room on the third level."[9] He visited the Hell Fire Club in 1982, one of the most decadent dens of iniquity in N.Y.C. All types of people go there. Guys and girls, straights and gays, cops, nurses, secretaries, pimps, hustlers, hookers, executives, leather types, and just anyone who can cough up the pretty stiff door fee to join in the madness. A bathtub with one or two fornicating in it in piss up to their necks was the only toilet. The screaming, beating, fucking, and sucking went on through thick smoke and dim red and black light bulbs sparsely situated. The smell of booze, piss and sex reeked about the joint.[10]

One of the more fascinating aspects of the diaries is their material relating to the New York fisting scene, an organized sexual culture in which Bowie was heavily involved. He also participated in the more public venues of the clubs—there are references to the orgy rooms of the Mineshaft and Ass Trick—but most such activity occurred in apartments and other private residences with small networks of aficionados, "the underground, private world of 'fist-fucking,'"[11] the venues that Gayle Rubin found central to San Francisco S-M.[12] "Unless one has experienced it," Bowie wrote, "there is no way to understand the experience . . . [it] puts your mind into the glorious state only approached by the most exotic, pure drugs which used to be available."[13] Apart from his attempt to evoke the intensity of the performance, something also stressed in Rubin's accounts, he described rather than analyzed such activity, with references to Crisco, poppers, slings, music (what Rubin called "Music to Fuck By"), and a suggestion that the whole experience was greater than the force of its sex: "Mario lives in a simple, clean, light apartment. A person's environment says so much about the individual and I thoroughly enjoyed this first visit to Mario's place. We had wild, fist-fucking, sperm sessions while listening to his great "Quad" sound system. Later I took a shower and had some of his homemade cheesecake. What a pleasure this evening was with Mario."[14] It is true that Bowie hinted at fisting's democratic possibilities: "The orgy contained the broadest spectrum of guys one could imagine such as a doctor, a minister and an ex prisoner with his parol[e] officer plus white, black and yellow races. It was one hell of a blast!"[15] But, generally, his descriptions lack philosophizing.

It is unfortunate that the 1983 diary is missing, for it must have covered the early days of AIDS. Bowie returned to the Mineshaft in 1984: "I couldn't get over how packed the place was . . . I was amazed by so many guys all 'doing-it.' Hasen't [sic] anyone heard of A.I.D.S.?"[16] (This entry is followed by an account he provides of having oral sex with an anonymous Italian youth.) By 1986 he was noting the effects of the virus on the world of more extreme sex (at least one of his fisting partners had succumbed, and another would a few years later), yet he still participated in such activity, as demonstrated by his account of attending a sex party: "Some precautions were taken such as the use of rubber gloves, avoiding swapping of sperm and frequent washing of hands. But the party was reminiscent of the promiscuity enjoyed during the peak years of gay liberation."[17] Indeed, Bowie's described experience varies from Rubin's claims for the inhibiting impact of AIDS on San Francisco practices.[18] He was still fisting while in the final stages of the deadly syndrome. He appears to have thought (mistakenly) that sex was safer if confined to those he knew: "I did lots of cruising . . . but not enough to take the risk . . . of bringing home a stranger . . . [because of] the A.I.D.S. risk of going to bed with someone you don't know."[19] He refers to invitations to "safe sex" orgies but does not elaborate on what that safe sex might have entailed.

There is certainly a great deal of described casual sex—between two and three hundred "sex episodes" or "sexperiences" in many of the yearly tabulations— with those only identified by their first names ("a guy named Jim," "a sexy, lean, black youth named Robbie," "a little Italian guy from Long Island named Carlo") or merely by physical or other characteristics ("a very young Hispanic with a perfect body," "a sexy, horny black youth," "street tuffy," a "big, black youth," "hungry mouth," "guy with a moustache"), what he labeled "many others where names didn't enter the encounter."[20] There were so many that it was easy to lose track: "I got home to bed at 0400 with a guy named Richard. My notes don't indicate if this was a new encounter or not."[21] However, there are named contacts and recurring partners, though the depicted sex was without commitment. His identified interactions included a renowned ballet dancer, a designer, a sculptor, a musician, a future male companion of a well-known New York socialite, and the model of a celebrated photographer.[22]

We should situate Bowie's behavior in its historical context, for his gay experience was not out of place in the urban United States of the 1970s and 1980s.[23] In 1983 a friend told the writer Samuel R. Delany to forget about press stories of one hundred to three hundred sexual contacts per year; the men that he knew had a lot more casual sex: "Three hundred a month *minimum* is a lot more like it."[24] As the authors of the 1970s classic *The Joy of Gay Sex* expressed it, "Sex is one of life's chief pleasures, and gay men have gained the reputation of being extraordinarily sexually active."[25]

It is also worth comparing the descriptive frugality of Bowie's journals with far more literary accounts of the Mineshaft and its associated sexual practices. The writer Edmund White's evocation begins before he even enters the club:

The Mine Shaft is located on a dark corner in the West Village meatpacking district. In the morning this area is noisy with hissing air brakes and quick with butchers in bloody white aprons guiding dead animals out of refrigerated trucks into cold storage. Traveling hooks swing sides of beef across sidewalks. On cold days metal oil drums blaze with fire and the men warm their hands over the flames. At night the streets are deserted, the pavement slick with blood. Everything smells of lanolin.[26]

White's Mineshaft is far more than a dark space with slings for fucking or being fucked. It represents a wider cultural moment where sex has become everything:

"our sole mode of transcendence and our only touchstone of authenticity."[27] Or there is the casual sex of Delany's trucks, involving up to a hundred strangers, a "libidinal saturation" that had to be experienced to be truly comprehended, not the predictable abandonment of pornographic representation but rather "hugely ordered, highly social, attentive, silent, and grounded in a certain care, if not community. At those times, within those van-walled alleys, now between the trucks, now in the back of the open loaders, cock passed from mouth to mouth to hand to ass to mouth without ever breaking contact with other flesh for more than seconds."[28] There was little such reflection—or describing of the indescribable—in Bowie's recording of acts.

We might also consider *Tricks*, Renaud Camus's 1981 recounting of homosexual sex in Greenwich Village at much the same time and doubtless in the same venues as those charted by Bowie.[29] Here, too, there were encounters without words, based merely on a smile and glance, male same-sex acts recalled in graphic detail without any theorizing about their significance, where, as I have observed elsewhere, the physical intensity and closeness of contact contrasts with the lack of intimacy of verbal interaction.[30] (Joel I. Brodsky said of the Mineshaft that it was a place "where cultural inhibitions were displaced, rather than discussed . . . an arena of critical practice, rather than critical discourse."[31]) Camus exhibited the ennui of excess and was remarkably indifferent to some of his casual sex. But Bowie never seemed world-weary.

The Joy of Gay Sex warned that one of the risks of one-night stands was compulsivity: "Everything about your sex life, including you, becomes routinized."[32] Indeed, there was nothing especially random—little that was casual—about the rituals of cruising, the chosen bars, and the private arrangements for the rites of fisting. Bowie always knew the names of those involved in fisting, apart perhaps from the spontaneous encounters in the Mineshaft. (Rubin has explained that because of the intensity and intimacy of fisting, "even casual encounters could lead to deep affection and lasting friendships."[33]) Moreover, contact was neither strictly anonymous nor arbitrary given that many of Bowie's (and Camus's) tricks were known by sight or by name (we will see that there were many Michaels). Bowie also had long-standing arrangements for no-strings, sexual contact, friendships that lasted for years. One such connection was married with children: "I've known Lenny since . . . he was only 16 . . . Since then he got married, worked . . . as a Corrections Officer at Reikers [*sic*] Island. . . . Our relationship has its ups and downs but it still goes on."[34] He described others as "friend, roommate, fuck-buddy, companion, lover, brother and confidant" or "boy-friend/sex-buddy."[35]

Though analysis of homosexual sex has tended to focus on public sites—bars, clubs, movie theaters, porn stores, restrooms, the trucks, piers, baths, and the "meat racks" found at certain beaches and parks—the Bowie diaries remind us of the importance of the private room, apartment, or house in this activity. The fisting sessions were usually in homes and apartments. His house in Queens, where contacts visited or came back with him after a night in the clubs and bars, was known as "cock castle."[36] Bowie constructed his personal space to reflect his sexual longings: his massive bed, pictures, paintings, pornographic collection, and sex toys (there was a rush to remove incriminating material when the police were called after his burglary). The paving of his garden with cobblestones taken at night from the streets of Chelsea, near the clubs and piers, symbolized this symbiosis between public and private.

Most of Bowie's sexual contacts were with males. But there are descriptions of heterosexual sex: one-to-one ("I may be gay but I'm straight enough to enjoy a nice hot pussy occasionally," he wrote next to his drawing of a vagina) and group (he referred to one such woman as "a sexy party pussy").[37] Moreover, some of Bowie's sexual interactions were with men who also engaged in sex with women and whose willingness to participate in homosexual sex was much like the heterosexual homosexuality described in my 2010 book *New York Hustlers*, though I knew nothing of Bowie when I wrote it. These were working-class men—white, Puerto Rican, and African American (Bowie was attracted by the lure of cross-class and cross-race sexual contact)—for whom sex was just sex regardless of the gender of their partner and who might trade their bodies occasionally. Strictly speaking, a hustler is a male prostitute, nearly always to men, who makes his body available in exchange for cash, but many men who traded on their looks or physical attributes did so for food, drink, clothing, or a room—as well as, of course, for pleasure's sake, without any monetary barter, though if there was also profit, so much the better. As I have argued elsewhere, a wide range of young working-class, heterosexual men in America's past were homosexually available, and hustling and trade should be seen in economic as well as sexual terms as a way of getting a living. *Some* of the young men who spent time with Bowie, enjoying his food and accommodation as well as sex, may have occasionally robbed him. He rarely called such men hustlers, indeed stating in his diaries that he avoided the dangers of hustler sex, but that is what a few seem like. The boundaries were more blurred than Bowie recognized.[38]

Bowie's promiscuity included interracial promiscuity. Race was a strong ingredient in Bowie's cross-class encounters. His diaries recount sex holidays to Rio de Janeiro, three trips in 1978 alone. Clearly, he eroticized these men of color, both in his sexual tourism and back in New York. There are repeated references to "little brown animals," "foreskinned, aromatic, Puerto Rican prick," "hot, Puerto Rican, male animals," and even a dildo called José ("it looked like so many of my friends"), as well as to "big, black, uncircumcised cock," "a beautiful black beast," and what he termed his "black period."[39] Bowie was obsessed with foreskins, as is clear from the hundreds of drawings of uncircumcised penises, and his race and foreskin fetishes were closely linked. This racial othering heightened his sexual contacts, yet we should guard against endowing these fancies with the power of more serious dehumanization.[40] They were fantasies: "My life is so blessed with Puerto Ricans and it is amazing the triangular and circular love affairs I get into with them."[41]

Bowie claimed that his diary was a record of gay life, but it was no direct account. Some entries were written soon after encounters, when memories were vivid and their writing was virtually a ritualistic part of the sex represented, as in this description of a visit to the Mineshaft in 1979, which is practically postcoital:

My first encounter was with an athletic looking, black youth who I fucked a load into. Then along came a very, young dark haired youth named Chuck who licked my still erect, oozing prick clean. I had a beer and then fucked another lean youth wearing leather pants, got my dick sucked some more by another guy with big nipples, sucked off a child with a perfect body, and finished up my morning with a very hot, moustached, lean youth who I fucked a load into. Whew!

I drove home feeling just great. I got in at 0530, *wrote in this diary* [emphasis added], had a bite to eat and went to bed at 0635.[42]

However, other entries occurred months after the described events: "I am writing this page on Saturday 17 January 1979 (almost 10 months after the date) so the information is quite sketchy . . . according to my sex calendar, I carried on with two guys on this date. Probably in The Mine Shaft."[43] "Since I have no notes for this date, most of the details have to be omitted. . . . But my social sexual calendar indicates that I carried-on with Michael on this date. Although I researched 17 Michaels from my past I could not place the one I was looking for."[44] He refers to taking notes for his journals that would be worked up years later. "My notes were sketchy . . . and considering how I partied during this era and the fact that I'm making this entry into this diary nearly ten years later, it is a wonder that I had as many details as I had here."[45]

Moreover, the care taken with his drawing, the constant drafting, the working and reworking, went on for years. (As has been hinted, the crafting was artistic rather than literary: he focused on his drawings rather than his prose.) The diaries have a fetishistic quality. They are sexual objects, Bowie's own sexual archive. He was aroused both by the memories they stored and by his textual and visual renderings. He refers to masturbating to his drawings—even while executing them. There was also a fetish within the fetish: Bowie's fixation on foreskins, referred to earlier. This is an archive imbricated in its chronicled sexual history in many intriguing ways.

Finally, the journals were a memorial to those friends he lost to AIDS, nearly fifty by the time of his own death. AIDS was, he reflected in 1987, "the Thorn in the side of the pleasure of life. . . . For me it has become a psychological burden on my sexual activity, social and daily life."[46] He described the indignities of dental work: "A young guy went to work on my teeth. He was very well garbed, gloved and shielded to protect him from me . . . he looked more like he was going to work with radioactive particles than another human being."[47] This was the limit to his deliberation. Bowie's AIDS reporting is very different from Eric Michaels's *Unbecoming*, a deeply reflective work written in the late 1980s and first published in 1990. The visual effects of AIDS written on Michaels's body (the sarcoma) prompted the script on the page as he assessed his life and his dying, his unbecoming, his social death before his actual physical departure.[48] Moreover, Michaels was aware that what he wrote might be published. With Bowie, however, AIDS was an unwelcome postscript to diaries long begun rather than an occasion for deep contemplation or savage observation. He had no expectation of publica-

In Memory of "Chipmunk"
12 May 1947 - 19 Jan.1986

Figure 3.

tion. Bowie was a chronicler rather than a diarist. Yet there is a quiet power in the account of his own travails with its unembellished referencing of chronic diarrhea, gastritis, vomiting, pancreatitis (caused by antiviral medication), hepatitis, bleeding toes, thrush and gingivitis, and transfusions to combat acute anemia.

The visual divergences between Michaels and Bowie are striking, too. *Unbecoming* begins with a photograph of its defiant author, revealing the disfigurement of his lesions. In contrast, Bowie's friends are remembered as healthy bodies. While his photographic commemorations, a steady stream from 1984 onward, are no different from the (beefcake) imagery of his Boys of the Year, this eroticization heightens rather than undermines their impact (fig. 3). The haunting image of "Chipmunk" rises from the sand and gazes across another image of himself (at another time) directly into the eyes of the viewer. It is a brilliantly poignant tribute.

We have Bowie's diaries because of the death of their creator. The volume for 1993 finishes with an entry for January 23. After that, the pages are blank. The chronicling stops; there are no more meticulous drawings. While it is tempting to read this whiteness as Bowie's own stark memorial, he should be remembered rather for the exuberant text that precedes this representational caesura: as the recorder of a lost culture in pursuit of sexual pleasure and creator of a wondrous example of sex in the archives.

Notes

I am most grateful to Richard Schaneman, the executor of David Louis Bowie's estate and the trustee of the diaries, for permission to consult the diaries and to reproduce the images that appear here. I would also like to thank Tal Nadan, reference archivist in the Manuscripts and Archives Division, for her help and encouragement during the preparation of this article. The images are reproduced by permission of the Manuscripts and Archives Division, the New York Public Library, Astor, Lenox and Tilden Foundations. Color version of figures 1 and 3 in this article are available in the online version, dx.doi.org /10.1215/01636545-2849558.

1. The New York Public Library, Humanities and Social Sciences Library, Manuscripts and Archives Division, David Louis Bowie Diaries, 1978–1993 (hereafter Bowie Diaries). When the collection was donated in 1993, the library closed it for seventy-five years because people were named in the diaries (Mary B. Bowling, curator of manuscripts, to Richard Schaneman, June 18, 1993). However, one of the archivists provided me with the donor's contact details, and I approached him for special permission to consult them, which was granted without reservation ("As a matter of fact, this is exactly the reason I made the effort to get them into the possession of the New York Public Library" [Richard Schaneman, e-mail message to author, June 8, 2010]). I have of course preserved the anonymity of those mentioned in the diaries.

2. Bowie Diaries, January 12, 1986.

3. Richard Schaneman, Bowie's former Queens neighbor, does not recall seeing any albums when Bowie's house was cleared after his death. Schaneman, phone conversation with author, April 12, 2013.

4. The 1991 painting *Cream of Mushrooms* features dripping penises in a mushroom patch. Leslie-Lohman Museum of Gay and Lesbian Art, New York. I am grateful to Wayne Snellen, deputy director for collections, for locating the Bowie file.

5. Bowie played with the words *festive* and *fistive* on more than one occasion. An entry for January 1, 1979, describing fisting, writes: "What a 'fistive' way to arrive into this New Year!" His homoerotic humor here is reminiscent of Carl Van Vechten's scrapbooks. See Jonathan Weinberg, "'Boy Crazy': Carl Van Vechten's Queer Collection," *Yale Journal of Criticism* 7, no. 2 (1994): 25–49.

6. Bowie Diaries, January 25, 1978.

7. Bowie Diaries, December 23, 1985.

8. Andrew Holleran, *Chronicle of a Plague Revisited: AIDS and Its Aftermath* (New York: Da Capo Press, 2008), 2.

9. Bowie Diaries, June 12, 1982.

10. Bowie Diaries, June 6, 1982.

11. Bowie Diaries, April 30, 1988.

12. Gayle Rubin, "The Catacombs: A Temple of the Butthole," chap. 9 in *Deviations: A Gayle Rubin Reader* (Durham, NC: Duke University Press, 2011). The essay was first published in 1991.

13. Bowie Diaries, March 19, 1984.

14. Rubin, "Catacombs," 231 (for music to fuck by); Bowie Diaries, February 14, 1978.

15. Bowie Diaries, March 8, 1986.

16. Bowie Diaries, October 6, 1984.

17. Bowie Diaries, March 8, 1986.

18. Rubin, "Catacombs," 236.

19. Bowie Diaries, February 8, 1986.

20. Bowie Diaries, October 31, 1978; September 24, October 7, December 30, 1979; August 13, 17, 19, 30, 1980.

21. Bowie Diaries, April 29, 1979.

22. For the privacy reasons discussed earlier, I cannot name these people.

23. The best discussion of this historical context is by Steven Seidman, *Romantic Longings: Love in America, 1830–1980* (New York: Routledge, 1991), 176–91. See also Ben Gove, *Cruising Culture: Promiscuity, Desire, and American Gay Literature* (Edinburgh: Edinburgh University Press, 2000).

24. Samuel R. Delany, *1984* (Rutherford, NJ: Voyant, 2000), 13–14.

25. Charles Silverstein and Edmund White, *The Joy of Gay Sex: An Intimate Guide for Gay Men to the Pleasures of a Gay Lifestyle* (New York: Simon and Schuster, 1977), 13.

26. Edmund White, *States of Desire: Travels in Gay America* (New York: Dutton, 1980), 282.

27. Ibid.

28. Samuel R. Delany, *The Motion of Light in Water: Sex and Science Fiction Writing in the East Village* (Minneapolis: University of Minnesota Press, 2004), 225–26. Delany's book was first published in 1988.

29. Renaud Camus, *Tricks: 25 Encounters*, trans. Richard Howard, with preface by Roland Barthes (New York: St. Martin's, 1981).

30. I discuss this at greater length in Barry Reay, "Promiscuous Intimacies: Rethinking the History of American Casual Sex," *Journal of Historical Sociology* 27, no. 1 (2014): 1–24.

31. Joel I. Brodsky, "The Mineshaft: A Retrospective Ethnography," *Journal of Homosexuality* 24, nos. 3–4 (1993): 248.

32. Silverstein and White, *Joy of Gay Sex*, 141.

33. Rubin, "Catacombs," 236.

34. Bowie Diaries, June 29, 1984.

35. Bowie Diaries, November 13, 1981; May 17, 1980.

36. Bowie Diaries, October 31, 1980.

37. Bowie Diaries, June 17, 1978; April 22, 1987.

38. See Barry Reay, *New York Hustlers: Masculinity and Sex in Modern America* (Manchester: Manchester University Press, 2010).

39. Bowie Diaries, July 16, 1978; January 1, June 4, 1980; July 4, 1987; February 9, 1980; January 1, 1988; October 22, 1980.

40. I have benefited here, and elsewhere, from reading Tim Dean, *Unlimited Intimacy: Reflections on the Subculture of Barebacking* (Chicago: University of Chicago Press, 2009), esp. chap. 3.

41. Bowie Diaries, May 3, 1979.

42. Bowie Diaries, March 4, 1979.

43. Bowie Diaries, April 26, 1978.

44. Bowie Diaries, May 24, 1978.

45. Bowie Diaries, August 19, 1980.

46. Bowie Diaries, notes at end of 1987 volume.

47. Bowie Diaries, October 24, 1991.

48. Eric Michaels, *Unbecoming* (Durham, NC: Duke University Press, 1997), 3. For a thoughtful analysis of this and other AIDS diaries, see Ross Chambers, *Facing It: AIDS Diaries and the Death of the Author* (Ann Arbor: University of Michigan Press, 1998).

Body, Sex, Interface

Reckoning with Images
at the Lesbian Herstory Archives

Cait McKinney

On a high shelf, in a small closet, at the Brooklyn brownstone that houses the Lesbian Herstory Archives (LHA), sits a Hollinger document case hand labeled "unprocessed 'porn'? and several snapshots." Available for any visitor to take down and browse, the box is full of photographs that remain "unprocessed," awaiting an interpretive sort by volunteers. Processing an archival acquisition involves several steps toward making materials accessible, including selection, appraisal, and creating a finding aid, means of description, and narration that are core sense-making epistemologies of archival science, with its rational roots in modernity. Processing materials is labor-intensive, resource-heavy, and time-consuming, more so in the digital era. Between acquisition and access provision, the interpretive act waits to be written; photographs are not yet mediated by a database form that attempts to pin down the stories they capture. But while processing a photograph of a well-known lesbian or event suggests a straightforward routine of identification and classification, the often-anonymous, amateur images of sexuality in the collection are more difficult to consider. As the LHA's photo collection moves online, volunteers must grapple with materials that have been waiting patiently in their boxes, and questions such as "How do you 'process' porn?" take on a renewed urgency.

Founded in 1974, the LHA is a volunteer-run, community archives that oper-

Radical History Review

Issue 122 (May 2015)   DOI 10.1215/01636545-2849567

© 2015 by MARHO: The Radical Historians' Organization, Inc.

ates on a shoestring budget funded mostly by individual donations—the archives will not accept state-supported grants and is skeptical of institutional partnerships.[1] An evolving, intergenerational coordinating committee of "archivettes" manages the archives, making decisions on a consensus basis. Most of these archivettes also work at the archives, staffing open hours, leading tours, and processing collections alongside a loyal group of interns and volunteers, many of whom are library science students in their twenties. Materials are spread over the basement and first two stories of the heritage home, while the top floor is home to the archives' "caretaker," who also serves on the coordinating committee. The collection includes vertical subject files on dozens of topics related to lesbian culture—bathhouses, fat liberation, matriarchy, nuns, utopia, a book collection, three thousand spoken-word cassette tapes, videos, "special collections" that are personal papers donated by individuals and organizations, periodicals, and all kinds of ephemera including sex toys, buttons, posters, and T-shirts. The space feels unlike a conventional archives in that there are cozy reading nooks and macramé adornments and visitors are allowed to access and handle any of part of the collection without prior request.

The archives' photography collection contains roughly ten thousand images, loosely cataloged according to volunteer-generated subject headings. Emphasizing the late twentieth century, the collection includes portraits, snapshots, documentation of nightlife and activism, porn, and scores of images that defy easy categorization under any of these terms. Images of sexuality are prevalent in the collection and range from elaborate S/M scenes, to the most willfully amateur self-portraits and snapshots of lovers, to work by professionals such as Del LaGrace Volcano and Tee A. Corinne. The scope of the collection is simply: any image that has been "relevant to the lives and experiences of lesbians."[2] A "National Lesbian Photography Drive" announced in the LHA's 1979 newsletter sought to build the foundation for the collection, asking "lesbians all across the country to send photographs of themselves, friends, children, homes, pets, activities," so that "our future sisters will be able to see us."[3] Lesbian visibility in its historical iterations guides the growth of this collection, and yet this is a category that many images seem to exceed; a case in point is the recently digitized work of gender variant Volcano, who identified as a lesbian at the time of acquisition.

Digitization of this collection began in 2010, the first self-directed project to offer extensive online access to the archives. Preparing this collection for an online database involves several factors. I consider digitization at the LHA an expansive process that is not conceptually limited to the creation of digital files from "analog" sources; to digitize also encompasses the design and implementation of an online user interface, the creation and assignment of descriptive metadata to images, and the selection of which images to offer online. The complexity of images of sexuality presents opportunities for reflecting on the cultural politics of this process, including the accessibility of sexual materials in lesbian, gay, bisexual, and transgender

(LGBT) archives as they move online. An archives' responsibility to provide access to images of sexuality is balanced with questions of legality, ethics, and propriety, creating a tension informed by the growing pressure of "queer liberalism" on these archives as they move further into public-facing roles mediated by the web.[4] This article draws on interviews, documentary research, and ethnographic observation conducted at the LHA to trace the process through which volunteer coordinators designed and began to carry out the digitization of the photography collection. The design of this project has generated moments of reckoning with various political contexts in which the archives moves, such as intergenerational feminism(s). Attending to these negotiations, I argue that the archives' approach to digitization is improvisational, open to revision and critique, and willfully imperfect in its management of considerations such as metadata. Digitization presents the archives with the opportunity to consider how historical representations of sexuality it houses challenge the normative imperatives that can accompany digital media practices, including the ways that all kinds of sex practices and gendered ways of being scramble the categorical logics of structured databases.

The photo collection is managed by Saskia Scheffer, who works in special formats processing at the New York Public Library and has been a volunteer coordinator at the archives since 1987. Saskia identifies the heterogeneous origins of the collection as one of its strengths. The subjects and photographers in many of the photos are unknown; donated by friends of the archives, these images hold stories that have been forgotten, or were never known. Unlike large institutions, the archives accommodates all kinds of donors as part of its inclusive politics of accessibility. Says Saskia, "We didn't have minimum requirements, and I don't mean for that to sound negative at all. If people had stuff, we took it. Still do. Not like if you don't give us a complete description with names and birthdates of everybody in the photo, we won't have it. We'll take it. We'll figure it out."[5] Though many of the photos resist attribution, the collection has been organized into subject files to facilitate browsing, in an interpretive practice aimed at access provision more familiar to libraries than archives. Digitization ultimately remediates categorizations already made by many volunteers. Most subject files are just the names of events or individuals, some famous, others just regular folks. More generally, descriptive subject headings are designed on an ongoing basis by volunteers when such headings seem like a logical addition to the taxonomy: these include "Military" and "Children of Lesbians." Many layers of "folksonomic" classification are at play here; rather than work with a standardized, controlled vocabulary of terms, as a librarian would in an institutional setting, the LHA allows the content of the materials and the judgment of volunteers to guide an evolving vocabulary.

Though subject headings offer a framework, what is contained in the folders often continues to perplex, especially the vernacular photographs of nonfamous lesbians engaged in everyday contexts. A fairly typical folder labeled with a first and last name contains undated snapshots, circa the 1980s, that depict an often-naked woman in all kinds of poses in the grass and in front of her motorcycle. What kind of record do these images offer when they make archival sense only because of their foggy relationship to the always-provisional identity category of lesbian?

The practical work of digitizing the photos is deceptively simple: Ronika McClain, a twenty-one-year-old volunteer working with Saskia, systematically sorts through the collection, creating a Google spreadsheet that describes each folder and indicates whether there is donor permission to place the images online. Saskia chooses images to scan using a high-quality scanner to which she has access off-site. She uploads them to a server hosted by the Metropolitan New York Library Council's low-cost Digital Collection Hosting Service, where they are accessed via CONTENTdm, digital collections management software that she trained herself to use. The "online photo sampler" currently includes nearly 650 images, to which Saskia assigns metadata fields for size, title, creator, and descriptive tags to make the photos searchable for research queries. There is no existing searchable catalog besides an offline word document; this project will produce the first robust, searchable database. Digitization responds to a desire for access that is as much about sorting and sense making as it is about offering scans through an online interface.

In explaining why it is difficult to sort the collection to prepare it for digitization, Saskia uses the example of the peculiar box of porn she didn't know what to do with. It is so emblematic of the challenge some photographs pose for the sense-making practice of digitization that another title for this article could be "An Ontology of the Unprocessed 'Porn' Box." With a bias to the 1980s, the nearly five hundred photographs stuffed into this box are from many eras, feature many subjects, and were likely taken by dozens of photographers. But this is all speculation; there is no provenance or donor agreement form for these images. Saskia has no idea how they got to the archives, their stories lost to fading institutional memory.

The dominant genre in the box is the self-portrait, an analogue version of the selfies one might text to a lover today. I sift through dozens of blurry prints of women masturbating, sometimes inscribed to a lover on the back, and many photos of couples and groups engaged in a range of acts; generally, they're blurry and composed haphazardly. Some photos defy the generic conventions of amateur porn: I'm intrigued by a series depicting a thin, white woman lying mostly naked on the floor of a garden shed, her head outside the frame, torso arranged alongside plants waiting to be potted, a gallon-size plastic jug, and a Shop-Vac. Inscribed on the back with a first name and the date "June 2 1985," these are vernacular photographs that most archives would not collect; they lack a clear subject or occasion, they don't adhere to formal or aesthetic conventions of "successful" photography, and they don't make sense to the modernist, epistemological desires of conventional archives, which search out photos with known photographers, subjects, locations, or time periods. The box's contents evoke art historian Geoffrey Batchen's description of vernacular photography as an "abject" genre, in the sense of being liminal, ambiguous, and difficult to categorize.[6] Yet the strangeness of these images, their very ambiguity, is part of what makes them compelling records of sexual subcultural style and its place in the archives.

Saskia tells me that the unprocessed porn box will likely never "see the light of day" that is the Internet.[7] Deselection—the process through which some materials are digitized and offered online, while others are not—has political implications for the evolution of LGBT archival collections, particularly in terms of the scope of an archives' online "holdings" in relation to its collection mandate. LGBT archives have a long history of collecting porn and other images of sexuality. Though some university collections

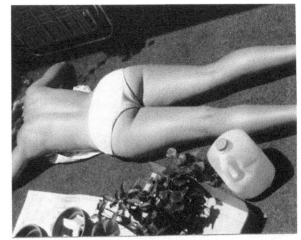

Anonymous photos from the unprocessed porn box, image courtesy of the Lesbian Herstory Archives photo collection

acquire porn today and have done so in the past, in a historical context, prioritizing porn has distinguished LGBT community archives from other institutions. The Canadian Lesbian and Gay Archives, another community archives similar in scope and age to the LHA, has a mandate of collecting gay male porn and erotica and has built an extensive collection.[8] Archives scholar Marcel Barriault describes collecting porn as a political act that challenges, deconstructs, and redefines what an archival institution can and should be.[9] Porn reflects more than the desires it portrays; as porn studies have shown, porn provides research "value" by illuminating the wider cultural frameworks in which it is produced and consumed.[10]

The porn at the LHA provides a critical record of lesbian subcultural moments in which power and pleasure have collided, such as the feminist S/M and porn debates—or "sex wars"—of the 1980s and 1990s. Despite the importance of

porn for constructing histories of LGBT subculture, sexual images tend to be preserved by these archives without necessarily being made easy to access, a trend
made more acute by the deselection of digitization.[11] As Barriault argues, there is a
need for community archives "to ensure that archives as bodies of knowledge also
reflect knowledge of the body."[12] As online interfaces become the primary mode
of encounter between archives and publics, this means ensuring that the body gets
digitized, as it were.

   Given the limitations of labor hours and server space, deselection at the LHA
is inevitable: the archives can't scan or pay to host all of its photos. Practicalities
aside, deselection has significant ideological effects, the politics of which can be too
readily justified by efficiency, or dismissed as inevitable; critical attention should
be paid to the conditions of possibility that shape the decision-making process of
digitization. The first reason the unprocessed porn is easier left in the box relates to
copyright, ethics, and permission to circulate, all guided by the archives' evolving,
feminist framework of consent and privacy.[13] It is difficult to acquire publication
permissions, and visitors to the archives are asked not to take photographs of images.
The photo files greet users with a notice: "Much of what was given to us came from
women who simply wanted their images saved, their lives remembered. They neither offered permission for publication, nor did we request it. . . . We are sorry that
the collection is so inaccessible to publication use. As explained above, it came out
of a different time and focus." Many photos were acquired during the sex wars and
reflect the conflicting politics of representing sex held by this archives' intergenerational public. For antiporn feminists, the problem of pornography was precisely the
mechanical reproduction of images, rather than merely the acts depicted in porn. As
a compressed form designed to create small file sizes that can be sent and received
with ease, the digitally reproduced image is constructed to circulate, formally biased
toward a politics of media that contravenes the sex wars prohibition on distribution.
Ultimately, consent to digitize is sought from donors and subjects, but as information
studies scholar Jean Dryden has shown, cultural heritage archives choose images
for digitization that are uncontroversial in their provenance to avoid complex, labor-
intensive searches for permission.[14] Deselection is critical as decisions about what
to put online shape what the archives becomes: images of sexuality can require discussions for which an archives run on a consensus model by volunteers has limited
capacity.

   The undescribability of many depictions of sexuality in the LHA's photo collection is the second reason these images stay in their box. Batchen's argument is
ultimately a suggestion that vernacular photographs do not articulate easily as evidence; they are the digital cataloger's "worst nightmare," as they evade attempts
to render them searchable. Vernacular images of sexuality can be particularly per-
plexing. I asked Ronika for an image that was difficult to add to the database, and
she thought of one of her favorites: "There's a woman who had a bunch of pictures

of herself. She was naked, and she had a bondage harness on. We pulled that out, looked at it, and we weren't really sure what we could say. We said something like 'playful photographs,' 'nude photographs,' like worked around the information," eventually settling on the description, "tough and topless."[15] Listening to Ronika describe this process as one of careful interpretive work is exemplary of the archives' improvisational digitization tactics. They involve anti-expertise, the accessibility of archival tools, and an ethos of finding solutions that are good enough to guide the project. This good-enough approach to description and metadata is not a disadvantage of the community archives; rather, as librarian-scholar Jen Wolfe has argued, even in large institutional archives, when it comes to metadata, "sometimes 'good enough' is good enough."[16] In the interest of getting materials online, catalogers must accept the provisionality of these standards.

Saskia describes the temporality of this approach as a practice of addressing issues when they arise, rather than waiting to have everything worked out in advance. She relates moving mindfully between the professional context of her day job and working at the archives using the metaphor of a cook who prepares the same meal in a professional kitchen and on a camp stove: "I'm realizing that I have to really give us the credit that what we do is actually really good. So what if it isn't perfect. . . . It is absolutely usable."[17]

Ronika's uncertainty about the image of the woman in the harness relates to an absence of contextual information about the subject's sexuality and relationship to being photographed and represents a moment when ethical concerns become intertwined with the challenge of description: "A lot of the times it's really difficult to categorize what people are doing in these photos, and there are a lot of instances where we open things and go, 'What do you say about this? . . . She's clearly expressing this part of her sexuality that may be sort of hidden . . . that's representative of a lot of the things that are in this collection, that sort of tentativeness to make this representation of yourself, especially in the sexual images.'"[18]

The images offered online have all been cleared to circulate in public, either through donor agreements or through careful judgment by Saskia and Ronika. Without a donor agreement, volunteers weigh the risk posed by publishing an image, asking whether there are recognizable women in the photograph, whether the image is donated or "found," and whether the subject matter of the photograph seems at all private or controversial, such as with an image that depicts nudity or explicit sexuality. These are ongoing, case-by-case decisions, and there is no overarching policy to follow. The LHA has made many efforts over the years to contact pre-Internet donors to request permission to list their materials online, but communication is often difficult to initiate. What is put online reflects the subjective feminist engagements that archives volunteers have with photography, the archives, and online media. Perceptions of the time in which a photograph was donated—how donors might have thought about the medium of photography then—are weighed in relation to common understandings of images and their circulation in the present, in which, for example, the sharing of "private" images via social media makes it easier to imagine these photographs as suitable for public consumption.[19] In an archives that describes itself as primarily by, about, and for "lesbians," the context of lesbian visibility and equal rights discourse is also critical. Art historian Carol Payne argues that photographic archives in cultural heritage organizations are technologies for constructing visual representations of imagined communities. The complexities of the collection at the LHA demonstrates how the imagined community of "lesbians" rests on an array of shifting, sometimes contested, boundaries and limits of that very category.[20]

The archives' approach to images of sexuality ought to be considered in relation to the larger role that LGBT archives play in constructing a liberal, palatable version of historical sexual subcultures. Much queer archival theory has celebrated LGBT archives as "counterarchival"—and thus inherently critical—spaces that house the eccentric materials other archives might not value.[21] Emphasizing the desiring attachments that queer publics form to historical objects, the queer archival turn in the humanities has often downplayed the implicatedness of archives in cultural "regimes of normalization."[22] LGBT archives are worlding technologies that can be called on to support homonational trends, in which the recognition of gay and lesbian citizen-subjects as rightly historical is tied to broader political agendas of gendered and racialized violence, exclusion, and empire in the present.[23] Photographic archives, in particular, shift this politics into a regime of visibility that associates being seen with being welcomed into the fold of liberalism. Online media is similarly implicated in the pedagogy of recognition; an example is the resiliency rhetoric of the It Gets Better project, in which Internet access rescues youth into a normative developmental narrative by modeling how to "come out." Critical archivists, archives scholars, and archives users are generally well aware of the formative influence that archives play in contemporary LGBT politics. Alexandra Juhasz has called this role "queer archive activism," where the archives does not just collect and preserve objects but also performs public-facing outreach and intervention.[24]

Information science scholar Tim Schlak has argued that postmodern critiques of photographic archives approach photos as "very difficult objects to talk about, let alone classify, describe, and essentially 'own' as archival evidence"; however, archivists often lack the time or resources to build digital interfaces in such a way as to accommodate the complexity of materials, especially at a volunteer archives.[25] After discussing my own investments in the photo collection as an important record of sexual subcultures, in which images depicting sexuality are key, I asked Saskia if she foresees a time when any of the images from the unprocessed porn box might go online. Her response reveals a nuanced understanding of these theoretical implications: "The only thing that I can imagine we would do with something like that is a little sampler of things we don't understand . . . have a page with ten photographs and then say these are ten samples of a box that came to us from an unknown source. . . . But I have other things to do." I ask her to explain what this unknown sampler would demonstrate about the collection. "It would show something about the sources of the material. It would show how we have organically grown. How we don't discriminate. That there's very interesting things here to be seen. Just the fact that we have that and we didn't throw it away. . . . That at some point in time some-body thought this might be appropriate here."[26]

Though rhetorical, Saskia's online mini-exhibition of unprocessed porn would digitize this material for circulation online while holding off on "processing" the images. The hypothetical act of description proposed here is one of refusing to describe, of leaving open the ambiguity that can characterize an archival encoun-ter with historical images of sexuality. The uncertainties, edges, provocations, and discomforts Ronika attributes to the image of the woman in the bondage harness are perhaps what give an otherwise innocuous portrait some of its charge in the first place. Though Saskia's idea is an intriguing thought experiment, she has "other things to do," a reminder that resource-strapped community archives must prioritize the needs users have for finding and accessing materials more easily through online interfaces. What Saskia and the LHA do make time for is a practice of self-reflexivity about their responsibility in shaping how the archives is encountered and an open-ness to revising how images are classified.

Information studies scholar Margaret Hedstrom calls the "archival interface" a "critical node in the representation of archives," through which archivists negotiate their role as intermediaries with the past.[27] Online interfaces are increasingly the most common mode of user engagement, forcing archivists to confront the interpre-tive nature of their role vis-à-vis digitization, in the wide sense of the term as I am using it here. Saskia describes creating the online catalog as a process of making sense of a thing that sometimes does not make that much sense—an opportunity to organize, classify, and render searchable. But how do you make sense of dozens of undated photographs of a naked woman with a perhaps tenuous relationship to the category lesbian, posed in front of her motorcycle? As librarian-scholar Marlene Manoff explains, "However much one refines one's tagging, one is still forced to impose a level of specificity and explicitness on texts that, in the humanities at least, defy such clear-cut distinctions."[28] The textual desires we have of archives are often exceeded by the "multiplicity of [LGBT] donors' identities" and the elusiveness of photographs as media.[29] Pulling a "what do you say about this?" image out of the photo drawer evokes wonder, because the ways these photos do not make sense are difficult to catalog and capture through mechanisms such as the searchable data-base form.

The digitization process creates an interface with palpable effects on user experience. The construction of the interface is evident in what is chosen for digi-tization, a practice Saskia describes as "completely subjective."[30] Often images are digitized because of researcher request, creating an emphasis on "research value." Selection can also be serendipitous, where Ronika flags compelling discoveries for Saskia. Both women described the intergenerational encounter of working together as personally fulfilling and an influence on the digital collection as it takes shape. For example, Ronika describes discussing the work of transgender photographers in ways that blended her emergence in a very recent queer scene with Saskia's long history at the archives as it has evolved to accommodate (or not) emerging trans politics. Saskia chooses images that evidence aspects of lesbian subculture she views as underrepresented. Images that make immediate visual sense take precedent; Schlak describes the emphasis on clarity as a textual paradigm, where photos obtain archival legitimacy once they can be described clearly as texts.[31] Says Saskia: "I also want it to look good . . . things have to be recognizable. Something nondescript, out of focus, in the distance, isn't going to be very helpful."[32] The garden shed portraits, for instance, do not "look good" in any conventional sense; their "deselection" from the LHA's online database contrasts with my academic and aesthetic affection for these pictures, which inevitably overemphasizes their significance in the collection.[33]

The photo sampler greets visitors with a graphic interface, the user-friendly "front-end" of a "back-end" database experience, that together mediate access and determine our connection to "history" as represented by this collection.[34] These complex virtual environments exert intellectual control over encounters once left open to more unstructured forms of in-person browsing in the photo folders; as Emily Drabinski warns, search functions can all but eliminate relational or happenstance "queer" browsing practices by classifying materials along firm identity-based lines.[35] The photo sampler is pleasant to look at and reasonably easy to search but is ultimately a structured database that creates culturally determined pathways to content. CONTENTdm is also designed for the creation of digital *collections*, which are necessarily partial and organized to cohere around an intelligible theme. The folksonomic naming of images through the assignment of descriptive metadata is another subjective process that shapes the interface. While fields for "date" and "creator" can be simple to complete, the field for "description" requires Saskia to summarize the subject of an image in one short phrase. The descriptive tags she assigns to each photo in the "keywords" field are a familiar process for anyone who has uploaded a photo to a site like Flickr. Though she does not work from a controlled vocabulary, Saskia associates the goal of precision with her choice of tags and is well aware that good tagging is what makes effective information retrieval possible in online photo-sharing interfaces.[36]

In tagging photos, Saskia practices a careful, improvisational self-awareness. For example, the archives has many of the papers of lesbian-feminist artist Corinne, including source photographs for her 1975 *Cunt Coloring Book*. Saskia put six of Corinne's less explicit images online after she found them in a small, handmade exhibition catalog from the mid-1980s. She assigned the tags "art," "erotica," and "labia." I asked her to describe how she chose these particular images and why she labeled them as she did.

I had absolutely no problem with this because there are no recognizable women in it. Those images are well known. . . . We have her permission to use them; nobody's going to make a big deal out of it. And, yes, it's art. You know, I called it "erotica"—why didn't I call it "sexuality"? At some point I just need to get stuff up [online], and I can't spend more time waiting for inspiration. If changes need to be made, that will happen. I think that discussion will come; clearly, we're having one now. And maybe you will make me aware of something, or I will make you aware of something, and something changes in the metadata. I have no problem going in the system and adding or taking something away in terms of description. The more I work with it, the more that actually happens, because I realize that I can be more exact, I can be more precise. It will be better, it will be easier to use, more informative.[37]

A work-in-progress approach to metadata description is an advantage of the feminist community archives' do-it-yourself approach, evoking the "liberatory descriptive standard" favored by information studies scholars Wendy Duff and Verne Harris. This database model "seek(s) ways of troubling its own status and its *de facto* functioning as a medium of metanarrative," to "push the capacity of description to accommodate partial or multiple rather than complete closure."[38]

The discussion of Corinne's work was a moment in my interviews with Saskia where my investments in the collection became explicit, as I relayed searching for "sexuality" without any results and searching for "porn" to find images of sex wars protests. Walter Kendrick argues that "erotica" lends images of sex a "specious aura of antiquity."[39] Writing long before the archival turn in the humanities, Kendrick is nevertheless engaged with questions of how classification and the archives define what

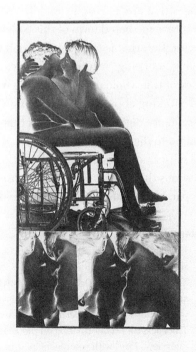

Untitled image tagged with the terms "art," "erotica," and "labia." Tee A. Corinne, image courtesy of the Lesbian Herstory Archives photo collection

is pornographic and what is fit for public consumption. To archive is to shape access in ways that delineate material as one thing or another. Linda Williams's notion of "on/scenity" extends the naming and classifying effects of prohibitive gestures to the contemporary ubiquity of sexual images online, where once-unspeakable acts are increasingly represented in public as diverse forms of sexuality.[40] The online interface, as a site of mediation, marks some material for public consumption, while porn must stay, quite literally in this case, in the drawer. Returning to Barriault's concern that LGBT archives go beyond preserving images of sexuality to improving access, the names given to images of sexuality matter for mediating access to that material, but naming can also have the effect of pinning down meaning in ways that images will always transcend.

Art historian Tom Normand has argued that to not classify images in vernacular photography collections is to "honor their variety and diversity" to allow these outlaw forms to be liminal, to occupy the "threshold between or in the margins of categories."[41] The theoretical and practical question becomes, How do outlaw archives with an investment in finding mediated forms that attend to the complexity of their collections design online interfaces that leave open the ambiguity of materials without falling back on the ease of deselection? Certainly, the desire for images that are as visually and historically legible as possible has implications for the future mediated form of this collection, whose drawers contain many "illegible" images. But what is critical in Saskia's words is the way she describes her process of "trying," of being "helpful," and of acknowledging and thinking through the contingency of this whole process. Moving with care, doing it yourself, deciding together, and thinking about the intersecting values of multiple archives publics, past and present, are digitization practices that constitute a feminist politics of getting by in relation to digital media. The LHA, with its willfully provisional, improvisational, and self-critical approach to digitization, is well equipped to engage with the urgent questions that images of sexuality pose in relation to digitization, questions that are inseparable from the archives as a mediated space in transition.

Notes

I am grateful to Saskia Scheffer, Ronika McClain, Rachel Corbman, and all the volunteer staff at the Lesbian Herstory Archives for their generosity, hospitality, openness, and time. Thank you to Susan Driver, Dylan Mulvin, Tamara Lang, Lisa Sloniowski, and the two anonymous reviewers for their careful readings and suggestions on the article. This research was supported by the Social Sciences and Humanities Research Council of Canada.

1. The background information on the LHA in this paragraph is assembled from unstructured interviews I did with volunteers in 2012 and 2013, my own observations at the archives during the three months I spent doing doctoral research there in this period, and the organization's history and statement of principles, available on its website, www.lesbianher storyarchives.org/history.html.

2. "Statement of Purpose," *Lesbian Herstory Archives Newsletter*, no. 1 (1975): 2.

3. "Announcing the Start of Our National Lesbian Photography Drive," *Lesbian Herstory Archives Newsletter*, no. 5 (1979): 3.

4. David Eng, *The Feeling of Kinship: Queer Liberalism and the Racialization of Intimacy* (Durham, NC: Duke University Press, 2010).

5. Saskia Scheffer, interview by the author, Brooklyn, NY, May 10, 2013.

6. Geoffrey Batchen, *Each Wild Idea: Writing Photography History* (Cambridge, MA: MIT Press, 2001), 57.

7. Scheffer, interview, May 10, 2013.

8. Marcel Barriault, "Hard to Dismiss: The Archival Value of Gay Male Erotica and Pornography," *Archivaria*, no. 68 (2009): 222.

9. Ibid., 226.

10. Feona Attwood, "Reading Porn: The Paradigm Shift in Pornography Research," *Sexualities* 5, no. 1 (2002): 91–105.

11. On the challenges that collecting porn poses for libraries and archives, see Lisa Sloniowski, "This Is Not a Love Story: Libraries and Feminist Porn," *Access: The Magazine of the Ontario Library Association* 18, no. 2 (2012): 14–17.

12. Barriault, "Hard to Dismiss," 225.

13. This framework is perhaps best exemplified by the archives' donor agreement forms, through which donors are invited to maintain ownership of their materials and design various privacy restrictions, some of which are unprecedented in archives; my search of these forms revealed restrictions such as "for lesbian eyes only" and "for pro S/M viewers only," both of which, the archives' staff admit, are impossible to enforce while maintaining open access to the collections.

14. Jean Dryden, "Copyright Issues in the Selection of Archival Material for Internet Access," *Archival Science* 8, no. 2 (2008): 123–47.

15. Ronika McClain, interview by the author, Brooklyn, NY, May 3, 2013.

16. Jen Wolfe, "Playing Fast and Loose with the Rules: Metadata Cataloging for Digital Library Projects," in *Radical Cataloging: Essays at the Front*, ed. K. R. Roberto (Jefferson, NC: McFarland, 2008), 71.

17. Scheffer, interview, May 10, 2013.

18. McClain, interview, May 3, 2013.

19. See Amparo Lasén and Edgar Gómez-Cruz, "Digital Photography and Picture Sharing: Redefining the Public/Private Divide," *Knowledge, Technology and Policy* 22, no. 3 (2009): 205–15.

20. Carol Payne, "Lessons with Leah: Re-reading the Photographic Archive of Nation in the National Film Board of Canada's Still Photography Division," *Visual Studies* 21, no. 1 (2006): 4–22.

21. Ann Cvetkovich, "The Queer Art of the Counterarchive," 32–35, and Judith Halberstam, "Unfound," 158–61, in *Cruising the Archive: Queer Art and Culture in Los Angeles, 1945–1980*, ed. David Frantz and Mia Locks (Los Angeles: ONE National Gay and Lesbian Archives, 2011).

22. Cvetkovich, "Queer Art of the Counterarchive"; Halberstam, "Unfound."

23. See Payne, "Lessons with Leah"; Ann Laura Stoler, *Along the Archival Grain: Epistemic Anxieties and Colonial Common Sense* (Princeton, NJ: Princeton University Press, 2010); and Jasbir Puar, *Terrorist Assemblages: Homonationalism in Queer Times* (Durham, NC: Duke University Press, 2007).

24. Alexandra Juhasz, "Video Remains: Nostalgia, Technology, and Queer Archive Activism," *GLQ* 12, no. 2 (2006): 319–28.

25. Tim Schlak, "Framing Photographs, Denying Archives: The Difficulty of Focusing on Archival Photographs," *Archival Science* 8, no. 2 (2008): 85–101.

26. Scheffer, interview, May 10, 2013.

27. Margaret Hedstrom, "Archives, Memory, and Interfaces with the Past," *Archival Science* 2, nos. 1–2 (2002): 22.

28. Marlene Manoff, "Archive and Database as Metaphor: Theorizing the Historical Record," *Portal: Libraries and the Academy* 10, no. 4 (2010): 394.

29. Angela L. DiVeglia, "Accessibility, Accountability, and Activism," in *Make Your Own History: Documenting Feminist and Queer Activism in the Twenty-First Century*, ed. Lyz Bly and Kelly Wooten (Los Angeles: Litwin Books, 2012), 85.

30. Scheffer, interview, May 10, 2013.

31. Schlak, "Framing Photographs, Denying Archives," 88–89.

32. Scheffer, interview, May 10, 2013.

33. In other words, the exemplary function of these images in this article enacts a form of "selection" that is just as political as the deselection processes under consideration here.

34. Manoff, "Archive and Database," 386.

35. Emily Drabinski, "Gendered S(h)elves: Body and Identity in the Library," *Women and Environments International Magazine*, nos. 78–79 (2009–10): 16–18.

36. Yi Kwan and Lois Mai Chan, "Linking Folksonomy to Library of Congress Subject Headings: An Exploratory Study," *Journal of Documentation* 65, no. 6 (2009): 872–900.

37. Scheffer, interview, May 10, 2013.

38. Wendy Duff and Verne Harris, "Stories and Names: Archival Description as Narrating Records and Constructing Meanings," *Archival Science* 2, nos. 3–4 (2002): 285.

39. Walter Kendrick, *The Secret Museum: Pornography in Modern Culture* (New York: Viking, 1987; Berkeley: University of California Press, 1996), 244. Citation is to the 1996 edition.

40. Linda Williams, "Porn Studies: Proliferating Pornographies On/Scene; An Introduction," in *Porn Studies*, ed. Linda Williams (Durham, NC: Duke University Press, 2004), 1–23.

41. Tom Normand, "Utility Photographs: Rethinking the Vernacular, Rereading the Archive," *Visual Culture in Britain* 13, no. 12 (2012): 325.

Privacy Anxieties

Ethics versus Activism in Archiving Lesbian Oral History Online

Elise Chenier

Queer archival projects are deeply political in nature. They advance "a political agenda aimed at social transformation"; they "challeng[e] discrimination"; they strive to counter the "alienating and distancing effects by being told you don't belong by being excluded from history."[1] Contesting queer oppression and empowering queer people by living out loud, however, conflicts with ethical standards that anchor oral history practice. In the oral history community, narratives are treated as one treats an individual's private papers: without the permission of the narrator or the narrator's estate, they should not be shared. The emergence of open-access digital archives raises new challenges for fulfilling the liberationist mandate to make stories public. Yet what should we do when protecting the personal and advancing the political collide?

This article examines this dilemma as it has emerged at the Archives of Lesbian Oral Testimony (ALOT), an open-access digital humanities archival project based at Simon Fraser University in Burnaby, British Columbia.[2] ALOT collects oral testimonies such as interviews conducted with lesbians and interviews that were produced for lesbian-defined projects, and digitizes those that were not born digital, produces transcriptions, and puts them online. The collection currently contains interviews generated for academic research, for documentary films, and for popular

Radical History Review
Issue 122 (May 2015)   DOI 10.1215/01636545-2849576
© 2015 by MARHO: The Radical Historians' Organization, Inc.

books. It also includes a small-town lesbian and gay cable television show produced in the 1980s. Not all of the narrators are living or can be located. Most signed over copyright to the interviewer at the time of the interview, but is it ethical to donate pre-Internet interviews to an open-access online archives? Is it ethical for archives to put online materials already in their collection?

Community-based lesbian archives have been essential to the development of the history of sexuality as a field of study and to the development of queer social and political community. As the South African Gay and Lesbian Archives put it, a lesbian, gay, bisexual, and transgender (LGBT) archives "give[s] substance to a community's right to its own memories," "[is] more overt in its mission to include those fragments and perspectives that ordinarily would not be recognized as valid or worth preserving," and "promotes community participation as a core principle." When tied to an "agenda of political transformation and anti-discrimination," the independent archival act "can only be understood in the context of the political nature of empowerment and recovery." Community archives are more than a space "where the past is documented and passively collected . . . ; [they] can become a significant tool for education, interpretation, argument and empowerment."[3] They also help reshape notions of citizenship and history. Institutional repositories such as these define which pasts matter and who counts as history's proper subjects.[4]

ALOT's aim is to build a community, not an institution. In practical terms this means the archives is nonproprietary. Using creative commons licensing and developing right-to-distribute agreements with existing (and grossly underfunded) archives and with oral testimony interviewers eliminates the need to retain ownership of the original material.[5] Rather than compete with existing archives, ALOT strives to assist them by helping digitize their collections and provide online data storage at no cost to them. In this way, A LOT supports rather than usurps the critical role archives play.

Making the Case
The passages at the start of this and the following two sections come from longer conversations, the audio files for which can be accessed as supplemental content to the online version of the article at dx.doi.org/10.1215/01636545-2849576. From sound file 1:

I felt we were unusual . . . because I hadn't labeled us lesbian, not knowing the word, I didn't know there were groups like this. But I also knew that the women I lived with . . . that we should try and keep the knowledge from them. . . . We didn't want to be caught.
—Helen Carscallen on the early 1940s when she lived in a house she shared with her lover, Bud, and two other women war workers in Toronto.

I interviewed Carscallen in 1995 for a research project on lesbian life in twentieth-century Canada. Carscallen lived a "double" life—she acted and appeared straight (or so she hoped) to everyone but her intimate partner, Bud. Carscallen and Bud did their best to hide the intimacy they shared from the rest of the world, which, they were certain, would condemn them. Like so many other lesbians, gays, and queers who lived in the 1940s, 1950s, and 1960s, discretion was mandatory.

Gay liberationists of the late 1960s and early 1970s were unwilling to pay the cost that remaining closeted exacted. For them, coming out was personally liberating and deeply political. It was a declaration, a challenge, *and* a celebration, never an explanation. Community-based historians and archivists played a central role in building this brave new "post-closet" world. Lesbians and gay men began the challenging work of searching newspapers, archives, and other traditional records to uncover evidence of same-sex experience.[6] Others grabbed tape recorders and microphones and began documenting gay life by gathering oral testimonies.[7]

At that time, oral history was more than a method; it was a movement. It was a means to "[break] through the barriers between the chroniclers and their audience; between the educational institution and the outside world."[8] Collecting and sharing testimonies was also a tool to empower marginalized communities by teaching everyday people how to tell their own stories so that they might write their own lives into the historical record, on their own terms. Thus telling life stories was about more than expanding the historical record to include the experiences of those who were excluded from history. By treating the experiences of everyday people as the building blocks for a new understanding of the past, oral testimony challenged traditional forms of knowledge and authority.[9] It was a counterforce against traditional history.[10]

For Will Roscoe, lesbian and gay community history "builds lives and identities, and provides both knowledge of the world and knowledge of the self. It is work that makes lesbian and gay living possible."[11] Educator, activist, historian, and archivist Joan Nestle shared Roscoe's vision for better living through history. In 1974 she cofounded the Lesbian Herstory Archives (LHA) in her Brooklyn, New York, living room. That it was named the "Herstory" Archives reminds us that feminism was half the foundation upon which lesbian history was built. Nestle was rescuing lesbian *and* women's history, including the history of women of color. For a variety of reasons, including that in most early gay organizations men occupied positions of leadership, lesbian and gay archives are typically dominated by material related to, and produced by, men. Only by making lesbian material a priority, and by having lesbians on staff to build relationships with members of the lesbian community, does a meaningful repository of women's material emerge.[12] Nestle shared Roscoe's view of the life-affirming role of the archives. The LHA, she once explained, is a place "for everyone, for surviving, a place to create a family album."[13]

The Lesbian Herstory Archives inspired countless lesbian history projects, including the Buffalo Women's Oral History Project founded in 1978 by Madeline Davis and Elizabeth Lapovsky Kennedy. The model they followed—to produce a written history of an urban lesbian community, to create an archive of oral history materials, and to give the history back to the community from which it came—implemented best practices in oral history work and inspired similar projects in cities across the United States and elsewhere.[14] The Toronto-based Lesbians Making History (LMH) collective gathered testimony from women who participated in lesbian communities in the 1950s, 1960s, and 1970s. LMH existed for only a short period, but its work provided the foundation upon which the acclaimed documentary film *Forbidden Love: The Unashamed Stories of Lesbian Lives* was created.[15]

Virgin Territory
From sound file 2:

IVY: She walks me along Dundas Street, and like, my mouth must have been dragging, I was in awe, I never went along Dundas Street, that was through Chinatown. . . . She took me into this place. . . . I walked in and I see all these guys sittin' there, and she goes in to talk to them, and this one guy says, comes out, and he says to me, "Are you with Rocky?," and I say, Oh no, no, no, no, I'm with Joan." "Who the fuck's Joan?"
Q: Was it mostly men?
IVY: IT WAS DYKES! IT WAS BUTCH BROADS!

Like Ivy Barber, many of those who undertook oral history projects traveled into regions for which there were no maps. Deemed too subjective and therefore too unreliable a source, critics dismiss oral history as popular storytelling.[16] Nevertheless budding lesbianologists created a substantial record of queer life from the perspective of queer people. The problem is few of them got around to archiving their work.[17] A recent ALOT investigation revealed that only three of fourteen lesbian oral historians surveyed deposited their oral history interview collections in archives. Even more troubling is that archives offer no guarantee that such material will be preserved: only one out of the three archived collections has been digitized. There are currently no preservation plans in place to ensure the future life of the other two sets of analog tapes.[18] Historians of the lesbian and gay past once lamented that centuries of oppression meant that our history was forgotten, silenced, and suppressed. Ironically, lesbian and gay history may now be in danger of disappearing yet again, though this time due to neglect.

With institutional support and federal funding in hand, ALOT is taking steps to preserve this rich source material for present and future purposes. The principal objective is to collect lesbian oral interviews from around the globe and make them as widely available as possible. The first step is to digitize those in analog and other formats and mount them on the website, where they can be accessed by anyone with a high-speed Internet connection. ALOT expects that the primary users will be researchers, but the online archives will also serve a general audience of nonspecialists interested in and curious about lesbian history. It could also serve educators who would integrate the material into lesson plans on the history of sexuality and oral history.[19]

Digital technology allows oral historians to engage new publics and contribute to the democratization of knowledge and cultural resources. By providing access to these interviews, ALOT expands the creative and intellectual commons. As seen in the example of the online version of this journal article, which unlike the print edition can incorporate sound files, the web also allows us to put the "aural" back into oral history. In nondigital brick-and-mortar archives researchers rarely listened to original recordings, preferring instead the written transcript. Where transcripts do not exist, material is rarely consulted. Aural history, by which is meant the original sound recording, brings material alive in ways that a transcript cannot.[20] In sum, then, there are four major advantages to making such material available online. It helps toward preservation; it allows for greater dissemination; it helps build community and supports a scholarly field of study; and it puts the aural back into oral history.

It's More Complicated Than You Think

From sound file 3:

Uh, well, I suppose I've had a kind of a live-and-let-live [attitude] when it comes to appearances. I guess what bothers me a lot about the butch and fem . . . mode is that when the violence comes as part and parcel of the role, and I mean: battered wives. Please, ladies, not in our communities, you know? Not in . . . So, that has really been an issue for me, and I get, I can get very angry when I see a lesbian couple in a butch and fem relationship and these roles are played out, you know, you know, and all the same bullshit that you might hear from a heterosexual couple come[s] out. Now, I have a lot of trouble with that, I just do. . . . I'm a rescuer and I'm a defender of the underdog.

Online archives, however, can exacerbate old problems and generate new ones. Copyright ownership of interview material is not established in law in Canada, the United States, or the United Kingdom.[21] But it is not only the law that is at stake. Oral historians abide by high ethical standards. For this reason, museums, archives, libraries, and researchers often turn to best practices written by experts in the field to guide them in determining if and how oral history interviews can be used.[22] Now that archives are no longer limited to brick-and-mortar structures and can put their holdings online, does "consent to archive" include consent to post online? When ALOT conducted a survey of archives holding predigital oral history materials in

2011 it found that best practices for posting oral history collections online were not yet established. Most respondents indicated that without explicit consent to archive the material, they would not accept the donation of oral interview material.[23] Given its extraordinary significance, what are the long-term implications of such a high ethical standard?[24]

Another problem is confidentiality. Oral historians and archivists have become even more cautious in light of increasing sensitivity to privacy concerns. Because the ways in which people are "out" can often be inconsistent and variable according to shifting contexts and individuals, lesbian, gay, bisexual, transgender, and queer (LGBTQ) material raises special concerns. Even if narrators are fully out, what about the people they name in their interviews? It is easy enough to have researchers working in traditional archives sign confidentiality agreements regulating the use of material, but can such measures be applied in an open-access environment, or does it require new technological solutions that allow us to deal with oral interview material differently? Putting anything online, even behind password-protected barriers that restrict access to those who have signed confidentiality agreements, makes many people uneasy, even when they themselves advocate barrier-free access. This reveals how brick-and-mortar archives rely on physical and geographic space to vet users. Should they?

Those who consider building online archives of lesbian and other oral history material are thus confronted with two fundamental questions. Is consent to archive the same as consent to archive online?[25] Does material of a sexual nature raise unique problems and issues that require different solutions? I think so, but not because it is sexual. The problem is the way in which sex and sexuality are political, and politicized, and how such iterations of politicized sex and bodies shift between the textual and the digital spheres, as questions of access radically shift as well.

In the early 1970s, gay and women's liberationists convincingly showed that by treating sex as a private matter its political dimensions were denied. They taught us how the privatization of sexuality denied women and queers basic citizenship rights to equality. Their trenchant critique has allowed us to see *the personal* as *political*. This insight is plainly evident to those on the sexual margins who find themselves subject to legal regimes that deem expressions of nonnormative gender and sexual behavior as, at best, a public nuisance and, at worst, a public danger. A liberationist approach would suggest that the answer to the dilemma posed by the ethics of privacy protection for narrators is clear: these stories must be preserved and made available to the greatest number of people. They should be treated on par with the Library of Congress Slave Narratives from the Federal Writers' Project, the United States Holocaust Museum Memory Project, and the Veterans Oral History Project, for example.

Best practices in the oral history community indicate that protecting the privacy of narrators takes priority over the political goal of using individual life stories to challenge oppressive social structures. This value is deeply ingrained in researchers who gather oral history testimonies. For example, one ALOT collection is the research tapes created by the filmmakers behind *Forbidden Love*. Though their narrators were prepared to tell their stories on-screen in a publicly funded feature-length documentary, the filmmakers hesitate to assume that this implies consent to post the research tapes online. What should be done with that material?

Oral interviews are often intensely intimate experiences. Narrators recount stories of abuse at the hands of parents, husbands, and lovers; they describe painful memories of children given up for adoption, of alcoholism, of being publicly shamed for being queer; and they recount the earliest moments of finding queer pleasure and the pride in deciding to pursue the same sex. They describe, sometimes in detail, their first masturbatory experience and their first time making love with a woman. They tell us these stories because they trust us, the interviewer.[26] They feel sure of our intentions.[27]

Interviewers work hard to build relationships of mutual respect and trust. Even if our narrators are deceased, it would be devastating to any interviewer to hear testimonies the interviewer collected being used in ways that do not honor what the interviewer feels is the narrator's truth. Is there, however, too much caution and not enough revolutionary spirit? When in the early 1990s I interviewed Lynn Crush and Ivy Barber, who were then in their sixties, they refused the option of anonymity and insisted that their full names be used in any publication. Both felt that it was critical that their stories be told, and although the Internet was not even imagined at that time, I believe that they would consent to their interviews being posted online. Is there really any difference, after all, between playing interview clips at conferences or publishing excerpts in journals and making them available online, as in the case of this *RHR* article being published in both textual and digital form and allowing for the access of sound clips?

There is. Recently, the Sophia Smith Collection at Smith College in Northampton, Massachusetts (see www.smith.edu/libraries/libs/ssc), posted a large donation of lesbian oral history material on its website. Although narrators had originally consented to the library's posting it online, once it was up on the web some were uncomfortable with their original decision. The oral historian responsible for the collection wrote:

I have found many LGBT narrators reluctant to have this kind of unmediated exposure. And even when they do sign a release giving permission to put their transcripts and/or clips online, they sometimes revoke that permission once they have the unsettling experience of googling themselves or other family members and have the transcript come up straight away. The material no longer feels like an archival document with any kind of gatekeeper but rather a trove of personal information available to the masses.[28]

Privacy concerns are also leading the Puerto Rican Community Archives at the New Jersey Hispanic Research and Information Center to consider pulling full PDF transcripts of their Latino Oral History: Justice collection offline and making them available by appointment or special request only.[29] The British Library also anticipated these problems. Its protocol requires reconfirmation of consent to post online before it actually does so, and each time it does so.[30] This provides narrators the opportunity to know the context in which their testimony will be available and just how accessible it will be. The approach demands greater labor resources than most archives have. What is needed is a policy that smaller-scale archives and community groups can implement as they make the transition to the web, and one that addresses the problem of the deceased narrator.

Experience indicates that permission to archive in a brick-and-mortar archives in not equivalent to permission to archive online. The Oral History Centre at Mary Immaculate College, Limerick, Ireland, is an example of a modestly staffed archives moving toward online access. In the process of clearing interviews for online availability, it finds that most narrators do not want their interviews posted online.[31] The evidence suggests that in cases where permission to archive online cannot be obtained from both interviewer and narrator, interviews should not be made available in an open-access online environment, at least not without anonymizing the material, which likely should mean access only to a transcript. Archives will traditionally release material after a period of time stipulated either by the donor or by legal custom. Different lengths of time apply to different types of materials such as census data, marriage registries, and personal materials housed in public libraries and archives. Should online oral testimony archives adopt similar practices?

Some oral history practitioners have found ways to protect narrators' privacy and reproduce some of the gatekeeping functions brick-and-mortar institutions provide. Open access to Suzy Subways's interviews with members of a radical left organization, the Student Liberation Action Movement (SLAM!), could cause considerable harm to informants, some of whom are immigrants, some undocumented, and others seeking to advance their professional careers. As Subways explains, she used "only the first names of the narrators along with the audio, no transcript, so what they said wasn't searchable. There is a PDF on the site with text, so that's also not searchable. . . . One of the narrators asked me to change the spelling of her first name so that the interview would not turn up in a google search, and I was happy to comply."[32] By taking these steps, one finds the collection because one is looking for the group, not the individual participant. Sometimes people who are fully aware of the web and how it functions nevertheless feel exposed once their material is online. That was the experience of Emma Kelly, a scholar whose father was involved in a gay New Zealand oral history project. Kelly participated in an interview with her father and in the process revealed her own bisexual orientation. Despite her political commitment to oral history and her personal investment in recording her father's story, Kelly feels deeply ambivalent about having her own sexual history exposed, in part because of biphobia within the political communities in which she participates, and in part because knowledge of her bisexuality may jeopardize current personal relationships. Perhaps this feeling of exposure is what the women whose interviews were put online at the Sophia Smith Collection experienced.

When participants in Kelly Anderson's Documenting Lesbian Lives project expressed misgivings about having their interview available online, the entire project was taken off the web. Currently it can only be accessed at the Smith College campus library. Anderson has since rewritten release forms "to be much more explicit about narrators' choices regarding access, privacy, anonymity, and copyright so that there is less room for interpretation and a much clearer sense of what [the narrator] wants done with the material."[33] As at the British Library, great attention is paid to each case. Now, Anderson states, "I am cautious and slow when placing oral histories online. [I am] watching and waiting to see what consensus emerges and [am] very reluctant to put another narrator in an awkward or even perilous position."[34] Perhaps it is still far too dangerous for queer individuals to have their stories online.

"Environments are not just containers," wrote communications theorist Marshall McLuhan, "but are processes that change the content totally."[35] Confronted with two competing imperatives—to treat oral testimonies as part of an "out and proud" political strategy and to protect the privacy of both narrators and interviewers— curators of oral history online are beginning to recognize that the Internet is not the same as a brick-and-mortar archives. Concerns about the abuse of material are real, but it should not deter us from capitalizing on the opportunity to expand the intellectual commons and democratize knowledge. Increased access has expanded the range of archives users. The web has generated new forms of discourse, some of which is uninformed of the politics and purpose of oral history.[36] It is not enough to adapt a traditional notion of archives to the online, digital environment. We must reimagine the archives as proposed and outlined below.

Drawing on emergent best practices for archiving oral history online and the need to reimagine archives as an online dissemination tool in light of new media forms and engagements, ALOT proposes the following dissemination policy:

1. Interviews will be allowed to be posted in open- or restricted-access spaces. Donors will determine where interview material will be stored and the degree of anonymization in accordance with the original agreement as set out between interviewer and interviewee. Requiring a paper application to access restricted archives will serve a gatekeeping function similar to that created by the mere fact of having to travel to an archives. Traditional legal agreements between ALOT and users dictating how material can and cannot be used will be adopted.

2.   The consent of both narrators and interviewers to post online will be sought, and both parties will be allowed to retract consent at any time. For example, while it might be okay to be gay today, tomorrow might bring new problems and challenges, as demonstrated by Russian historians of sexuality who are currently having to transition into new areas of research.[37] Having queer oral history materials online could jeopardize narrators' and researchers' future—or present in the case of Russia—safety. Such political shifts cannot be anticipated; an ethical practice must acknowledge that being queer or engaging in activities that might lead someone to assume that you are queer remains risky business.

3.   Where narrators cannot be located, or are deceased and family members and/ or executors of a narrator's estate cannot be located, interviews will not be posted online in their entirety; edited clips will be permitted for materials deemed to be low- or no-risk as determined by ALOT and interviewers.

4.   Web sites are not archives; they engage new publics in potentially new ways. Open-access materials are curated in a manner similar to archival displays aimed at the informal visitor. Curation in this context means creating short, edited audio and video clips with transcripts from those materials deemed low- to no-risk, and for which both interviewer and narrator have given permission to share in an open-access environment. A simple application to the archives and a signed agreement to abide by ALOT's policies concerning use, reproduction, and dissemination of archival materials will allow researchers and other interested publics to access the entire collection and will prevent discovery from random searches.

5.   Data management practices will be implemented that prevent identifying information from turning up in web searches. Just as an acid-free box is a tool to prevent the deterioration of paper materials, new technologies allow us to protect our archival materials from misuse, insofar as archives are able. This includes developing new editing tools that increase our ability to more easily anonymize both aural and transcribed materials where narrators desire it.

ALOT's objective is to, as Andrew Flinn puts it, "give substance to a community's right to its own memories; [to] include those fragments and perspectives that ordinarily would not be recognized as valid or worth preserving; and to hold community participation as a principle of our mission."[38] However, one cannot empower a community by disempowering the individual. Even gay liberationists understood that coming out was a deeply personal choice, and no matter how critical it was to the success of the movement it was ultimately an individual choice to do so.

Open access shares important parallels to gay liberation and oral history movement objectives. By rejecting the monetization of data, of research, and of knowledge in favor of diverse public interests, open access rejects the individual consumer and liberal individualism for the collectivity and democratic publics. The politics of oral history is to resist everyday oppression by empowering subjugated people and communities to tell and share their stories and, in this way, to restore human dignity. As collections shift to online environments, the politics of the personal must be rethought anew.

Notes

1. Andrew Flinn, "Archival Activism: Independent and Community-Led Archives, Radical Public History, and the Heritage Professions," *InterActions* 7, no. 2 (2001): 4; Andrew Flinn, "Independent Community Archives and Community-Generated Content: 'Writing, Sharing, and Saving Our Histories,'" *Convergence: The International Journal of Research into New Media Technologies* 16, no. 1 (2010), excerpted from Andrew Flinn, Archival Activism, February 25, 2011, Information Studies Colloquia Series, Graduate School of Education and Information Studies, University of Los Angeles, itunes.apple.com/gb/itunes-u/information-studies-colloquia/id434135345?mt=10.
2. ALOT, www.alotarchives.org.
3. Flinn, "Archival Activism."
4. Stuart Hall, "Whose Heritage? Un-settling 'the Heritage,' Re-imagining the Post-Nation," in *The Third Text Reader: On Art, Culture, and Theory*, ed. Rasheed Araeen, Ziauddin Sarda, and Sean Cubitt (New York: Continuum, 2002), 72–84.
5. Jack Dougherty and Candace Simpson, "Who Owns Oral History? A Creative Commons Solution," in *Oral History in the Digital Age*, ed. Doug Boyd et al. (Washington, DC: Institute of Museum and Library Services, 2012), ohda.matrix.msu.edu/2012/06/a-creative-commons-solution.
6. Jonathan Ned Katz, *Gay American History: Lesbians and Gay Men in the U.S.A.: A Documentary* (New York: Crowell, 1976); John D'Emilio, *Sexual Politics, Sexual Communities: The Making of a Homosexual Minority in the United States, 1940–1970* (Chicago: University of Chicago Press, 1983).
7. Madeline Davis and Elizabeth Lapovsky Kennedy, "Oral History and the Study of Sexuality in the Lesbian Community: Buffalo, New York, 1940–1960," *Feminist Studies* 12, no. 1 (1986): 7–26; Allan Bérubé, *Coming Out Under Fire: The History of Gay Men and Women in World War Two* (New York: Free Press, 1990).
8. Paul Richard Thompson, *The Voice of the Past: Oral History* (New York: Oxford University Press, 1978), 26.
9. Lynn Abrams, *Oral History Theory* (New York: Routledge, 2010).
10. Sherna Berger Gluck and Daphne Patai, *Women's Words: The Feminist Practice of Oral History* (New York: Routledge, 1991); Thompson, *Voice of the Past*.
11. Will Roscoe, "History's Future: Reflections on Lesbian and Gay History in the Community," in *Gay and Lesbian Studies*, ed. Henry L. Minton (New York: Haworth, 1992), 176.
12. Joan Nestle, "The Will to Remember: The Lesbian Herstory Archives of New York," *Feminist Review*, no. 34 (1990): 87.
13. Ibid., 87–88.
14. Davis and Kennedy, "Oral History"; Elizabeth Lapovsky Kennedy and Madeline Davis, *Boots of Leather, Slippers of Gold: The History of a Lesbian Community* (New York: Routledge, 1993); Lesbians Making History, "People Think This Didn't Happen in Canada," *Fireweed: A Feminist Quarterly*, no. 28 (1989): 95–114. Other examples include the

Archives lesbiennes de Montréal—Traces in Montreal; the June Mazer Lesbian Archives in Los Angeles; the Ohio Lesbian Archives in Cincinnati; the Pacific Northwest Lesbian Archives in Seattle; and Glasgow Women's Library's Lesbian Archive.

15. Lynne Fernie and Ann Weissman, *Forbidden Love: The Unashamed Stories of Lesbian Lives* (Montreal, Quebec: National Film Board of Canada, Studio D, 1992), VHS.

16. Thompson, *Voice of the Past*.

17. Elise Chenier, "Hidden from Historians: Preserving Lesbian Oral History in Canada," *Archivaria*, no. 68 (2009): 247–70.

18. Ibid.

19. Lisa Snider, *Archives of Lesbian Oral Testimony (ALOT) Survey Report* (Burnaby, BC: Simon Fraser University, May 2011), alotarchives.org/system/files/ALOTSurveySummary.pdf.

20. Siobhán McHugh, "The Affective Power of Sound: Oral History on Radio," *Oral History Review* 39, no. 2 (2012): 187–206.

21. John Neuenschwander, *A Guide to Oral History and the Law* (New York: Oxford University Press, 2009).

22. Oral History Association, "Principles and Best Practices," www.oralhistory.org/about/principles-and-practices (accessed July 14, 2013).

23. Azin Mirsayah, "A Report on Access and Privacy Policies in Specific Cases of Oral History Interviews," unpublished paper, Simon Fraser University, April 2011.

24. Increasing pressure on researchers to make their data available in open-access repositories has led to valuable explorations of the implications for qualitative research materials. See, e.g., Jane C. Richardson and Barry S. Godfrey, "Towards Ethical Practice in the Use of Archived Transcripted Interviews," *International Journal of Social Research Methodology* 6, no. 4 (2003): 347–55; and Odette Parry and Natasha S. Mauthner, "Whose Data Are They Anyway? Practical, Legal, and Ethical Issues in Archiving Qualitative Research Data," *Sociology* 38, no. 1 (2004): 139–52, doi:10.1177/0038038504039366.

25. See Mary A. Larson, "Potential, Potential, Potential: The Marriage of Oral History and the World Wide Web," *Journal of American History* 88, no. 2 (2001): 602; and Mary Larson, "Steering Clear of the Rocks: A Look at the Current State of Oral History Ethics in the Digital Age," *Oral History Review* 40, no. 1 (2013): 36–49.

26. Annamaria Carusi and Marina Jirotka, "From Data Archive to Ethical Labyrinth," *Qualitative Research* 9, no. 3 (2009): 287; Brigitte Halbmayr, "The Ethics of Oral History: Expectations, Responsibilities, and Dissociations," in *Oral History: The Challenges of Dialogue*, ed. Marta Kurkowska-Budzan and Krzysztof Zamorski, Studies in Narrative 10 (Philadelphia: John Benjamins, 2009), 195–204.

27. On the use of interview material by someone other than the original interviewer, see Richardson and Godfrey, "Towards Ethical Practice."

28. Kelly Anderson to H-OralHist mailing list, July 6, 2012, h-net.msu.edu/cgi-bin/logbrowse.pl?trx=vx&list=h-oralhist&month=1207&week=b&msg=hDeOWWhvU%2BDKZN%2BKa2EUuQ&user=&pw=.

29. Yesenia López, e-mail to the author, July 9, 2013. Participants in a local community history project raised similar concerns about putting personal narratives of any kind online. John Riley, personal communication with the author, December 26, 2012.

30. Mary Stewart and Robert Perks, "Oral History: Exploitation, Ethics, and Exposure" (paper presented at the Eighth European Social Science History Conference, Ghent, Belgium, April 15, 2010), h-net.msu.edu/cgi-bin/logbrowse.pl?trx=vx&list=h-oralhist&month=1307&week=b&msg=to5bOPsw%2by8jslzLXNaA5w&user=&pw=.

31. Maura Cronin to H-OralHist mailing list, July 10, 2013, h-net.msu.edu/cgi-bin/logbrowse. pl?trx=vx&list=h-oralhist&month=1307&week=b&msg=to5bOPsw%2by8jslzLXNaA5w &user=&pw=.

32. Suzy Subways to H-OralHist mailing list, July 9, 2013, h-net.msu.edu/cgi-bin/logbrowse .pl?trx=vx&list=h-oralhist&month=1307&week=b&msg=H6fUb0qjuvhoY16OEM89pQ &user=&pw=.

33. Kelly Anderson to H-OralHist mailing list, July 9, 2013, h-net.msu.edu/cgi-bin/logbrowse .pl?trx=vx&list=h-oralhist&month=1307&week=b&msg=xizdMBD1YreJq2pA5Fo3lw &user=&pw=.

34. Ibid.

35. Marshall McLuhan, *Essential McLuhan*, ed. Eric McLuhan and Frank Zingrone (New York: Routledge, 1997), 275.

36. Steve Cohen, "Shifting Questions: New Paradigms for Oral History in a Digital World," *Oral History Review* 40, no. 1 (2013): 154–67.

37. Saul Kanowitz, "Russian Duma Criminalizes LGBT Movement: Legislature Endorses Anti-gay Violence," *Liberation*, June 15, 2013, www.pslweb.org/liberationnews/news/russian -duma-criminalizes-lgbt-organizing.html.

38. Flinn, "Archival Activism."

Queering the LDS Archive

K. Mohrman

Behold, there shall be a record kept among you.
—*Doctrine and Covenants*, 21:1. See figure 2.

He shall continue in writing and making a history of all the important things
which he shall observe and know concerning my church.
—*Doctrine and Covenants*, 69:3

It is the duty of the Lord's clerk, whom he has appointed, to keep a history, and
a general church record of all things that transpire in Zion.
—*Doctrine and Covenants*, 85:1

Entering the heavily surveilled, but immaculately kept, Church of Jesus Christ of
Latter-day Saints (LDS) Church History Library is, to say the least, an intimidating
experience. The library may look to an outsider like simply another run-of-the-mill
office building, but on closer inspection this structure is anything but ordinary. Or,
perhaps, it is *too* ordinary. In many ways the library is the embodiment of the religion itself, with its spotless facade and pristine interior as simply the physical mani-
festations of LDS belief and practice.[1] Situated cornerwise from Temple Square,
the actual and figurative center of the religion as well as the historic and geographic
center of Salt Lake City, the library's placement symbolizes a long legacy of Mormonism in American culture, a legacy in which the church and its members have

Radical History Review
Issue 122 (May 2015)   DOI 10.1215/01636545-2849585
© 2015 by MARHO: The Radical Historians' Organization, Inc.

Figure 1. Outside the entrance to the LDS Church History Library, which was completed in 2009

been paradoxically, and oftentimes simultaneously, characterized as dangerously outside but also perfectly encapsulated within the US nation-state.[2]

The commonly regurgitated account of LDS history that neatly packages Mormon resistance to the federal government in the nineteenth century and its stark program of assimilation in the twentieth into a progressive narrative culminating with the church's global expansion, which many LDS and Mormon studies scholars themselves reiterate, is unable to account for this legacy of contradiction. Perhaps what is most interesting and ultimately problematic about this narrative is that the account troublingly parallels narratives of American exceptionalism that characterize US history as a movement away from isolationism toward its current status as a morally superior global superpower and glosses over interconnected histories of colonialism, imperialism, political economy, race, gender, and sexuality that complicate such liberal representations. While there may be a certain truth to this linear historical narrative of Mormonism (after all the church's protracted resistance to federal regulation eventually did give way to an expansive program of assimilation), consideration of the contemporary cultural landscape suggests that Mormons have never fully been able to shed the specters of their past. Here I am of course referring to nineteenth-century Mormon polygamy, in addition to their lesser-known history of economic communalism, but I am also alluding to the ways in which contemporary Mormons have so successfully conformed to the norms and expectations of American life.[3] In fact, their assimilation into the nation has been so seamless that it borders on the bizarre; contemporary representations of Mormonism highlight the extent to which many Americans are unsettled by the Mormons' peculiar ability to so perfectly perform their "Americanness."

One need look no further than the unprecedented success of the musical *The Book of Mormon* to see that the American imaginary has yet to reconcile the history of the LDS Church with its integration into mainstream American culture. What is so striking about many popular representations of Mormonism as both essentially

American and essential Other is that they rely on a camp aesthetic that explicitly evokes a queer history of performance. It is no mistake that these representations rely on such an aesthetic or that they often draw parallels between Mormon and gay identity, as was so famously done in *Angels in America*. Rather, these cultural texts bring to the surface what underlies American anxieties about Mormonism: that the religion, its followers, and their practices are essentially and lastingly queer.

As someone who grew up in Salt Lake City and was surrounded by Mormon religion and culture I was all too aware of the misconceptions and assumptions that the majority of non-Mormons had come to associate with the religion, its people, and their practices. Looking back, my impulse to study the religion was originally stimulated by the knowledge that Mormonism was different in some way from other religious traditions, that the discomfort it sowed in some was a product of more than just rumors about special underwear and planets.[4] But I was also keenly aware of the powerful hold that the church had on the social and political landscape of both the city and the state. As I began to study the queer community in my hometown I was forced to reconsider these two facts: that there was something peculiar about the church, but that there was also something resoundingly normative about it.

So when I entered the Church History Library I knew that its impossibly clean walls and manicured lawn, part of an approximately seven-block radius owned and operated by the church in downtown Salt Lake City, was one element of a larger project of Mormon assimilation and dominance that the leaders and its members are continually engaged in. Encompassing not only the religious, administrative, and business arms of the church, but also a brand-new commercial operation,[5] these seven blocks are indicative of the power and influence of a church that has grown to exemplify what Lauren Berlant and Michael Warner describe as "the project of normalization that has made heterosexuality hegemonic," a project that includes "those material practices that, though not explicitly sexual, are implicated in the hierarchies of property and propriety that [are] heteronormative."[6]

In this way I see the symbolic (hyper)normativity of the library and its surrounding environment, embodied in the impeccably groomed physicality, as an expression of the standards that the church has come to not only accept but to integrate into its history and system of belief—including a full-fledged embrace of capitalism, a long-standing investment in whiteness, and a heteropatriarchal familial and church structure. What I find most interesting about Mormonism's normativity, however, is its extremity—I suspected, and my time in the archive confirmed, that it is not a product of the church's long-standing conservatism but rather a response to a queer past that has been too resilient to be completely eradicated from popular memory, history, and the archive itself. Despite the widespread public interest in Mormonism (especially as that interest relates to the church's opposition to same-sex marriage) and its rich and unique history, far too little has been done on the LDS Church and histories of sexualities.[7] Although there has been much work on and around polygamy, especially as it relates to gender norms and family structure, there has been less work on Mormonism in histories of sexualities.[8] Moreover, none of the scholarship on polygamy has considered how this nonnormative sexual practice related to or influenced the church's approach toward same-sex sexualities.

Spurred by this lack of attention to Mormonism and same-sex sexualities, I made the decision to embark on a research project at the LDS Church History Library beginning in the summer of 2012. Rather than be put at ease by the never-ending waves of smiling security officers, volunteers, and librarians, each with his or her own neatly pinned name tag, I was filled with a rising sense of apprehension and not the usual wave of excitement that I had come to expect on crossing the threshold of an archive. Walking into the library and announcing my intention to research the development of the LDS Church's attitude and policies toward same-sex sexualities would certainly have raised red flags and could have resulted in my (permanent) expulsion. My fears were not unfounded given the church's past decisions to ban certain individuals from using their facilities after their research agendas were discovered.[9] My trepidation, however, was not simply due to the church's critical stance toward same-sex sexualities but also stemmed from the notoriously tight grip that the church continues to maintain over the production of academic work about its own history.[10]

From its inception, the LDS Church has prized archiving as a divinely ordained practice, one that is not only required for the pursuit of essential religious rituals but that has become a technology for the reproduction of the church itself.[11] As any Mormon studies scholar will tell you, the church has sought to influence, if not control (and has largely succeeded, although by no means completely), the production of history about itself, its people, and Mormonism more generally. Perhaps more pointedly than any other religious tradition, Mormonism privileges history

Figure 2. Entryway to the publicly accessible section of the LDS Church History Library

as proof of its correctness and as a guide for the beliefs and practices of both its members and leaders. As one prominent scholar of Mormonism, Jan Shipps, has observed, "Mormonism does not have a theology; it has a history."[12] As with any institution, religious or otherwise, the struggle to control the knowledge that is produced by and about it is central to both its continued operation and the maintenance of its power.

As with many privately owned and operated libraries, the LDS Church exercises control over access to its collection, which includes over 4 million items.[13] Private collections, whether they be religious, corporate, nonprofit, or personal, can pose an acutely difficult challenge to researchers, especially to those of us who seek to conduct research that is at odds with the agendas and purported objectives of the institutions that fund and manage them. In addition to the laundry list of challenges around access, with which researchers already grapple (whether they be lack of funds, poor organization, damaged materials, or special permission—to name only a few examples), private archives pose yet another set of hurdles that often prove impossible to negotiate for scholars and for historians of sexualities in particular. Because our lines of inquiry often, but certainly not always, chafe against the officially sanctioned accounts and representations of institutions, governments, and societies, our ability to access material is especially precarious. But as I argue below, it is imperative that we do gain access to these collections, not because they may provide us with some hitherto unknown fact (which they always of course might) or will allow us to identify some "truth" about something or someone, but rather because they can help us explore the ways that queerness was, and is, contingent on and complicit with dominant formations.

Scholarship in the history of sexuality has all too often taken the route of praising nonnormative sexualities as always already resistant and oppositional and has paid much less attention to how nonnormative sexualities—their emergence, collectivity, and very survival—have depended on their relationship to hegemonic configurations.[14] Moreover, the extensive attention paid to the development of certain sexual identities and communities, as well as the contexts that made them possible, has made it much harder to "interpret[] a wide range of associations and transient relationships," as queer.[15] Viewed in this light, Mormon polygamy, for example, cannot be discarded as a purely patriarchal religious anomaly but can instead be understood as a nonnormative sexual, marital, and familial practice that both relied on *and* challenged dominant formations. Thus I take seriously Jasbir Puar's appeal to think queerness not as "an identity nor an anti-identity, but an assemblage that is spatially and temporally contingent."[16] Puar's formulation is particularly apposite and thorny for historians since "queerness as an assemblage moves away from excavation work," a practice, it may be argued, that the very foundation of history has been predicated on.[17] This practice has proved more difficult to abandon than historians of sexualities would care to admit, as Anjali Arondekar notes in her examination of the turn to the colonial archive in sexuality studies: "[Scholars] continue to privilege the reading practices of recovery over all others."[18] Puar's challenge, then, is not an easy one to meet; utilizing the archive, especially one that has sought to erase particular subjects, practices, and communities, without engaging in the process of recovery, requires a theoretical and methodological approach that forces us to rethink the very premise of "queering the archive." Such an approach must grapple not only with the instability of (archival) subjectivity but also with the narratives of domination and resistance that have become hegemonic in critical histories of sexualities, especially since many of those narratives highlight religion as a singularly oppressive force.

The limited work on Mormonism and same-sex sexualities has been no exception to this trend of recuperation. In response to the highly repressive and violent actions taken by the church against lesbian, gay, and bisexual (LGB) people, scholars who have addressed the subject of same-sex sexualities and Mormonism have sought to identify Mormon gay and lesbian subjects as well as illuminate the church's attitude toward them. Both D. Michael Quinn's groundbreaking *Same-Sex Dynamics among Nineteenth-Century Americans: A Mormon Example* and Rocky O'Donovan's "'The Abominable and Detestable Crime against Nature': A Brief History of Homosexuality and Mormonism, 1840–1980" are based in part on materials from the LDS Church History Library.[19] Quinn, one of the September Six, a group of LDS academics who were either excommunicated or disfellowshipped from the church for publishing scholarship that was at odds with official church doctrine and/or criticized the church's leadership in the fall of 1993, provides an extensive, if conservative, analysis of Mormonism and its treatment of LGB individuals in the nineteenth century.[20] Quinn concludes that while there was little evidence of actual same-sex sexual activity among nineteenth-century Mormons, the church itself was relatively tolerant of both sodomy and homosexuality prior to the turn of the twentieth century. O'Donovan's piece, by contrast, asserts a much more explicit polemical argumentation, insisting that the church has always been an overtly homophobic institution, one that sought to hide the "true" nature of its gay and lesbian members.

The attention that these two authors bring to the history of same-sex sexualities and the Mormon Church cannot be discounted. On the one hand, their pioneering work in the field has done what many historians of sexualities have simply neglected to do—attend to a rich history that has for too long gone unwritten, accessing an archive that has long been the provenance of only "official" histories. On the other hand, however, their adherence to the archival strategies of recovery and recuperation has led to a disturbingly limited focus that not only labels individuals according to anachronistic terminology and modes of understanding but also claims to know and give voice to those who are more likely than not forever lost to the archival record. As Michel Foucault so cogently notes,

All those lives destined to pass beneath any discourse and disappear without ever having been told were able to leave traces—brief, incisive, often enigmatic—only at the point of their instantaneous contact with power. So that *it is doubtless impossible to ever grasp them again in themselves*, as they might have been "in a free state"; they can no longer be separated out from the declamations, the tactical biases, the obligatory lies that power games and power relations presuppose [emphasis added].[21]

To recognize that the individuals who appear in archival materials are often only the mere traces of actual lives is to recognize that what is most useful about these accounts is what they can reveal to us about the currents of power that leave those traces. Attention to power rather than subjectivity not only shifts our lens away from identity toward process, but it also allows for a more complex acknowledgment of the shifting boundaries of normativity. Scholarship that relies completely on identifying or recovering subjects in archival material reinforces a positivist approach to history, one that stakes the legitimacy of scholarship on the ability to identify definitively the exact thoughts, actions, and practices of individuals, a veritable impossibility.

Quinn attempts to do exactly this throughout his book. For example, he relies on a single diary entry from one nineteenth-century Mormon man to discuss a case of what he calls "female homoeroticism." According to him, this early case

was an allegation of attempted sex between women. While fulfilling a special preaching assignment from Brigham Young, Richard Ballantyne referred in December 1856 to an unnamed woman in Salt Lake City who "was trying to seduce a young girl." This married LDS woman admitted to adultery with a man, but she "denied having any hand in trying to seduce Brother West's daughter, though the testimony seems plain against her." This was the first reference to female-female eroticism among nineteenth-century Mormons. However, it involved only an attempted seduction, rather than actual sexual acts between women.[22]

Quinn's fixation on the occurrence of actual sex functions as a blinder to the more interesting implications of this diary entry. On reading the full paragraph from which Quinn takes this case, it becomes clear there may be more complicated issues at play:

We found some [ward members] that had committed Adultery, and one woman that was still practicing such wickedness, and trying to seduce a young girl of Brother West's family. She confessed to Brothers Johnson and [illegible name] that she had had unlawful sexual connection with Judge Styles but denied having anything to do with any person else, except her husband. Denied having any hand in trying to seduce Brother West's daughter, though the testimony seems plain against her. She had promised to confess to Brother Kimball.[23]

In the broader context of the entry, Richard Ballantyne is describing a larger epidemic of sin that was sweeping his local ward, which he was hoping to squelch by counseling individuals through home visits he undertook with other stake leaders.[24] Earlier in the entry he states that "the women did not love the order of a plurality of wives and that they ruled the Ward."[25] When the totality of the woman's reported conduct is taken into account, as well as its context in the full diary entry, other equally valid interpretations become evident.

While it is certainly possible that this woman was trying to sexually seduce this young girl, it is just as possible that this woman was trying to "seduce" this young girl into opposing polygamy (what Ballantyne refers to as "the order of a plurality of wives"). The general "sinfulness" of these women, that is, their resistance to polygamy, as described at the beginning of the entry seems to be what in fact instigated the home visits in which individuals were asked to confess their sins to church leaders. This woman may have been confessing to both adultery *and* resistance to the testimony of "a plurality of wives." This reading is further supported by the fact that Ballantyne saw fit to separate her denial of "having anything to do with any person else, except her husband" from her denial of "trying to seduce Brother West's daughter" in the diary entry itself. Yet another interpretation might be that this woman's sexual seduction was sinful because of the age ("young girl") rather than just the gender of the victim. The majority of recorded cases (whether legal, sectarian, or secular) of same-sex sexual encounters in Utah during the nineteenth century are cases in which either violence or a significant age difference between the participants is involved. This suggests that Mormons were more likely to ignore same-sex sexual activity if it was between consenting partners of a similar age.

My objective in reinterpreting this archival material is not meant to discredit Quinn or his work more generally. In fact, many of his observations about the church leadership and its motives are insightful; however, it is meant to demonstrate that what is significant about this entry is not whether sex between two women actually took place but rather if the local Mormon authorities understood the possibility of such activity and, if they did, how they chose to deal with it. If the existence of "men and women" such as the one mentioned in Ballantyne's diary "comes down to exactly what was said about them[, then] nothing subsists of what they were or what they did."[26] What is left, then, is what was (or was not) done to them. In the words of Ann Laura Stoler, we might be well advised to "explore the grain and read along it first" rather than hurriedly jump ahead to "read against the grain," as the refrain so familiarly goes. To read along the grain first allows us to examine our assumptions not only about what we are reading but about what we chose to read in the first place. My own experience in the LDS archive speaks to Stoler's warning that "assuming we know th[e] scripts rests too comfortably on predictable stories with familiar plots."[27]

As my research progressed, my own assumptions about the historical bed-rock of the LDS Church's views on homosexuality were significantly undermined. When I began my research I had presumed that I would find a long and consistent history of homophobic action and policy on the part of church leaders, but as it turns out there was surprisingly little evidence to support this conjecture. It was only between the late 1880s and the 1890s that references to same-sex sexualities began to appear with any regularity in the archive. Even in the references that do exist they are usually couched in general discussions of sexual sins. For example, one of the first public references to sodomy came from President George Q. Cannon at a major church gathering called general conference in October 1897.[28] Referencing the famous case of Oscar Wilde, which had intrigued Utahans since Wilde's visit to Salt Lake City not long before, Cannon decried the "abominable crime" of Sodom and Gomorrah, but did so in reference to the multitude of sexual crimes that were being committed in the community.[29] While this church leader was quite clear about his abhorrence of sodomy, he was by no means solely focused on it as the only or the most grievous sexual crime. Cannon's invocation of Wilde's trial seemed to have been more about demonstrating the depravity of the world outside of Utah, than it was about condemning homosexuality in particular.

Overall, what I have found suggests that while the church has always been stringent about the sanctity of marriage, condemning any sexual activity outside the bonds of matrimony, it had never been overtly concerned with homosexuality; in fact, it had been, comparatively, quite disinterested in it. As Quinn argues, Mormons were more tolerant of homoerotic behavior "than they were of every other non-marital sexual activity" before the turn of the century.[30] For example, the church called for blood atonement for a whole host of sexual sins including incest, rape, pedophilia, bestiality, adultery, and fornication, but sodomy was surprisingly absent from this list. This begs the question: Why the omission? This lack of interest in or anxiety over same-sex sexualities is in striking contrast to other histories that recount the increasingly strong attention that was being paid to same-sex sexualities by medical, legal, and religious authorities during this period.[31] I find this lag in Mormon attention to homosexuality particularly queer—while identities and communities were beginning to solidify around a homosexual identity both in Utah and across the United States, the LDS Church was distinctly disinterested in regulating it on any sort of consistent basis.[32] The evidence suggests that the Mormon hierarchy was not unaware of these sexual practices in their midst but rather that they were more concerned with other issues. In particular, they were concerned with regulating the church's marriage and economic practices as well as protecting those practices from the ire of the federal government.

What is even more intriguing about the church's lack of interest in same-sex sexualities is that, by and large, this attitude of toleration lasted throughout the first thirty years of the twentieth century. Although sodomy trials began to appear on the books in Utah more or less regularly starting in 1880, it appears that Mormons were reluctant to prosecute one another for sodomy, and those individuals who were prosecuted were given relatively light sentences. And, as I alluded to previously, the vast majority of cases involving sodomy were ones dealing with violent crime and/or pedophilia, again suggesting that those practices were more concerning than the same-sex sex itself.[33] It was not until the late 1940s that the church and its leadership began to take a consistent stance on homosexuality as a problem, and it was not until the late 1950s that they saw it as a significant one.[34]

This pattern departs remarkably from other accounts of same-sex sexualities during the late nineteenth and early twentieth centuries, a departure that indicates the extent to which the LDS archive houses the potential to queer the prevailing historical narratives regarding same-sex sexualities and religion. Despite this departure, there is one striking similarity between the Mormon and national contexts: increased media coverage of and documented engagement in same-sex sexual practices coincided with the absorption of Utah's economy into the larger workings of American capitalism, which accompanied the completion of the railroad in the state in 1869. This overlap recalls John D'Emilio's contention, in his seminal piece "Capitalism and Gay Identity," that "it has been the historical development of capitalism—more specifically, its free labor system—that has allowed large numbers of men and women in the late twentieth century to call themselves gay, to see themselves as part of a community of similar men and women, and to organize politically on the basis of that identity."[35] This is certainly true for homosexuals in Utah starting in the late 1800s—ironically, D'Emilio even cites what Quinn calls "the earliest community study of lesbians and gay men in America" to support his claim.[36] Mildred Berryman, herself a lesbian and a Mormon, conducted this ethnographic survey for her honor's thesis while in college in Salt Lake City between 1916 and 1922.[37] Putting aside the implications and importance of Berryman's study and D'Emilio's reliance on it to support his groundbreaking argument, I highlight the fact of Utah's nascent, but nonetheless thriving, gay and lesbian community between the 1880s and the 1920s because it demonstrates how attention to archives, like those of the LDS Church, can provide new insight into the ways that queerness exists in relationship to various configurations and invocations of power.

As I spent more time in the LDS archive, the relationship between the consolidation of homosexual identity and community (largely ignored by the church) and the onslaught of industrial and consumer capitalism in the United States (adamantly resisted by the church) became more apparent in part because this relationship was both prefigured and mirrored by the relationship between the church's dual practices of polygamy and economic communalism. The material support I found for D'Emilio's claim spurred a realization that I needed to take a different approach to my archival research, one that more purposely reflected Puar's call to think of queerness as an assemblage. Such an approach relieved the need to self-consciously probe the archive for traces of queer lives, a tactic already exhausted by O'Donovan and Quinn, but it also allowed for a more fluid and dynamic approach to thinking about queerness in the context of archival research. In shifting my focus to how the church's nineteenth-century economic ideologies and practices, specifically its communalist and socialist policies and experiments, related to its nonnormative sexual and marital practices, I was able to reconsider not only the constitutive relationship between (non)normative sexualities and economic configurations, but I was also able to challenge the prevailing account of religion as an oppressive threat to nonnormative sexualities.

This new approach to my research, which was in part a product of the challenges posed by working in the LDS archives (one cannot simply search for "homosexuality" or "sodomy" in the library catalog, for example), not only helped relieve the pressure of conducting taboo research in an unfriendly institution, but it also pushed me to develop alternative theorizations of queerness. As with most unexpected turns taken in the course of archival research, this path of inquiry has opened up a much more complicated and fascinating story than I could have ever imagined. What I have discovered thus far suggests that the interrelated and contingent relationships between the hard-fought political battles over polygamy (with its ties to and implications for the racial order of US empire) and the extensive, but failed, experiments of Mormon economic communalism can actually tell historians of sexualities a great deal about both the constitutive and oppositional elements of sexual identities and practices in relation to capitalism. For example, Mormon resistance to federal attempts to destroy the church's marital as well as political and economic practices indicates the potent possibilities for both critiquing and building alternatives to prevailing systems of economic and political domination vis-à-vis alternative sexual and familial formations.

Had I simply maintained my original focus on uncovering the history of the church's homophobia, ready to "read against the grain" and "queer the archive," I would have never encountered the ways in which the LDS archive is *already* queer. It houses materials that challenge assumptions about the role Mormonism, and by extension religion in general, plays in defining, policing, and constituting sexualities, particularly nonnormative ones. Despite the church's contemporary status as a homophobic institution that has been at the forefront of the battle over gay marriage, its early history, as revealed by the materials in its own library, reflects a vastly different stance toward nonnormative sexualities. The sheer lack of attention paid to same-sex sexual practices in the nineteenth and early twentieth centuries suggests that its move to police and shun homosexuality in the mid-twentieth century was part of a larger shift, a shift that I see as intimately connected to its economic ideology. The disruptive potential of the materials the archive houses (disruptive to both official church history and histories of sexualities) suggests that like same-sex sexualities, queerness flourishes under the very conditions that it is often assumed to oppose. Of course, it is not only academic narratives that are being challenged here. The materials I encountered disrupt many carefully constructed and widely distributed discourses, perpetuated by the church itself, but also readily accepted by the public. It can no longer be assumed that the church has maintained a consistent policy of condemning homosexuality. On the contrary, the lack of documentation before 1950, combined with the plethora of documentation after that date, suggests that the church leadership has only recently identified homosexuality as a "problem." Moreover, it has, since the mid-twentieth century, continually worked to refine its policies and approaches toward same-sex sexuality, in essence helping to define what it only purported to describe and condemn.

But my conclusions, as I have indicated, were not solely derived from the materials that I did examine; those that I could not access were equally telling. In other words, I take Stoler's contention that "insights into the social imaginaries of colonial rule" can be "gained from attending not only to colonialism's archival content, but to the principles and practices of governance lodged in particular archival forms" one step further, arguing that historians can gain a great deal from attending to what collections do not house.[38] The ways in which collections are managed, regulated, and restricted, how materials are organized, coded, and, perhaps most importantly, censored, can tell historians just as much as the materials themselves. In my own case, what I learned from the church's selective pattern of censorship helped me to interpret what I *was* allowed to read. For me the church's effort to represent LDS teachings as having consistently "held that sexual acts are morally appropriate only between husband and wife [and that] all other sexual relations, whether they are heterosexual or homosexual, have *always* been seen as violations of moral discipline" (emphasis added) and condemned by church authorities suggests an active campaign on the part of the church to create a particular representation of its history that is in line with current teachings.[39]

Since 1947 when Spencer W. Kimball was appointed to deal with cases of sexual misconduct, Mormon leaders have increasingly dealt with homosexuality as a public issue.[40] While proof of the church's increasing interest in and obsessive need to curtail same-sex sexual activity among its members is available both online and in the Church History Library itself, any evidence of the church's stance on the subject before 1947 is extremely difficult to find. Beyond a few scattered references in speeches, there are no available archival materials that point to the church's official or unofficial position on the matter. I was able to find only a single reference to the church's official position prior to 1947. In a 1977 biography of Kimball, it is revealed that Charles A. Callis, a member of the Quorum of the Twelve Apostles from 1933 until his death in 1947, was assigned to deal with a "flow of interviews with Church members involved in fornication or adultery or homosexuality."[41] Despite my attempts to locate materials on Callis and his calling, I was stymied at every turn. The catalog declared any and all promising materials "closed to research." According to the LDS Church History website, materials are censored in the collection because they contain information that is sacred, confidential, or private.[42] As I was personally informed, any information that consists of correspondence between church authorities about individual members is often censored to protect the privacy of that member and/or his or her family, especially if the record deals with an excommunication. While I cannot wholly discount this explanation's validity, it would be naive to assume that the church is not using this explanation as a way to censor materials that could possibly contradict its current official teaching on homosexuality.

I find this stark shift in the archival record, marked by the year 1947, quite revealing. The church moves from relative privacy and silence on the issue, in the era of Callis, to a much more vocal and increasingly cataloged response to homosexuality, under Kimball's leadership.[43] This shift indicates that the church may be hiding an earlier, less polished, and perhaps more inconsistent policy toward same-sex sexualities before 1947. That is not to say that before that year the church was not concerned with regulating and discouraging same-sex sexual activity among its members. To do so would ignore the evidence that points toward the church's disapproval of both sodomy and homosexuality in its earlier history. Yet the development of a strict and refined policy took time to solidify, reflecting not only the changing attitude toward homosexuality in the United States but also the slow-moving program of assimilation that the church was engaged in after 1890, the year in which the church officially abandoned polygamy and that marked the decline of economic communal experimentation by the church.[44] The dearth of accessible documents relating to Callis, while extremely frustrating, is in itself telling of the church's desire to maintain control over its history, in this case the representation of how it has dealt with the issue of same-sex sexualities. This shift is an example of the ways that archives, despite the efforts of librarians, religious authorities, and bureaucrats, can still retain traces of the potential queerness that lies within.

The assumptions we make as historians about what is contained, or is not contained, in an archive have a significant impact on the stories that we tell. My research in the LDS archives tells me that we, as scholars, need to be extremely careful about when and why we make those assumptions. Private collections, such as the one discussed here, pose a number of challenges, not all of which I have enumerated. To meet these challenges is to submit to the possibility that what we may find in them is not what we expect, that the materials we encounter have the potential to unravel our narratives, undermine our investments, and wreak havoc on our intellectual stability. Instead of immediately attempting to queer the archive, perhaps we should simply submit to the organic ebbs and flows we find there, bearing witness to the already queer forms and practices that are housed within them.

Notes

1.   An ordered and immaculate aesthetic characterizes both the system of belief and the material practice of the twenty-first-century LDS Church. It is evident in the standardization and routinization of religious practice and worship, the careful maintenance of LDS property, and the formulaic architecture and interior design of temples and wards. This aesthetic is largely a product of Correlation, a formal program of organization and routinization for the Mormon priesthood system implemented during the twentieth century. For further explanation, see Matthew Bowman, *The Mormon People: The Making of an American Faith* (New York: Random House, 2012), esp. chap. 7.

2.   For the purposes of this essay, the use of *Mormonism* and *Mormon/Mormons* will refer only to the LDS Church and its adherents and no other religious denomination.

3.   Technically, Mormons engaged (before 1890) in polygyny, or the practice of plural marriage, where a man has more than one wife. However, the term *polygamy*, which indicates a marriage with more than two partners of either gender, has become synonymous with the Mormon marriage system. I use the widely accepted term *polygamy* for the purposes of this essay.

4.   "Special underwear" refers to what LDS members call a "garment," which is a type of undergarment that is worn by adult members of the church in connection with temple rites and ordinances, specifically the endowment ceremony. References to planets are distorted explanations of Mormon cosmology, specifically the Mormon belief regarding heaven.

5.   Opened in March 2012, City Creek Center is a mixed-use development that incorporates commercial, dining, and residential components. The two and a half blocks, on which it rests, as well as the development itself, are privately owned and operated by the church and its partner Taubman Centers.

6.   Lauren Berlant and Michael Warner, "Sex in Public," in "Intimacy," ed. Lauren Berlant, special issue, *Critical Inquiry* 24, no. 2 (1998): 548.

7.   While I have chosen to highlight the lack of discussion about Mormonism in the history of sexuality for the purposes of critiquing recuperative archival practices that privilege the excavation of queer subjectivity, I also wish to point out that there is an equally surprising shortage of scholarship about Mormonism in other areas as well. For example, there has been little work done within ethnic studies on Mormonism, nor has there been much written on the role that Mormonism has played in the consolidation of US empire. A notable exception to both of these is Hokulani Aikau, *A Chosen People, a Promised Land: Mormonism and Race in Hawai'i* (Minneapolis: University of Minnesota Press, 2012).

8.   I do not wish to discount the work of numerous scholars (some of whom identify themselves as historians of sexuality and others who do not) who have contributed significantly to the discussion of Mormonism and histories of sexualities. For a few works among many in this area, see Bruce Burgett, "On the Mormon Question: Race, Sex, and Polygamy in the 1850s and the 1990s," *American Quarterly* 57, no. 1 (2005): 75–102; Nancy Bentley, "Marriage as Treason: Polygamy, Nation, and the Novel," in *The Futures of American Studies*, ed. Donald E. Pease and Robyn Wiegman (Durham, NC: Duke University Press, 2002), 341–70; Julie Dunfey, "'Living the Principle' of Plural Marriage: Mormon Women, Utopia, and Female Sexuality in the Nineteenth Century," *Feminist Studies* 10, no. 3 (1984): 523–36; and Lawrence Foster, *Religion and Sexuality: Three American Communal Experiments of the Nineteenth Century* (New York: Oxford University Press, 1981).

9.   For example, historian Connell "Rocky" O'Donovan was purportedly banned from the archive by LDS authorities.

10. The church's reputation in this regard is well known and accepted among academics, Mormon and non-Mormon alike. See, for example, news coverage of the church's excommunication of the September Six, such as Dirk Johnson, "As Mormon Church Grows, So Does Dissent from Feminists and Scholars," *New York Times*, October 2, 1993, www .nytimes.com/1993/10/02/us/as-mormon-church-grows-so-does-dissent-from-feminists-and -scholars.html.

11. For a discussion of the archive as a technology for the reproduction of the state, see Ann Laura Stoler, *Along the Archival Grain: Epistemic Anxieties and Colonial Common Sense* (Princeton, NJ: Princeton University Press, 2009), 28.

12. Jan Shipps, *Sojourner in the Promised Land: Forty Years among the Mormons* (Urbana: University of Illinois Press, 2000), 381.

13. This number is as reported on the LDS Church History website: churchhistorylibrary.lds.org /primo_library/libweb/static_htmls/custom/CHL/pages/general-about.jsp. This number does not include the materials in the Family History Library collection, also owned and operated by the LDS Church, which vastly outnumbers those in the Church History Library.

14. My aim here is not to disparage the work that has been done on the history of gay and lesbian subjects. Rather, I wish to point out that in the rush to recuperate subjects "lost" to history, not only has this scholarship helped to create them, but it has also helped to erect boundaries around certain subjects and to erase others. In trying to identify subjects and communities, opportunities have been squandered for encountering the less tangible and more ephemeral moments, exchanges, and formations that could be considered a part of histories of sexualities.

15. Nayan Shah, *Stranger Intimacy: Contesting Race, Sexuality, and the Law in the North American West* (Berkeley: University of California Press, 2011), 8.

16. Jasbir Puar, *Terrorist Assemblages: Homonationalism in Queer Times* (Durham, NC: Duke University Press, 2007), 204.

17. Ibid., 205.

18. Anjali Arondekar, "Without a Trace: Sexuality and the Colonial Archive," in "Studying the History of Sexuality: Theory, Method, Praxis," ed. Julian Carter and Lesley A. Hall, special issue, *Journal of the History of Sexuality* 14, no. 1/2 (2005): 12.

19. See D. Michael Quinn, *Same-Sex Dynamics among Nineteenth-Century Americans: A Mormon Example* (Urbana: University of Illinois Press, 1996); and Rocky O'Donovan, "'The Abominable and Detestable Crime against Nature': A Brief History of Homosexuality and Mormonism, 1840–1980," in *Multiply and Replenish: Mormon Essays on Sex and Family*, ed. Brent Corcoran (Salt Lake City: Signature Books, 1994), 123–70.

20. Since excommunication records are closed to the public, it is impossible to know exactly why Quinn was banned from the church, but *Same-Sex Dynamics* was not published until 1996, three years after his excommunication. For more information on the September Six, see Johnson, "As Mormon Church Grows." For a brief history of Quinn's career, see Peggy Fletcher Stack, "Noted Historian Still Believes in Mormonism, but Now as an Outsider," *Salt Lake Tribune*, October 1, 2013, www.sltrib.com/sltrib/news/56899817-78/quinn -mormon-lds-church.html.csp.

21. Michel Foucault, "Lives of Infamous Men," in *Power*, vol. 3 of *Essential Works of Foucault, 1954–1984*, ed. James D. Faubion (New York: New Press, 2000), 161.

22. Quinn, *Same-Sex Dynamics*, 269.

23. Richard Ballantyne, "Sabbath Dec 21 1856," Diaries and Reminiscences, microfilm, MS 467 1, LDS Church History Library, Salt Lake City, UT.

24. A ward is akin to a parish in other Christian faiths. A stake, made up of several wards, is roughly comparable to a diocese.

25. Ballantyne, "Sabbath Dec 21 1856."

26. Foucault, "Lives," 162.

27. Stoler, *Along the Archival Grain*, 50.

28. In the LDS Church two conferences are held every year, one in April and one in October. These meetings are composed of several sessions in which church leaders deliver sermons to the entire church. Many Mormons gather in Utah for general conference, but the proceedings are broadcast via radio, television, and the Internet and can be accessed internationally.

29. "President George Q. Cannon: Mission of the Saints—How Satan will be bound—Approaching Judgments—Wickedness of the world—Cleansing process in progress—Who are the children of God?—The Spirit of Revelation with the Church—Return of the Ten Tribes," in *Conference Reports October 1897–April 1900* (Salt Lake City, UT: Deseret News Publishing Company, 1897), 64, M204 .1 Al 18971900, LDS Church History Library.

30. Quinn, *Same-Sex Dynamics*, 265.

31. See, e.g., George Chauncey, *Gay New York: Gender, Urban Culture, and the Making of the Gay Male World, 1890–1940* (New York: Basic Books, 1994); and John D'Emilio and Estelle Freedman, *Intimate Matters: A History of Sexuality in America* (Chicago: University of Chicago Press, 1988).

32. See Quinn, *Same-Sex Dynamics*, esp. chaps. 9–10.

33. Ibid.

34. This timing, of course, overlaps with the McCarthy-era persecution of homosexuals. It is interesting to note that Mormons, both locally and nationally, were some of the first to persecute and vehemently oppose homosexuality during the Lavender Scare.

35. John D'Emilio, "Capitalism and Gay Identity," in *Queer Economics: A Reader*, ed. Joyce P. Jacobsen and Adam Zeller (New York: Routledge, 2008), 183.

36. Quinn, *Same-Sex Dynamics*, 195.

37. See Vern Bullough and Bonnie Bullough, "Lesbianism in the 1920 and 1930s: A Newfound Study," *Signs* 2, no. 4 (1977): 895–904.

38. Stoler, *Along the Archival Grain*, 20.

39. George L. Mitton and Rhett S. James, "A Response to D. Michael Quinn's Homosexual Distortion of Latter-day Saint History," *FARMS Review of Books* 10, no. 1 (1998): 143.

40. For examples of the church's public stance on homosexuality after 1950, see Spencer W. Kimball, *The Miracle of Forgiveness* (Salt Lake City, UT: Deseret Book Company, 1969); and Boyd K. Packer, *To Young Men Only: An Address Given at the Priesthood Session of General Conference, October 2, 1976* (Salt Lake City, UT: Intellectual Reserve, 1976), www.lds.org/bc/content/shared/content/english/pdf/language-materials/33382_eng .pdf?lang=eng.

41. Edward L. Kimball and Andrew E. Kimball Jr., *Spencer W. Kimball: Twelfth President of the Church of Jesus Christ of Latter-day Saints* (Salt Lake City, UT: Bookcraft, 1977), 271. The Quorum of the Twelve Apostles is the second-highest ruling body in the LDS Church.

42. For further explanation of what falls under each of these categories, see the Church History Library website: history.lds.org/article/access?lang=eng.

43. The late 1940s and the early 1950s also marked a larger shift on the part of church authorities to modernize in various ways. Kimball was one of several church leaders who participated in this campaign of modernization. The regulation of homosexuality during this

period and the explicit rejection of socialism and communism that the church leadership advocated in the 1930s tell an important story about the style and types of assimilatory practices that were engaged in by the church and its members during the mid-twentieth century.

44. For a discussion of how the federal government's campaign against polygamy was connected to its campaign against the church's economic practices, see Sarah Barringer Gordon, *The Mormon Question: Polygamy and Constitutional Conflict in Nineteenth-Century America* (Chapel Hill: University of North Carolina Press, 2002), esp. chap. 6.

Beyond Accountability

The Queer Archive of Catholic Sexual Abuse

Anthony M. Petro

The entire issue of "Child Sexual Abuse," whether . . . categorized as pedophiliac, homosexual or heterosexual, is displayed prominently across the front pages of newspapers where it shall remain for at least the balance of the decade (having replaced the sexual issue of the seventies, homosexuality).
—Confidential 1985 report, "The Problem of Sexual Molestation by Roman Catholic Clergy," by F. Ray Mouton and Rev. Thomas P. Doyle, OP, JCD

BishopAccountability.org describes itself as "an archive of archives" that seeks to document the sexual abuse crisis in the Roman Catholic Church.[1] Founded by Terence McKiernan and registered as a nonprofit organization in Massachusetts, its mission is twofold: to offer a full "account" of the bishops' responsibility in the sexual abuse crisis "both collectively and individually" and to hold accountable "bishops who have caused the abuse of children and vulnerable adults."[2] To this end, the archive publishes online the records of church administration and abuse for hundreds of dioceses across the United States dating back to the mid-twentieth century.[3] In addition to diocesan and religious order documents, much of them released through court order, it holds criminal investigation records, accounts from survivors and their families, and media coverage of the crisis. The layout of the archive overwhelms through its many options for accessing documents, allowing users to search

Radical History Review
Issue 122 (May 2015)   DOI 10.1215/01636545-2849594
© 2015 by MARHO: The Radical Historians' Organization, Inc.

by keyword, through a database of accused priests, by diocese, by legal or media accounts, by survivor accounts, or through frequently requested documents. And the digital archive continues to grow, aspiring to include "every relevant diocesan and Vatican document" representing "every conceivable perspective on the crisis."[4]

By design, BishopAccountability.org underscores how bishops mismanaged allegations of abuse. Statistics compiled by the site detail both the scope of sexual abuse and the long histories of negligence and cover-up by church officials.[5] Between 1950 and 2011, the Catholic Bishops of the United States received allegations of abuse committed by 6,115 priests, about 5.6 percent of the 109,694 priests active over this period. Conservative estimates report allegations from about sixteen thousand survivors of abuse. But others place the total number between 25,000 and 280,000. To date, nineteen bishops in the United States have been accused of abuse, and about two-thirds of sitting bishops have been accused of enabling abuse by protecting priests, often by moving them to new assignments. Of all these allegations of sexual abuse, less than 2 percent have proved false.[6] While these alarming numbers point to the broader scope of the crisis, the records of local dioceses detail the misconduct of specific church leaders in handling allegations of abuse.

Consider the case of "Priest A," identified in the media as Joseph Mundy, who comes up in the 2003 grand jury report of the Suffolk County Supreme Court, which covers allegations of abuse in the Diocese of Rockville Centre, New York. In the 1980s, a fourteen-year-old altar boy confided to religious educator Pat McDonough that he had grown close to Mundy, who told the boy he struggled with celibacy and that the two needed each other. McDonough suspected the priest was grooming the boy for sexual abuse and addressed the matter with Monsignor Alan Placa, the point person for sexual abuse at the diocese. According to McDonough, he retorted: "It is not my responsibility to worry about the boy. My job is to protect the Bishop and the church."[7] The grand jury report and news coverage of this case emphasized the failure of religious leaders to address allegations of abuse.[8] Such failures have dominated coverage of Catholic sex abuse since it first gained national attention in the 1980s.[9] Over the next two decades, a number of book-length exposés, including journalist Jason Berry's groundbreaking 1992 account *Lead Us Not into Temptation*, would document the wide-ranging sexual abuse of minors and vulnerable adults that leaders within the Catholic Church covered up to avoid scandal.[10]

BishopAccountability.org advances this political endeavor. But its rich archive also invites different kinds of analysis, including queer readings that could augment the rhetorical and political power of exposé by moving from the scandal of cover-up toward the difficult stories beneath. Much of the material proves painful to read, given the often-jarring stories of abuse the archive reveals and because of the bureaucratic languages and organizational forms—legal, religious, journalistic— through which these stories struggle to speak and through which their speech so often is produced. Moreover, most descriptions of abuse arise in legal records and survivor accounts that remain in the form of allegations, often made public years or even decades after the events they purport to recall. Here, I read with and against the rhetoric of allegation in order to suggest the broader stories these accounts make possible. And there are many stories here to tell, including those of priests who abused teenage girls, the abuse of younger children, abuse committed by religious sisters and nuns, and the abuse of adults. This essay emphasizes testimonies from men abused (usually) as adolescents, which constitute the majority of cases in the archive, and from priests accused of abuse. These cases suggest an anthropology of relationships that is attentive to dynamics of power between and among survivors and their alleged abusers that moves beyond the narrative of cover-up.[11]

Let us return to the story of that fourteen-year-old boy in Rockville Centre, who was interviewed by *Newsday* in 2002. By then, he was twenty-two, living in Manhattan, and working as a musician and artist. Between the article and the grand jury report, more of his story unfolds. "In eighth grade my mother found out I was gay," he explains. "She insisted I speak with (*Priest A*) to have him make me not gay." The young man recalls his surprise at Mundy's reaction: the priest admitted to working through similar issues and suggested that "maybe they could help each other out."[12] In the following months, the young man described, Mundy took him to movies, on ski trips, and to Broadway shows in Manhattan. He explained how, after a trip to Lincoln Center, they stopped by the Limelight, a gay club located in the deconsecrated building that was formerly the Episcopal Church of the Holy Communion. They visited a back room where men were having sex. Looking back, the young man described to the grand jury how "he was both terrified and excited at what he saw."[13] After getting a drink, the report continues, he began having sex with some of the men in the room while Mundy watched. Eventually, the priest pushed them aside and began touching the teen, who became "very angry and confused." After he refused the priest's advances, they left the club. According to the grand jury report, over the following months, Mundy continued to pressure the teen for sex until he finally gave in.[14]

This case demonstrates the pernicious role played by the church hierarchy. In 2002, the young man mentioned being even angrier at Placa than at Mundy for doing nothing to prevent the abuse. "I think he wanted to make sure I wasn't going to say or do anything," he reported. "And once this passed, it opened the floodgates, because Joe [Mundy] thought it was safe."[15] But this account also suggests the more complicated interplay of religion, sexuality, and abuse to be found in this archive. When, for instance, does an introduction to one form of gay life become a case of religious and sexual abuse? What can we learn about the histories of sexuality and Catholicism from this story and others like it? What kinds of political work can queer analysis of the history of Catholic sexual abuse do—for the survivors of abuse, for the abusers and those who protected them, and for all of us trying to make sense of this case and so many others now accessible through this archive?

To begin addressing such questions, this essay offers two interventions. I take up BishopAccountability.org as a queer archive, demonstrating both its effort to "liberate" victims from the clerical closet (transforming them into "survivors," the preferred term in this community) and its insistence on the political act of making these stories about sex public. This push to make Catholic/abusive sex public underscores my second argument: queering this archive challenges the normative politics of queer history itself. Historians have been attentive to "queering" nonnormative sex that we find laudable, often precisely because it is countercultural, across historical contexts. But historians of sexuality have largely avoided discussions of child sexual abuse, perhaps anxious to resist conflations of homosexuality with pedophilia. And the Catholic Church appears largely as an enemy in histories of queer politics in the United States, a site for proscriptions against gay sex rather than a location for the production of queer forms of sexuality. What would it mean to take up the conjunction of these two sites—sexual abuse and Catholicism—as queer and to account not only for sexual practices we value politically but also for those we might stringently contest? This essay suggests how reading the accounts of the abused and abusers as queer demonstrates the entanglements of religion and sexuality that expand the kinds of stories that we must tell about the historical diversity of sexual practices in modern American history. Including Catholic sexual abuse in queer history also complicates existing accounts of the historical and social contexts through which the crisis unfolded and revises reductive explanations issuing from both conservative and liberal interpretations.

Catholic Sexual Abuse as Queer History

Queer accounting for Catholic sexual abuse would consider more carefully the contours of Catholicism, sexuality, power, and abuse. It would ask how they come together in the lives of survivors and abusers as well as in the relationships between them. This approach challenges readings that position sexual abuse and Catholicism as essentially distinct from each other. In this model, the institutional church *facilitates* sexual abuse, whether by mandating clerical celibacy, placing sexually repressed priests in positions of authority over vulnerable people, failing to screen out homosexuals or pedophiles, or covering up abuse and transferring priests to new locations. Berry, in his account, thus asks whether Jesus would approve of "an ecclesiastic culture [that] *harbors* child molesters [and] *tolerates* homosexual activity."[16] This rendering overlooks how the ecclesiastical, cultural, or theological practices of Catholicism not only enable but also produce the kinds of subjects who commit (and who experience) acts of abuse.

Other interpretations of sex abuse grant this claim but characterize it as a distortion or perversion of some ostensibly authentic Catholicism. Church leaders and many Catholics certainly have a vested interest in making this argument. But as Robert Orsi and other historians of religion have argued, the tendency to protect "good" religion from those forms we deem "bad" too often places scholars in the position of protecting some forms of religion (usually liberal Protestantism) over others (which historically have included Catholicism, evangelical Protestantism, and Islam). This approach overlooks the full range of religious history, whether good or bad.[17] From what historical vantage point can we refer to instances of Catholic sexual abuse as "bizarre distortions of tenets of Catholic faith," as one clinical expert of sexual abuse put it?[18] As historians of the family have demonstrated, there is nothing bizarre about the sexual abuse of children, which, historically speaking, has been all too common, however terrible.[19] Queer studies—being "more attuned to the vagaries of sexuality," as Ann Cvetkovich puts it—helps us both to avoid pathologizing sexual abusers or the survivors of abuse and to think through how these subject positions are shaped culturally and religiously.[20]

The admixtures of the religious and the erotic found in the archives of modern Catholic sexual abuse have much longer histories.[21] We must account for the homosocial and homoerotic contexts through which priests encounter other priests as well as parishioners, young and old—encounters often defined through unequal relations of religious and political power. Mark Jordan captures the religious erotics of this obedience:

The Son who is faithful to the point of death will be glorified by the Father. Within the structures of Catholic power, this means young men who submit to the totalized authority of older men will inherit the older men's power. This power is totalized as "orthodoxy." By means of "orthodoxy," abject submission will be "redeemed" as untrammeled power. One of the principal expressions of orthodoxy is the obedience of young male bodies to the sexual prescriptions of older men. It is the exchange of young male bodies for older male power. How could that exchange not be a homoerotic transaction—a version of what the Greeks meant by "pederasty"?[22]

Following Jordan, we begin to see the eroticism of such encounters working through relations of power that queer politics would want to critique, even as cases of Catholic sexual abuse unsettle common presumptions about the proper boundaries of sexuality, religious practice, and abuse. Two stories from BishopAccountability.org demonstrate this entanglement.

The first comes from a 1995 letter from an anonymous survivor of abuse to his alleged abuser, the Reverend Lawrence C. Murphy. The author describes the lasting effects of abuse he experienced as a student at St. John's School for the Deaf in St. Francis, Wisconsin. The second example, recorded in a 2004 affidavit, introduces the story of John Doe III, who reports being molested by Father James Janssen and two other priests starting when he was twelve, in Fort Madison, Wisconsin. Here is how they describe their instances of abuse:

Anonymous survivor: Do you remember that first time? I came to confession and you asked if I had been masturbating. Then you told me to pull down my pants. I will always feel the horror of that moment. The conflict inside. Telling me to go to the bed and lie down. Touching me. Letting me believe that it is not a sin if you are the one masturbating me. I would not go to hell because you are a priest. And then continuing to allow me to believe that garbage for years![23] . . .

. . . *John Doe III:* At Janssen's direction as my priest, he heard my confessions. This would be done face to face and not in the confessional. I would confess to him after abuse by him that "I blew someone" (which was Janssen). He would giggle and forgive me for my sins. He made a point of having the altar boys confess their "sins" of sexual abuse by him before he would clear them for serving mass. I was also afraid of having to explain to my parents why I would not have been fit to serve mass, so I blindly followed his directions. I witnessed Janssen, Bass and Geerts confessing their sins to each other face to face.[24]

In these accounts, the sacrament of confession becomes a site for sexual abuse. Michel Foucault has famously described confession as one of the first modes of power in the hermeneutics of the self, through which one comes both to decipher oneself and to denounce that truth of oneself.[25] Certainly, we must ask what understandings of the self could possibly emerge for the boys in these cases. But this Foucauldian analysis only interprets the person offering confession. We could also ask what forms of knowledge this ritual of interaction offers the priests, who stage the confessions to elicit what they already know. The ritual does not aim toward producing new knowledge; it repeats previous behaviors, now rendered into the language of confession. It reproduces obedience and control. It also becomes a site of religious and sexual play, evidenced by the instance of a giggle. Here eroticism, Catholicism, and abuse constitute one other. We see this again in descriptions of abuse:

Anonymous survivor: I can't keep our secret about your life as a terrible molester. . . . I must tell the truth to Archbishop Weakland about how you ruined mine and many other children's faith in God and Jesus. You made us hate the Catholic church because we couldn't understand how you could be such a hypocrite of a priest who taught us about God while you were a secret molester.[26] . . .

. . . *John Doe III:* These priests (Fathers Janssen, Geerts and Bass) took from me my religion and most regrettably my belief in God![27]

Both accounts, like many others, narrate how sexual abuse robbed survivors of religion. I want to emphasize this point. It is far more common to hear in stories *about* Catholic sexual abuse that children were robbed of their innocence.[28] Innocence here signifies not only the lack of sin but more specifically the lack of sexuality. It is through abuse, according to such narratives, that children are introduced to sex. The abuse in this telling must be sexual to fit the narrative of lost childhood innocence. But this anonymous survivor and John Doe III, like many survivors, tell a somewhat different tale of loss. They emphasize how their experiences of abuse damaged their faith in the Catholic Church, in Jesus, or in God. They prompt us to question the modifiers in "Catholic sex abuse": Is the abuse sexual or is it Catholic?

This is not to say that sexual abuse is unique to the Catholic Church—such an argument would ignore obvious histories of abuse in other religious traditions, in secular organizations, and within families.[29] Rather, this interpretation resists pathologizing sexual abuse as a universalizable medical, psychological, or criminological condition while it insists on the continued interrogation of the very categories that define this crisis. By unsettling assumptions about good or authentic religion versus bad, this approach likewise points to the need to analyze religion alongside family as a crucial domain of sexual power and abuse. This is one queer political and historical project opened up by BishopAccountability.org.

BishopAccountability.org and the Queer Politics of Speech

Silence is a recurring theme in the history of Catholic sexual abuse. This includes the silence of the church hierarchy in responding to allegations of abuse, but also the silence of survivors, compelled to keep their abuse secret. Breaking silence becomes a key political act for a number of survivors and often their only means of recourse. As a digital archive, BishopAccountability.org provides a unique site for survivors of abuse to share their stories. A preface to data on the "human toll" of sex abuse states: "Thousands of Catholic clergy and religious have raped and sodomized tens of thousands of children—perhaps more than 100,000 children—since 1950. These crimes were committed in secret, and bishops nurtured that secrecy. Nearly 15,000 survivors have broken through the silence, and their accounts have created an in-depth picture of the crisis, both in their own writings and in the work of journalists and law enforcement officials."[30] Most survivor accounts were produced many years or decades after abuse and come filtered through legal documents and from support groups like Survivors Network of Those Abused by Priests and Other Clergy (SNAP). They speak through language shaped by years of psychological and psychiatric counseling. I offer them not as evidence for children's experience but to show how survivors themselves narrate their experiences and name their losses. For many, telling their stories has proved exceptionally difficult, often bringing back traumatic memories and sometimes even contributing to emotional and psychological breakdowns, substance abuse, and thoughts of suicide.[30] But for some, like David Coleman, the political risks of silence are far worse.

Coleman details how his three years of sexual abuse began in 1957, when he was eleven. After playing basketball on Friday evenings, he reports in a 1993 affidavit, Father Richard Coughlin, a priest at St. Patrick's in Stoneham, Massachusetts, would sometimes take a group of boys for pizza and then drop them off at home, one by one. Coleman recalls that he was often "the 'lucky one,'" meaning the last boy dropped off.[31] "I can't tell you how I felt during the episodes when he would fondle me," Coleman writes in a personal account, called "Living on a 'Fault' Line," which he faxed to the Archdiocese of Boston in 1992.[32] "I can tell you how I think I should have felt, how I hope I felt, wish I felt, but there's no certainty I felt any of those things." Coleman did not seek out these sexual experiences, he writes, though he did work hard to gain acceptance from Coughlin and the other children around him. "I had worked to become part of the group," he explains, "to be accepted by them and especially by him since I felt unaccepted and unwanted at home. . . . I must be at least partly to blame for what happened. Or so I felt." In 1993 Coleman contacted his alleged abuser "to tell him how much he had hurt me, how confused my life had been, to have him take responsibility for what happened, to tell me it wasn't my fault." He explains that Coughlin first denied that any such "relationship" had occurred. Once he recounted specific locations of abuse, Coleman describes how the priest acquiesced: "If that's what you remember, it must be so." But, Coleman insists, "he never said it was so."[33]

With little recourse to legal justice (the statute of limitations in his case had run out) or recognition of the alleged abuse from Coughlin or the Archdiocese of Boston, Coleman turned to "public disclosure." "To do otherwise is to perpetrate a second victimization," he explains, "to let Coughlin escape the public justice that accompanies this accusation. He has become an old man, respected in his community, respected because of my silence, a silence that has to end."[34] For Coleman, like so many other survivors of abuse, breaking the silence remains central to both personal and public redress, raising for queer historians the question of what work these accounts do politically and what they might share with the goals of queer politics.

Publicizing stories of abuse augments the prevailing legal and therapeutic means of redress. It takes part in the formation of a public culture that resists the privatizing tendencies of clinical approaches while at the same time inciting new traumas of memory. These shared stories of abuse form what Cvetkovich, in her book by the same title, has described as "an archive of feelings." BishopAccountability .org both facilitates and produces this archive by allowing survivors not only to share their stories but also to read the stories of others, organized by individual dioceses and even specific priests who were alleged to be serial abusers.[35] We might follow Cvetkovich's lead in treating the trauma of sexual abuse reported in these stories as a "social and cultural discourse that emerges in response to the demands of grappling with the psychic consequences of historical events." Defining the experiences of Catholic sexual abuse in cultural terms, rather than clinical ones, also opens the archive of Catholic sexual abuse to broader forms of queer historical and political engagement.[36]

Catholic Sexual Abuse in Queer History

Opening the archive of Catholic sexual abuse to queer history is not simply about turning our analytic attention to another form of nonnormative sexual practice. In fact, I would argue that some efforts to "queer" various forms of sex too easily lose sight of the hidden limits of inclusion itself—that is, the queering scholar might find deserving of inclusion, at various moments, bisexuals, celibate nuns, or "welfare queens," but not evangelical ex-gays, polygamous Mormons, or contemporary pedophiles. This list has become more conservative, not less, as marriage has increasingly monopolized discussions of gay politics. Moreover, interest in queering sexual encounters—particularly with those we would recognize today as minors—appears to dissolve as historians move from premodern to modern historical contexts.[37] For *queer* to signify something meaningful, in a political sense and as a hermeneutic approach, we cannot lose sight of its particular historical emergence in the late twentieth century and its politics of sexuality.[38] In contrast to mainstream lesbian and gay politics, queer politics has balked at the need for state authorization, called for antiassimilationist politics and critiques of heteronormative assumptions that appear natural, and advanced projects geared toward making queer sex public while increasing the range of practices one may find sexual and pleasurable.[39] Taking up Catholic sexual abuse in queer history makes sense, then, for its potential to interpret this crisis in ways that contribute to such antihomophobic and antiheteronormative projects.

Efforts to explain the history of Catholic sexual abuse abound, though most historians of religion and of sexuality have yet to take it up themselves.[40] In one of the few academic histories, conservative scholar Philip Jenkins describes how both liberal factions and traditional and conservative groups within the Catholic Church have used the crisis to very different political ends. Liberals, like Berry, the Catholic journalist, point to patriarchy and institutionalized celibacy as the mechanisms leading to abuse—a church out of line with modernizing trends in gender and sexuality becomes pathological, a symptom expressed through sexual abuse with minors. Traditionalists and conservatives, in contrast, point to the radical changes in Western cultural values since the 1960s, including the popular acceptance of homosexuality. They lament the growing number of homosexuals accepted into the ranks of the institutional church and often blur the line between homosexuality and pedophilia.[41] Bill Donohue, president of the conservative Catholic League for Religious and Civil Rights, articulates this position in a 2010 ad printed in the *New York Times*. It decries the newspaper's failure to recognize that the "pedophilia crisis" has actually always been a "homosexual crisis."[43] In 2004, the United States Conference of Catholic Bishops (USCCB) commissioned the "Bennett Report," which targeted poor screening procedures for failing to weed out homosexual priests, as another key factor to consider: "Although neither the presence of homosexually-oriented priests nor the discipline of celibacy caused the crisis, an understanding of the crisis is not possible without reference to these issues. There are, no doubt, many outstanding priests of a homosexual orientation who live chaste, celibate lives, but any evaluation of the causes and context of the current crisis must be cognizant of the fact that more than eighty percent of the abuse at issue was of a homosexual nature."[43] While this statement reverses the direction of Donohue's charge, characterizing the "more than eighty percent" of cases of abuse involving same-sex interactions as stemming from "homosexual nature" that leads to pedophilia, both ultimately posit homosexuality as the underlining factor.

Orsi points to the failures of such liberal and conservative explanations of sex abuse. "The overriding tendency," he writes, "has been to sexualize the problem, to see it as the consequence of the celibate body or of sexual perversion. Defining the crisis as one of biological urges works to take it out of history and culture." He offers one exception: the charge from the Vatican and conservative Catholics that the sex abuse crisis is particularly *American*, in that it has grown out of the American acceptance of homosexuality and gains for gay rights. In such accounts, he concludes, "the abused bodies of children are being appropriated and mobilized to substantiate a critique of liberal Catholicism and of homosexuality in the United States, and many Catholics fearfully anticipate a crackdown on gay priests."[44] Orsi powerfully redirects analysis of this crisis to children. "Whatever else this moment was about in the history of Catholicism," he insists, "it has fundamentally been about *children*, about children's vulnerability to adult power and adult fantasy in religious contexts and about the absence of real children in these settings—real children as opposed to 'children' as the projection of adult needs and desires or 'children' as extension of adult interiority." Could we take Orsi's point about children without abandoning claims that this crisis is also about sexuality? This move would require a historical approach to sexuality that avoids the biologization Orsi fears but also acknowledges the sexuality of children.[45]

The shifting visibility of Catholic child sexual abuse, including the explosion of allegations of sexual abuse and their emergence as national news in the 1980s, offers the best reason why we need a historical approach to make sense of it.[46] Recent studies commissioned by the USCCB and released by John Jay College have mapped patterns of incidence and reports of abuse between 1950 and 2010.[47] They describe a spike in cases of abuse in the 1960s and 1970s that peaked in the late 1970s and then dropped off after 1985. The 2011 John Jay report on the historical context of Catholic sex abuse suggests that "social influences on sexuality" in the 1960s contributed to this increase, which it describes as "similar to the rise in other types of 'deviant' behavior in society," like increasing rates of divorce, illegal drug use, and crime.[48] The studies also describe a spike in the *reporting* of incidents of abuse (usually occurring decades before) in the 1980s, with significant increases in 1993 and 2002 as well.[49] They explain away the lag in reporting abuse simply as "typical." Jenkins offers a better assessment of the historical reasons for the surge of reports in the 1980s, citing more willingness among the courts to hear cases of abuse and less reluctance among members of the press to criticize sites of institutional authority, including the Catholic Church.[50] The psychological and medical community also took greater interest in sexual abuse in this period. Historians of sexuality could augment this explanation. Linda Gordon's historical analysis of family violence offers a useful guide.

According to Gordon, models employed to understand family violence, including incest, shifted from 1880 to 1960 between psychological explanations that arose in conservative times and sociostructural interpretations during periods marked by progressive politics and stronger movements for social reform. "The presence or absence of a strong feminist movement," she explains, "makes the difference between better and worse solutions to the social problem of child sexual abuse." It also shapes the interpretations offered for sexual abuse. "Without a feminist analysis," Gordon continues, "evidence of child sexual abuse means that danger lies" not in families shaped through patriarchy but "in sex perverts, in public spaces, in unsupervised girls, in sexually assertive girls."[51] Cultural explanations and policy recommendations that emphasize these sites of danger—including injunctions against speaking to strangers that became the hallmark of elementary school programs created in the 1980s to reduce cases of sexual abuse—appear to demonstrate commonsensical concern for children, argues Gordon. But instead they betray the weaknesses of conservative responses to abuse. They fail to account for one statistical fact that has remained consistent over the past century, which is that "the most dangerous place for children is the home, the most likely assailant their father."[52]

Gordon calls instead for a political interpretation of child sex abuse that "demystifies the family" and focuses on male power, including education programs aimed at teaching boys about male sexual aggression.[53] Gordon's feminist intervention could be quite instructive in the Catholic case. Rather than overemphasize celibacy as repressive, the decline of family values, or the rise of homosexual rights as the causes of Catholic sexual abuse, we should locate the problem, at least partly, in the hegemony of male power within the church and in relationships of family intimacy, which, for much of the twentieth century, included families' relationships with priests. The political solution in this case would focus less on the elimination of gay priests or on celibacy than it would on the male stranglehold on power within the institutional church. This approach is hardly anti-Catholic; it is certainly antisexist and antihomophobic.

Queer studies of American political and sexual culture since the 1970s extend this analysis. The conservative revolution of the 1980s and 1990s witnessed the formation of what Lauren Berlant has called the "intimate public sphere," which elevated private life over public forms of living and activism.[54] This shift placed the child (or even the fetus)—imagined as innocent, desexualized, and in need of protection—at the center of American political and sexual life. Against this background, the national attention given to the Catholic sex abuse scandal must be read not only as part of a larger criticism (sometimes anti-Catholic or anticlerical) of the institutional church but also as a ritual for renewing our faith in childhood innocence and its need for protection, whether from would-be abortionists or from homosexual pedophiles.[55] Given the long history of sexual abuse against women and girls, we have to ask how national anxieties about the sexual violation of young (white) boys in particular fueled this attention, not because girls or boys of color escaped such abuse, but because white boys became the dominant face of the "victim." In this light, the national response to Catholic sexual abuse might be read as no less than a spectacle of threatened heterosexuality. To pursue this interpretation, only sketched here, of course takes nothing away from the real pain of sexual abuse. But we still have to pose the question: Why do some victims matter (publicly) more than others, and how ought a queer analysis challenge this economy of concern?

Confronting the archive of Catholic sexual abuse as an academic project of this sort comes with some risk. As Kathryn Lofton writes, it "could suggest that we might wish to think away its awfulness" or "that we seek to argue away its visceral trauma."[56] This risk becomes all the more alarming if we take up not only the abused but also the abusers in these accounts.[57] Queering this archive suggests a desire to reclaim sexual abuse, first, *as sexual* (rather than merely a practice of power or violence). This archive powerfully demonstrates how sex becomes imbricated in, and produced through, relations of piety, power, and coercion. Second, it might imply that sexual abuse is something we ought to celebrate for its departure from heterosexual norms. I fully endorse the former claim but want to suggest that we both *queer* and claim *as queer* the culture of Catholic sexual abuse without recourse to the latter. Claiming the Catholic sexual abuser as part of queer (and Catholic and American) history is not the same as condoning abusive behavior. But it does resist sidelining those aspects of nonnormative sexuality that queer and mainstream gay politics find so threatening. This move refuses to construct, in the words of Heather Love, "a positive genealogy of gay identity," one that excludes those darker figures in the history of queer sexuality and politics.[58]

In "The Curious Case of Paul Richard Shanley," Kent Brintnall suggests one direction for this kind of analysis. Held at BishopAccountability.org, the archive of one of the most infamous priests accused of abuse in the Archdiocese of Boston challenges how we narrate the march of gay history. Paul Richard Shanley was ordained in 1960 and according to media and legal records began abusing boys the following year. With one exception, his reported victims were all male and ranged in age from six to twenty-one, most of them over the age of thirteen. In 2005 he was found guilty of raping a member of his parish from the time the boy was six until he was eleven. Brintnall reads Shanley's history as an abuser alongside his success as one of Boston's most well-known street priests.[59]

During this period, Shanley ministered to drug users and to young people on the margins of sexual culture. He challenged church teachings on homosexuality and birth control through lectures and political appearances, including a trip to Wichita, Kansas, to fight against the repeal of a gay rights ordinance during the heyday of Anita Bryant's Save Our Children campaign. Shanley was also one of three members of the clergy who attended a meeting of about 150 men and boys held in a church basement to "consider the legal, psychological, moral, and social issues related to man-boy love." The next day a separate group met (this time without Shanley) to form the National Man-Boy Love Association, or NAMBLA. Mainstream gay rights activists bristle at groups like NAMBLA, which fall outside the code of gay respectability, as they seek to erect a firm boundary between homosexuality and pedophilia. But, as Brintnall clarifies, "we must remember that Shanley's mutual interrogation of the condemnation of homosexuality and man-boy love was fully consonant with gay liberation discourse" in the 1970s. Indeed, at the time, mainstream and gay press alike lauded Shanley for his charismatic presence and radical politics.[60]

But by 2002 Shanley's reception had soured. A cover story in *The Advocate* warned: "Paul Shanley's compassion was just a part of a scheme to abuse vulnerable boys and young men." Here Shanley's activist past becomes little more than a pathological ruse to gain access to more victims. Brintnall pushes against this reading: "I would like to find a way to speak about Shanley as *both* a sexually abusive priest worthy of disdain *and* a pioneering voice for gay rights worthy of admiration."[61] Brintnall not only challenges the practices of forgetting that remove once-lauded gay activists like Shanley from narratives of the gay rights movement. He also reanimates the political and historical overlap between mainstream gay rights activism and movements supporting man-boy love. We could take Brintnall's call even further by including Shanley and other participants in the sex abuse crisis within narratives of sexual and Catholic history regardless of their particular contributions to gay political activism. In this sense, they become part of the larger histories of sexuality and Catholicism—including histories of homosexuality, pedophilia, and child abuse—that go beyond merely celebrating the progress of gay lives. They dwell in the far more ambivalent mix of desire, power, and eroticism that shape modern American sexual history.

The archives of Catholic sexual abuse and of queer history necessarily overlap in the projects I have sketched here. These include efforts to create a public culture around sexual experiences of abuse, one that refuses the privatizing pressures of conservative politics since the 1980s, as well as historical analysis of sexual abuse that resists conservative interpretations of and solutions to sexual violence. The archive of Catholic sexual abuse also demonstrates alternative cultures of sexuality, including those defined through religious and abusive sex acts, that both challenge and extend queer political projects that aim to contest normative accounts of (hetero)sexual history. We are only beginning to tell the history of Catholic sexual abuse. The archival collections of BishopAccountability.org suggest that we need not look far to see queer history there.

Notes

I am grateful for feedback from the Religion in the Americas Colloquium at Princeton University, especially to Gill Frank, Wallace Best, and Judith Weisenfeld. I also thank the two anonymous reviewers and Nathan Ha, Christienna Fryar, and Patrick McKelvey for their excellent suggestions.

1. BishopAccountability.org (hereafter BA), "Introduction to the Archives," bishopaccountability.org/Introduction_to_the_Archives (accessed June 30, 2014). I first encountered this archive at the "Sex Abuse and the Study of Religion" conference at Yale University in 2011 led by Robert Orsi and Kathryn Lofton. Several participants, to whom I am greatly indebted, have written about the archive for the blog *The Immanent Frame* (blogs.ssrc.org/tif/sex-abuse-in-the-catholic-church). Given that this archive records allegations of abuse, the author takes no position here on the truth or falsity of any allegations explicitly discussed, including those recorded in legal proceedings, media coverage, and survivor accounts.

2. BA, "Who We Are," bishop-accountability.org/WhoWeAre (accessed June 30, 2014).

3. The archive also includes some records from outside the United States. McKiernan has written on the global reach of this crisis, in Terence McKiernan, "Governments Must Step into Priest Sex Abuse Cases," CNN, March 19, 2010, cnn.com/2010/OPINION/03/19 /mckiernan.catholic.sex.abuse.

4. BA, "Who We Are."

5. It included tabling a 1985 report by F. Ray Mouton and the Reverend Thomas P. Doyle, OP, JCD, which survivors have since cited as a sign of the church's negligence. Thomas C. Fox, "What They Knew in 1985," *National Catholic Reporter*, May 17, 2002, www.bishop -accountability.org/news/2002_05_17_Fox_WhatThey.htm.

6. BA, "Data on the Crisis: The Human Toll," bishop-accountability.org/AtAGlance/data.htm (accessed June 30, 2014).

7. Suffolk County Supreme Court, Special Grand Jury, *Grand Jury Report*, CPL190.85(I) (C), January 17, 2003, 10, www.bishop-accountability.org/reports/2003_02_10_ SuffolkGrandJury/Suffolk_Full_Report.pdf; Eden Laikin and Steve Wick, "Chapter and Verse of the Accusations," *Newsday*, February 11, 2003, www.bishop-accountability.org /news/2003_02_11_Laikin_ChapterAnd.htm; Carol Eisenberg, "Misconduct Concerns: Diocesan Official's Role in Complaints Eyed," *Newsday*, June 3, 2002, www.bishop -accountability.org/news/2002_06_03_Eisenberg_MisconductConcerns_RC.htm.

8. See Laikin and Wick, "Chapter and Verse"; and Eisenberg, "Misconduct Concerns."

9. For journalistic reporting on Catholic sex abuse, see BA, "A Documentary History of the Crisis," bishop-accountability.org/AtAGlance/timeline.htm (accessed June 30, 2014).

10. Jason Berry, *Lead Us Not into Temptation: Catholic Priests and the Sexual Abuse of Children* (New York: Doubleday, 1992); Frank Bruni and Elinor Burkett, *A Gospel of Shame: Children, Sexual Abuse, and the Catholic Church* (New York: Perennial, 2002); Investigative Staff of the *Boston Globe, Betrayal: The Crisis in the Catholic Church* (Boston: Little, Brown, 2002); A. W. Richard Sipe, *Sex, Priests, and Power: The Anatomy of a Crisis* (New York: Brunner, 1995). On media coverage, see Philip Jenkins, *Pedophiles and Priests: Anatomy of a Contemporary Crisis* (New York: Oxford University Press, 1996), 53–76.

11.   I am indebted to an anonymous reviewer for this language.

12.   Suffolk County Supreme Court, *Grand Jury Report*, 6.

13.   Ibid., 7.

14.   Ibid., 8.

15.   Quoted in Eisenberg, "Misconduct Concerns."

16.   Berry, *Lead Us Not into Temptation*, 367 (italics mine); Jenkins, *Pedophiles and Priests*, 103.

17.   Robert Orsi, *Between Heaven and Earth: The Religious Worlds People Make and the Scholars Who Study Them* (Princeton, NJ: Princeton University Press, 2006), 177–204; Kathryn Lofton, "Sex Abuse and the Study of Religion," *The Immanent Frame*, July 6, 2012, blogs.ssrc.org/tif/2012/07/06/sex-abuse-and-the-study-of-religion.

18.   Mary Gail Frawley-O'Dea, *Perversion of Power: Sexual Abuse in the Catholic Church* (Nashville: Vanderbilt University Press, 2007), 4.

19.   Linda Gordon, *Heroes of Their Own Lives: The Politics and History of Family Violence; Boston, 1880–1960* (New York: Viking, 1988); Steven Mintz, "Placing Childhood Sexual Abuse in Historical Perspective," *The Immanent Frame*, July 13, 2012, blogs.ssrc.org/tif/2012/07/13/placing-childhood-sexual-abuse-in-historical-perspective.

20.   Ann Cvetkovich, *An Archive of Feelings: Trauma, Sexuality, and Lesbian Public Cultures* (Durham, NC: Duke University Press, 2003), 29.

21.   John Boswell, *Christianity, Social Tolerance, and Homosexuality: Gay People in Western Europe from the Beginning of the Christian Era to the Fourteenth Century* (Chicago: University of Chicago Press, 1980); Mark Jordan, *The Invention of Sodomy in Christian Theology* (Chicago: University of Chicago Press, 1997); Jordan, *The Silence of Sodom: Homosexuality in Modern Catholicism* (Chicago: University of Chicago Press, 2000); Richard Rambuss, *Closet Devotions* (Durham, NC: Duke University Press, 1998); Judith C. Brown, *Immodest Acts: The Life of a Lesbian Nun in Renaissance Italy* (New York: Oxford University Press, 1986); Carolyn Dinshaw, *Getting Medieval: Sexualities and Communities, Pre- and Postmodern* (Durham, NC: Duke University Press, 1999).

22.   Jordan, *Silence of Sodom*, 220. See, e.g., the case of Robert Van Handel at St. Anthony's boarding school in Santa Barbara, California, in Gillian Flaccus, "Church Sex Abuse Exposed by Release of Franciscan Files," *Huffington Post*, May 22, 2012, huffingtonpost.com/2012/05/22/franciscan-files-church-sex-abuse_n_1537772.html.

23.   Letter from a survivor to Lawrence C. Murphy, February 12, 1995, BA, bishop-accountability.org/docs/milwaukee/murphy_lawrence/ARCH_MARSHALL_00146_00152.pdf.

24.   Affidavit of John Doe III (Law No. 101428), May 11, 2004, 5, BA, bishop-accountability.org/ia-davenport/archives/johndoeiii-docs.htm.

25.   Michel Foucault, "Pastoral Power and Political Reason" (1979), in *Religion and Culture*, ed. Jeremy Carrette (New York: Routledge, 1999).

26.   Letter from a survivor to Murphy.

27.   Affidavit of John Doe III, 7.

28.   Kevin Ohi, "Molestation 101: Child Abuse, Homophobia, and *The Boys of St. Vincent*," *GLQ* 6, no. 2 (2000): 195–248.

29.   Hilary Kaiser, "Clergy Sexual Abuse in U.S. Mainline Churches," *American Studies International* 34, no. 1 (1996): 30–42.

30.   BA, "Data on the Crisis: The Human Toll."

31.   David Coleman, Affidavit, July 18, 1993, Addendum Doc. No. 0126, BA, bishop-accountability.org/ma-boston/archives/PatternAndPractice/0126-ColemanAffidavit Coughlin.pdf.

32. David Coleman, "Living on a 'Fault' Line," December 16, 1992, Addendum Doc. No. 0106, BA, bishop-accountability.org/ma-boston/archives/PatternAndPractice/0106-Coughlin-3-6.pdf.

33. Ibid.

34. Ibid.

35. For a collection of survivor accounts, see BA, "Accounts by Survivors and Their Families and Friends," bishop-accountability.org/accounts (accessed June 30, 2014).

36. Cvetkovich, *Archive of Feelings*, 18.

37. See note 21 above.

38. On the limitations of queer politics, see Cathy Cohen, "Punks, Bulldaggers, and Welfare Queens: The Radical Potential of Queer Politics?," *GLQ* 3, no. 4 (1997): 437–65.

39. Lauren Berlant and Michael Warner, "Sex in Public," in *Publics and Counterpublics*, by Michael Warner (New York: Zone Books, 2002), 187–208; Michael Warner, *The Trouble with Normal: Sex, Politics, and the Ethics of Queer Life* (Cambridge, MA: Harvard University Press, 1999).

40. Catholic sex abuse receives only passing attention from several important American histories of sexuality and of Catholicism. See Michael Bronski, *A Queer History of the United States* (Boston: Beacon, 2011); John D'Emilio and Estelle Freedman, *Intimate Matters: A History of Sexuality in America*, 2nd ed. (Chicago: University of Chicago Press, 1998); John T. McGreevy, *Catholicism and American Freedom: A History* (New York: Norton, 2003), 289–94; and Scott R. Appleby and Kathleen Sprows Cummings, eds., *Catholics in the American Century: Recasting Narratives of U.S. History* (Ithaca, NY: Cornell University Press, 2012).

41. Jenkins, *Pedophiles and Priests*, 95–112.

42. Nicholas Graham, "Bill Donohue: Catholic Sex Abuse Scandal Is Not a Pedophilia Crisis but a Homosexual Crisis," *Huffington Post*, May 31, 2010, huffingtonpost.com/2010/03/31/bill -donohue-catholic-sex_n_520187.html.

43. Robert S. Bennett et al., *A Report on the Crisis of the Catholic Church in the United States* (Washington, DC: USCCB, 2004), 8.

44. Orsi, *Between Heaven and Earth*, 15.

45. On the queerness of childhood, see Kathryn Bond Stockton, *The Queer Child, or Growing Sideways in the Twentieth Century* (Durham, NC: Duke University Press, 2009); and James Kincaid, *Erotic Innocence: The Culture of Child Molesting* (Durham, NC: Duke University Press, 1998). On Catholic childhoods and sex abuse, see Robert Orsi, "Close Formation," *Boston College Magazine* 64, no. 1 (2004): 32–37, bcm.bc.edu/issues/winter_2004/features .html; and Orsi, "A Crisis about the Theology of Children," *Harvard Divinity School Bulletin* 30, no. 4 (2002): 27–33.

46. Here I paraphrase Linda Gordon's claim about the historical study of family violence. Gordon, *Heroes of Their Own Lives*, 2.

47. Jenkins, *Pedophiles and Priests*, 53–76; John Jay College of Criminal Justice, The City University of New York, *The Nature and Scope of the Problem of Sexual Abuse of Minors by Catholic Priests and Deacons in the United States, 1950–2002* (Washington, DC: USCCB, 2004); John Jay College of Criminal Justice, The City University of New York, *The Nature and Scope of the Problem of Sexual Abuse of Minors by Catholic Priests and Deacons in the United States, 1950–2002: Supplementary Data Analysis*, prepared by Karen Terry and Margaret Leland Smith (Washington, DC: USCCB, 2006); Karen Terry, et al., *The Causes and Context of Sexual Abuse of Minors by Catholic Priests in the United States, 1950–2010*, prepared by the John Jay College of Criminal Justice (Washington, DC: USCCB, 2011).

48. Terry et al., *Causes and Context*, 46.

49. Ibid., 27.

50. Jenkins, *Pedophiles and Priests*, 33–52.

51. Linda Gordon, "The Politics of Child Sexual Abuse: Notes from American History," *Feminist Review*, no. 28 (1988): 61.

52. Ibid.

53. Ibid., 62.

54. Lauren Berlant, *The Queen of America Goes to Washington City: Essays on Sex and Citizenship* (Durham, NC: Duke University Press, 1997).

55. Jenkins, *Pedophiles and Priests*, 19–32.

56. Lofton, "Sex Abuse."

57. Mark Jordan, "Abusing Rhetoric," *The Immanent Frame*, July 27, 2012, blogs.ssrc.org/tif /2012/07/27/abusing-rhetoric; and Kent Brintnall, "The Curious Case of Paul Richard Shanley," *The Immanent Frame*, August 3, 2012, blogs.ssrc.org/tif/2012/08/03/the-curious -case-of-paul-richard-shanley.

58. Heather Love, *Feeling Backward: Loss and the Politics of Queer History* (Cambridge, MA: Harvard University Press, 2007), 32.

59. Brintnall, "Curious Case"; also see the Shanley files at BA, bishop-accountability.org /ma-boston/archives/PatternAndPractice/doc-list-1.html (accessed June 30, 2014).

60. Ibid.

61. Ibid.

Archival Justice

An Interview with Ben Power Alwin

K. J. Rawson

As the curator of the Sexual Minorities Archives (SMA) since 1977, Ben Power Alwin has been a longtime activist for queer history and has extensive experiential knowledge of queer archiving. Ben and I first met in the summer of 2008 when I was conducting research for my dissertation at the SMA. Throughout my research process, I was continually struck by the stark differences between the SMA and the more institutional archives maintained by universities and historical societies where I was also researching. The SMA is a grassroots archive with an activist edge—it has endured nearly four decades in a rapidly changing political climate; it has a unique organizational system that implicitly critiques traditional descriptive systems; it includes sexually explicit materials that are often not collected in other archives; it has a growing emphasis on recent history, people of color, and the working class; and it is maintained in Ben's personal residence and funded purely by donations.

Founded in Chicago in 1974 by a lesbian-feminist organization known as the New Alexandria Lesbian Library, what is now the SMA has been located in western Massachusetts since 1979. When the lesbian collective that created the collection dissolved in 1978, Ben took it into his personal apartment in Chicago and then moved it with him to Massachusetts the following year. From 1978 until early 2011, Ben served as the sole caretaker for the collection until he established a nonprofit organization, the Sexual Minorities Educational Foundation, whose board of directors currently oversees the SMA. Though the SMA has been maintained by

Radical History Review
Issue 122 (May 2015) DOI 10.1215/01636545-2849603

Ben in his private residence for the majority of its existence, he has always treated it as a community-owned collection, built entirely from community donations and steadily used by about five hundred visitors per year.

Whether run by a radical collective, an individual archivist, or a nonprofit organization, the SMA has had a long-standing political purpose that resonates with a broader queer archival impulse. The ability to control the histories of sexual and gender minorities is an important motive for the SMA, not merely because it responds to the systematic misrepresentation and omission of queer histories in traditional archives (and in our culture more broadly), but also because it creates a domestic, anti-institutional environment for queer researchers. As Ben explains below, "I am constantly being imposed upon by my oppressors; the last thing that I want to do personally is go into an institutional archive where I feel that it's run by my oppressors." Even as the systematic neglect of queer historical materials increasingly (and thankfully) erodes, Ben argues for the continuing need for grassroots queer archives in a way that suggests that queer archival projects can simultaneously critique and reify particular aspects of identity politics. The SMA's archival model of collecting historical materials by community donation, maintaining them in a personal residence, creating an in-house organizational system from the ground up, and welcoming visitors by appointment presents a significant contrast to institutional archives, and it provokes important considerations about privatization, access, and long-term preservation.

Beyond its grassroots method of archiving, the SMA is also distinguished by the unconventional relationship that exists between Ben and the collection itself. In the early 1990s, when Ben transitioned from female to male, he also transitioned the collection from an exclusively lesbian-feminist collection to an all-inclusive lesbian, gay, bisexual, transgender, queer, and intersex (LGBTQI) archives. Historically, the SMA's shift also mirrored what was happening on the national level as many organizations began committing to a more inclusive spectrum of queer identities. But perhaps more poignantly, the parallel between Ben's transition and the transition of the SMA suggests that just as individuals develop and change the ways we identify, archival collections can also have an identity that is equally adaptable.

As the only trans man who curates a national queer collection (to our knowledge), Ben's curatorial influence highlights the adaptability and political responsiveness of an archive. If the focus and scope of a collection like the SMA can be so explicitly and radically altered, we might wonder: in what ways are all archives shaped by the archivists who maintain them? While Ben's influence on the SMA can be seen in the shift in the identity of the collection and even in some of the idiosyncratic holdings, there is a mutual influence between Ben and the collection that extends beyond these surface-level qualities. Ben's relationship with the SMA might be better understood as symbiotic—as Ben lives in the collection, his transgender body has become an everyday part of the archive and the archive has become an everyday part of his body. During our interview, Ben describes this element of the archive as the "lifeblood of queerness," a powerful description that suggests the incredible potentiality of archival queerings that centralize the queer body and queer bodily experience.

In the following June 21, 2013, interview, Ben discusses his archival activism, and he offers some provocative challenges to many accepted norms of archival practice and the role of archives in our culture.

K. J. Rawson: *We're sitting in your living room right now completely immersed in books and archival materials. This is your home and it's also the home of the archive. To get us started, I was wondering if you could talk a bit about the significance of this collection being maintained in your personal residence?*

Ben Power Alwin: The archive was started in 1974 as part of the Lesbian Feminist Center, which was a storefront that was rented by a collective of lesbians. That was a very bold thing to do, literally coming out of the closet and onto the streets by renting this big windowed storefront on the north side of Chicago to have a bookstore and then this little nascent library in the back. When it closed four years later, it was by default that I took it into my apartment, because it really would have been thrown out into an alley in Chicago. I wanted to save it. It was an impulse to rescue the history and literature that was being collected by lesbians, for lesbians.

I had a role model for having an archive in one's home and that was the Lesbian Herstory Archives, which was started seven months before the New Alexandria Lesbian Library. So I didn't feel like what I was doing by rescuing it was completely foreign. In that era, in the seventies and really into the mid-eighties, there was a tremendous backlash to anything gay or lesbian, and there were issues about where a queer collection would be safe. For many years, I felt like the only safe place to do an LGBT collection was in my home. That level of safety and privacy was mandatory if this collection was going to grow and be accessible to our people. I've always considered myself the bulldog at the door of the archive. That photo shows it [points to wall] .

Figure 1. Ben Power Alwin in front of a 1988 photograph of himself, "the bulldog at the door of the archive." Credit: K. J. Rawson

I am literally standing in front of the books in that photo, and I am protecting them. So we start there with this sense of place and why this is in my home. The other reason it's in my home is because, financially, it was a way to be able to keep it. I devised a way in my life to be able to provide this space affordably and economically, by myself being the rent payer on the space. I would go out and earn money working in the corporate world, and I brought the money back to support this archive. Also, it's a matter of control and being in my hands, which are transgender hands.

What impact do you think the domestic nature of this collection has on visitors and researchers?

The personal and private nature of LGBT materials in someone's home fosters, to me, a real sense of comfort and being at ease for visitors and researchers who come here. It also fosters discovery. We have everything available, so people can handle materials, browse, take things off of the shelf or out of the file cabinets, and find materials they didn't even know they were looking for. You don't need to put on gloves and ask me to go get it. You can open the file cabinets, you can go through the periodical stacks, and you can see for yourself. I think there are comparisons to be made to museums. Some museums are very staged, and everything's behind glass, very protected, and your experience is highly structured. Other museums are interactive discovery museums where you can actually go up to an exhibit, you can press buttons and make things happen, and you can pull things out and look at things. I always feel like people learn more when they do the latter, and it's just a more enjoyable experience.

In what ways does the geographic location matter to the identity of the SMA?

The setting that it's in is geographically beautiful. The house is located on the bank of the Connecticut River, about two miles from the center of downtown Northampton, Massachusetts, which is in itself a small town—sophisticated, but small. It's no coincidence that it's on the bank of the Connecticut River, a powerful river. I read all these books about the history of the Connecticut River and the romance and the paintings and the poetry about the river, all told from white heterosexual eyes. For once it's empowering queers.

Figure 2. The first book room, which is also Ben's living room.
Credit: K. J. Rawson

You can't separate the internal safe space from the geography surrounding it. I know that individuals who visit here and do research here can feel that outside environment as well as the inside space, and it just is really, to me, the most perfect and beautiful and comforting setting to have LGBTQ materials in. It's like a cushion of support and safety for people who have been so harshly dealt with. When we think of how our bodies have been battered and people have been killed, all of the groups we collect on have been so oppressed and physically battered and unsafe, and the minute we walk out the doors of our homes we're under attack. And so this setting, this archive, is like the antidote to that. It provides the comfort and the support and a healing experience as well as an educational experience to come here and to either work here or research and study here or to volunteer here. And it is strengthening. It is strengthening spiritually as well as academically and intellectually.

What is it like for you to live in this archive?

It's incredible. It's amazing. It's an honor to live here. I try to imagine myself not living here and just living in the world like most queers do . . . every day living in a world that is not queer, being affronted by what is presented to me in the media images of people like me, being affronted on the street with whatever catcalls or even violence that I might encounter, being affronted if I go to work, being affronted if I go to school. When I was fighting the corporate wars in my career I'd go out to battle every day being a trans man in corporations in the seventies and eighties and nineties. I would have evenings when I would come home entirely depleted, and I would sit in this room and just soak in the strength from the books, from the visuals on the walls, and from all the people who have visited here over the years. There is definitely a spiritual strength here. It's the way that I continue, after all these years, to be empowered myself. And I know that if I am empowered, anyone who comes here is empowered.

It seems like there's a symbiotic relationship between you and the collection, which may be one of the queerest things about this archive. How has the SMA adapted and changed as your life and identity have changed?

[*Laughs.*] Well, it's a profound place. It's a very personal archive because my body is in it. My body is living in it every day, and I have a transgender body. I live here, eat here, sleep here. That's an interesting and very human and dynamic aspect that is very warm and full of the lifeblood of queerness, to have somebody who's curating who's from one of the groups that are the subjects of the materials, to have that person's lifeblood literally be there with it.

It started as a lesbian collection, and I was, at the time, in the lesbian community. I worked on it and came into it in 1977, so it had already been established by a lesbian collective for three years. By 1979, I was moving it out here because it was in my home already for nearly two years. The aspects of myself that surfaced in 1986 were transgender, because that was the year in which I had met Lou Sullivan, and I also came out as leather/BDSM[bondage/discipline/sadomasochism]. By 1990, I started to become uncomfortable as a trans man curating a lesbian archive. I was at a crossroads. I said to myself, I am either going to have to find lesbian leadership for this archive or I am going to have to expand it to the diverse rainbow of communities that we have who are queer, and then I can stay with it. I chose the latter, and on January 1, 1992, I renamed it the Sexual Minorities Archives.

When I looked at what was already in the collection, I knew that it was already more than lesbian holdings, so I just had to make the leap in identity for the archive. Renaming the collection allowed me to stay on as a curator, and because I personally am transgender and BDSM, it allowed me to be in a position of knowing in the early 1990s to go after and acquire materials that were trans and that were BDSM, in particular. Consequently, this collection has strong holdings for those communities.

I am what I call a street collector, which is, wherever I go, I've got my eyes open for collections. If I see a poster that's related at all to the LGBT community that's posted in a public space and that's out-of-date, I take it for the archive. When I go to conferences or workshops, I browse all the free literature tables and I take materials for the archive. I've traveled in leather/S-M circles, and I travel in transgender circles, and I collect there. The collection is then almost an extension of my body and where my body goes, I am finding materials that I can bring back. That's a minor way in which materials are acquired, but that's an important aspect of my body living here and being the curator.

One reason why I felt very strongly about evolving the collection into LGBTQISM, the complete spectrum of the rainbow, is because I have a personal politic that says that my trans community or any of the queer communities that are in that rainbow label are going to get somewhere farther faster if we're all united and working for each one of those communities actively. If we're all pulling the boat the same way, it's going to get there faster. So in this collection it's all the communities living on the shelves side by side, peacefully coexisting, and it's powerful.

Why did you choose the name Sexual Minorities Archives?

It needed to be a name that opened the archive up to reflect all the categories of people that we're collecting on. It had outgrown its lesbian name. I thought that the LGBT acronym itself was too long for a title: lesbian, gay, bisexual, transgender, queer or questioning, intersex, SM, BD, fetish archives wouldn't work [*laughter*]! So I thought, what summarizes it all? There wasn't one individual to name it after, and I didn't want to name it after myself. To call us "sexual minorities" is true. I think to be a little more accurate it would be Sexual and Gender Minorities Archives. But for now it's the Sexual Minorities Archives because what we have in common is that our sexuality is different from cisgender heterosexuals'.¹ I also think that the word *minorities* puts us closer to racial and ethnic minorities as a coalition effect, which is what we want in this archive.

Why not queer?

Some people in the LGBTQISM community are comfortable with the word *queer* and others are not. I like it. I say I'm as queer as a three-dollar bill. But some of us are not comfortable with the word *queer* as an overarching word to summarize all of us, and that's the reason why it isn't in the name. I also think because that word comes from Queer Nation, which has more of a homosexual meaning, that doesn't summarize the whole spectrum that we're dealing with here. *Queer* is expanding and changing in its meaning, and especially with the advent of *genderqueer* it's really taking another path than [the one] Queer Nation started it [on] with white gay men.² It's getting more rich and complex, but I still don't think it encompasses all the groups that we're collecting on.

Similar to your careful selection of the name of the collection, the SMA has a unique organizational structure that was built from the ground up and uses language in a very political way. How does the organization and classification function to represent and interpret the materials collected here?

We know that naming is powerful. Language is powerful. Words are powerful. So when the collection was the New Alexandria Lesbian Library, there was some basic naming for books [in sections] such as "Fiction," "Lesbian Fiction," "Women's Fiction," "Nonfiction," "Lesbian Poetry," "Herstory," and so on. There was already the beginning of a different naming in using "Herstory" for the history books that were collected. I got why that was important: to change that word to "Herstory" was political naming. It was naming that was more appropriate for lesbian women.

So over the years, with the book categories, for example, we keep adding political naming. For example, the books that we have about the psychiatric world are [in a section] called the "Mental Illness System." We could have called that the "Mental Health System," but many of them deal with the struggles of homosexuals, lesbians, and others being incarcerated, and so that's a political name to identify a system of oppression as the mental illness system. Or the "Bullshit" section—that's a collection of books that are hateful or homophobic or lesbian-phobic or trans-phobic and that are full of lies. We should collect them, but we should warn people by naming them [based on] what we think of these books. The "Herstory" book section is now called "Ourstory" because it houses the stories of LGBTQIs and it's all encompassing, so it's "Ourstory." Now that we have a "Transgender" section, we can start looking at some of the figures who were traditionally included in "Lesbian Lives" and make decisions about whether they should be moved to "Transgender Lives."

Radclyffe Hall comes to mind. The names on the shelves for books are getting more and more numerous, and they do reflect changing language in the communities that we serve, and they also reflect a radical perspective on the world around us and an interpretation of the content of the books that we collect.

I will also say that in the naming for the subject files area we have an anti-racism policy in which we are fighting racism and racial invisibility by consciously deciding to label people of color materials as such and placing them physically first in the file cabinet drawers so that they are visible first, to any researcher, so that they are easily found. That is one of the active ways that we fight racism. The collection is a political collection, and it needs to live up to its own moral and political ethics.

So in that light, then, how would you compare this collection to broader, non-LGBT institutional archives that collect queer materials?

Let's just talk about institutional collections that are controlled by cis-heterosexuals, which are the majority of them. What is being applied there is the collection [and] preservation [of] and accessibility to our content through the lens of people who are outside of our community and who are part of the group in society that has traditionally oppressed our community, cis-heterosexuals of a certain class. So right there, that becomes problematic. It's the antithesis of queer bodies walking and living in the collection and handling and making and processing the materials and providing levels of access. It's people from the oppressor class doing those functions. I am constantly being imposed upon by my oppressors; the last thing that I want to do personally is go into an institutional archive where I feel that it's run by my oppressors.

In many cases, institutions may have a wealth of our materials as property, but the access is greatly reduced, and in some academic settings one must have credentials to use and access them. In the Sexual Minorities Archives, there are no credentials needed. Everyone is welcome. Some of the locations of institutional archives are locations where people of color queers or working-class queers either can't or won't go, because either it's out of the realm of their experience or it is unsafe and they would be denied access or treated with discomfort.

I also think that in an academic setting with cis-heterosexual curators and directors, they lack the experience and the knowledge base of our queer experience to be able to adequately direct researchers who are queer to view and to understand the significance of the materials they are even viewing. Is the curator telling them, "Oh, this is what you should look at"? I guide them, and I give them stuff, and then I let 'em loose. I'm queer, the curator, [and] you're queer, the visitor—that's the perfect environment for growth because we're asking our own questions about our own lives. Nobody's telling us how to look at our lives. We're looking at it from queer angles. There's just no comparison in the experiences. And to me it's very political.

The SMA is saying that a strategy of queer residence–based and queer community–based location and control for a national LGBTQ archive is the most effective one in collecting, preserving, protecting, and making accessible the true evidence of queer lives. Queer materials in queer hands is the strategy that, through education, helps get our people closer to equality.

One of the ways that you are distinguishing the SMA from other archives is because it is overtly political, perhaps even activist. How do you think the SMA relates to the broader queer movement?

I believe that our queer archives are the underpinning of what happens in the movement. The statement that the SMA makes by being so inclusive of the whole spectrum is an underpinning to support a united queer movement. Traditional archives are, for the most part, collectors of what has happened in the past. That's an aspect of what we do here, but we're also very much collecting in the present moment as the LGBTQ movement has been happening.

From day one, this collection has been collecting in an activist way, as its workers and the curator have involvement in the very movements on which it's collecting. I've often asked, does this collection reflect the politic of the time, or does this collection influence the politic of the future? I think it's both. I really believe that our archives are what give strength to the movement. They always have. The ONE Archives started along with the beginnings of the homosexual movement because people who are thinkers understand that education has to come first. I don't believe that without the ONE Archives and the ONE Institute coming earlier in US history we would have had a Stonewall. We wouldn't have been educated or proud enough to rebel.

Each issue of the *ONE Magazine* had a cover theme that was about something that had never been examined from the lens of having pride. One of those cover issues was on transsexualism in a prideful way. One issue was about homosexual marriage. Can you see where I'm going with this? Without the *ONE Magazine* cover issue "Homosexual Marriage?" (August 1953), would we have marriage today? I don't think so. It takes the intellectual examination of what equality looks like and it takes publishing about it and it takes educating and teaching about it before it can be achieved. That's why this is an activist place.

I tell the volunteers who work here, when they label one subject file and they catalog one book, it's a political act. It's a political act because the way that oppression works, especially for us queers, is silencing and erasure. Everything that we can do to erase the erasure and to give voice where there was silence, that's what we're doing with this archival work every single day. Everything I do in here every day is a political act because it's bringing to light information that has been suppressed.

I feel like it's archival justice—telling the truth about people who are alive today and about people who are already dead, for God's sake. The pre-Stonewall queer figures in New England whose histories we're telling for the first time through the SMA, for example. It's about justice, it's about making it right. Not just to remember but to make it right. The core of my oppression is suppression. Is silencing. And it's also lies. It's hateful tellings about who we are, about who I am. It's stereotyping. It's misinformation. And it's hate. So what we're doing here is we're bringing the truth to light and we're speaking the stories that had never been told. We're breaking the silence. The motto of the SMA is Never Again the Silence, because we learned from the ACT UP movement that "silence = death." It's as true today as it was true in the eighties. If there's a gap in knowledge about us, it will be quickly filled by the homophobes and the haters, and they will tell lies about us. So we're building out the truth. This is a house of truth. And the bigger it can get, the better. The more programs that we do, the more history walks, and history talks where we're speaking, and we're doing show-and-tell about the truth, it's breaking the silence. That's what this is about. It's not just a bunch of materials sitting static in a cold place in an institution waiting to be stumbled upon or just being preserved for the hell of it, just because it's property. Uh-uh, no, no, no. This is changing the movement, and this is changing the world. It's changing the conditions of life for our people. The goal of this archive is to achieve equality for our people. That's the goal of this archive.

You're making me wish that we could publish this as a sound interview, because the passion that you are expressing right now will be very difficult to capture in text. You are moving me emotionally in the ways that you are talking about this collection and its political function, and I think that's incredibly important.

It's my life's work. By 1977, I knew why I was born. I knew why I was on this planet. I was put on this earth for one reason: to leave this legacy. To build it, to make a difference in my life, and to leave it behind in a way that, when I'm gone, it can do nothing but get bigger. That's why I'm on this planet. The queer archival movement is so important. It is the basis for political activism. It is the basis for queer pride. It all started with our archives, and it continues because of our archives.

Queer archives initially began out of an impulse to preserve history that was not being collected elsewhere, and it was very oppositional and political in that function. But now we find ourselves in a very different climate, as queer history has become a hot topic and countless repositories are actively seeking out queer materials. How do you see the continuing function of the SMA in relation to that changing climate?

I think there has to be a voice out there countering all this drive to place stuff in institutions and to assimilate it. There's got to be a counterpoint, because we've got to think about what we're doing with our materials. We've got to help the community think about what they're doing with their materials. I think the core question is, who owns our movement? The work of the LGBT movement is never going to be over, completely, until we've really reached equality. So what happens in the meantime? If we have institutions absorbing our literature, history, and art, are they delaying our movement in some way? Are they extending our arrival at freedom longer? How could it be making it shorter? How could their acquisition of our materials make us closer to freedom? It's only if one looks at success as being assimilation. But what happens is that queer culture gets lost in the process. When you absorb culture you can erase it. I want to control my own story, and I want people like me, other queers, controlling their stories. Straight cisgender people haven't had the oppression we've had. They haven't had the struggles we've had. And we don't have the equality yet that they have. So it becomes a political thing to me to give over control of our lives to the oppressor class.

Who do you imagine as the audience for this collection? It seems as though most archives imagine their audience as researchers who have specific informational needs, but much of what you've said also hints at the emotional needs of visitors to this collection.

On the intellectual level there are some really practical needs that occur. There is research that has definite questions that need to be answered and documented with sources and maybe a theory established or a bold analysis that never had been made. That's the intellectual level. But then, on the emotional level, there's the aspect of people who want to come and visit and see it. Some of them come back once or twice and they want to just hang out or listen to music or watch a video. Those people want to be surrounded by their own materials. They want to be in a queer space. They want to be surrounded. They want to discover things. They want to learn. They want to learn what they're not learning in high school and college. It nurtures them the way it nurtures me to live here. It makes them feel strong to soak up all this information and this environment, which they never get to walk in. I forget that people don't get to walk around in this every day like I do. I don't know how I would feel if I didn't have this. I wouldn't feel strong, I know that. I may not have survived my life unless I had this to come to. This is a survival-level nurturance place. It's an empowerment place.

Notes

1. *Cisgender*, in contrast to *transgender*, refers to people who identify with the gender that they were assigned at birth. As a shorthand, *cisgender* is often spoken and written as *cis-* or *cis*, the Latin prefix meaning "on this side of."
2. *Genderqueer* is an identity category or a catchall term for people who challenge binary gender categories and norms.

"Queering the Trans* Family Album"

Elspeth H. Brown and Sara Davidmann, in Conversation

Elspeth H. Brown and Sara Davidmann

Sara Davidmann is a photographer working in London, and Elspeth H. Brown is a US cultural historian who lives in Toronto. Both of us are engaged in the creation of queer archives concerning recent lesbian, gay, bisexual, transgender, queer, and intersex (LGBTQI) history, with an emphasis on trans* and queer archives.[1] Brown is currently describing trans* activist Rupert Raj's collection for the Canadian Lesbian and Gay Archives (CLGA) as a volunteer, while also conducting an oral history project concerning the histories and experiences of partners (cis and trans*) of trans* men in the United States and Canada. Davidmann has been photographing her queer and trans* community in London for fifteen years, while also interviewing her image collaborators about their lives. Together, we developed a few questions that allowed us to address the intersections between our various projects. The conversation that follows concerns our ruminations concerning archives, photography, ethics, queer methods and bodies, and trans* lives.

Radical History Review
Issue 122 (May 2015)   DOI 10.1215/01636545-2849612
© 2015 by MARHO: The Radical Historians' Organization, Inc.

Elspeth H. Brown: *Can you describe the archive you are making, your methods and archival ethics?*

Sara Davidmann: The archive that I'm making is really about trans° partnerships, relationships, families. So it's not just about trans° people; it's also about the people who are involved in their lives as significant others in those families. The archive is through photography primarily, though I always make recorded interviews. Having worked with Elizabeth Edwards for my PhD in practice, I am deeply aware of photography's long history as a technology of colonialism and scientific racism, especially in relationship to late nineteenth- and early twentieth-century physical anthropology and ethnology. As a result, I am very sensitive to the power dynamic inherent in the making of photographic images. So I started to work with people directly in terms of making the images in different ways. Sometimes people would suggest ways that they wanted to be photographed, and I would work to that. I give people the power to say yes or no as to whether images can be reproduced for exhibition, for online purposes, or for publishing. So the people I photograph have quite a lot of control over not only how they're represented in the image but also in terms of whether or not that image can be seen—which as a photographer is a very hard thing to do because I have a huge investment in making images. But the collaborative aspect has been hugely important in terms of allowing people self-representation through my photography. It's really, really important that people have control over these images because it's their decision whether to be out or not or to what extent they feel comfortable having this image shown in public, as it might potentially out them as queer or trans° or both.

EHB: The issue of control is also central to my oral history work, which is really a form of collaboration. I've been very influenced by feminist and queer critiques of oral history and ethnography as methodologies, and I do what I can to allow the narrator's control over the process.[2] The confidentiality issues are intense, since the people I am interviewing discuss not only their own lives, of course, but also those of partners, children, ex-lovers, parents; some of the trans° men are stealth, which means that the partners are as well. To accommodate confidentiality issues, one narrator and I even conducted an entire interview in the past tense, even though we were discussing the present, an agreement that is decidedly queer in the context of normative historical methodologies. Everyone has an opportunity to edit or annotate or even eradicate the interviews, working with the transcript. Historians continue to grapple with the ethical complexities of LGBTQI oral histories, especially at our current moment when activists, artists, scholars, and archivists are actively digitizing collections and making sensitive and personal material available online.[3]

What's "Queer" about Your Archive?

Both of us consider ourselves to be queering the archive, in different though complementary ways. At the level of identity politics, we are both creating archives that include "queer" subjects, many of whom self-identity this way. For example, in Brown's archive, the vast majority of interview subjects currently identify as queer, even if their partners do not, as an easy shorthand to "cis-gendered women who once identified as lesbian or dyke, whose partner is now genderqueer or male, but who do not see themselves as heterosexual." But at the level of methodology, we see our artifacts as queer as well, whether gestures, silences, hair, or tattered envelopes marked "to be destroyed": our continued interest in archiving these nonnormative historical traces mark us as queer in relationship to traditional historical methods, which continue to privilege written texts.[4] Both of us are deeply interested in the visual, which certainly in history circles is still considered a queer (as in nonnormative) evidentiary form, despite recent interventions.[5] Our bodies (we do not identify as trans°, lesbian, or male) are often a queer incursion into normative archival spaces, gay or straight, as when Brown, who reads as female and white, used a male name to describe her partner in the front office of the Canadian Lesbian and Gay Archives, a wonderful organization whose very name suggests the absences that our subjectivities represent. We are, in other words, archival queers, bodies that do not often fit in the archival spaces we inhabit.[6] Finally, we see our archival projects as fundamentally queer. Both of our projects consider trans° men and trans° women in relationship to queer kinship structures, which are central to the process of transition but which are often rendered invisible in the neoliberal discourse of "individual" transition; in this way, we consider our projects to be queer interventions into what can sometimes be a normative trans narrative.[7]

Queering the Trans⁑ Family Album

The family photograph album has been, historically, one of the most pernicious of affective technologies.[8] Proliferating since the late 1880s, when Kodak perfected roll film and began marketing its cameras and film to women and children as an instrument of normative domesticity and heterosexual family life, family snapshots and the albums in which they appear have routinely been a site of anxious disidentification for queer and trans° family members.[9] Yet photography's instrumental, affective capacity can also be harnessed to produce connection and belonging—feelings that can be considered queer in relationship to normative family formations. We know this, of course, in relationship to queer and trans° art photography, where many projects of the past twenty-five years—from Catherine Opie to J. J. Levine to Zanele Muholi—have taken queer kinship networks as their subject. But almost all of us have domestic snapshots, so-called family photographs, whether bound in albums, thrown into boxes, or monopolizing memory on our smart phones. These images, so central to the affective production of trans° family, however defined, have not been the site of sustained discussion. Our collaboration begins this conversation, with specific reference to two sets of images from Davidmann's work: one from her own family of origin and one from her (queer and trans°) family of choice.

Album One: "K: To be destroyed"

SD: When my mother moved into a nursing home in 2010, while going through my mother's paperwork I found two large envelopes and a large brown paper bag in a chest of drawers in the garage. Written on the front of these were "Ken. To be destroyed," "Letters from Hazel re Ken," and "Ken's letters to Hazel. To be destroyed" (fig. 1).[10] The handwriting on the envelopes belonged to my mother—not to Ken.

Ken (K) was my "uncle." K had married my mother's sister Hazel in 1954 and died in 1979 at the age of fifty-nine. Several years earlier, because of my own relationships with trans° people, my mother told me that K had lived as a woman in the home and as a man outside the home. My mother said that I was to keep this a secret and not even to tell my siblings—both of these I refused to do. I was upset by the fact that there was such shame in my own family attached to someone being trans°. I later carried out an oral recording with my mother talking about K.

At the same time as I discovered the envelopes and bag (full of letters and documents in K's handwriting), I also came across a photograph of K and Hazel on their wedding day (fig. 2). Looking at the photograph and envelopes together, it seemed to me that, in one hand, I was holding an emblem of what in the case of trans° people a conventional family album allowed—the erasure of the trans° life—and, in the other, evidence of the experiences that would have been erased.

EHB: It's not just the letters that were to be destroyed, of course, but K's feminine persona as well. The dearth of trans° archives is a testament of such erasures. The word *proof* at the bottom of figure 2, which you mentioned had been written on the image by the wedding photographer, has an irony to it: Proof of what, exactly? And the illegibility of the word in its entirety suggests the contingent nature of photographic visual evidence, which seems to offer so much certainty, but which in fact tells us quite little.

SD: Absolutely. From the letters and notes I learned that K had known from long before getting married that she was trans° but that K only dared share this—privately, only with Hazel—in 1958, four years after their wedding. The letters revealed that, at first, Hazel was shocked to learn that K was trans°. But eventually she came to accept it, and K and Hazel renegotiated their marriage, family expectations, public personas, and hidden private lives. Hazel did not want K to transition to live full-time as a woman, and they were able to reconcile their relationship to encompass K being trans° by K living as a woman in the home but never outside.

EHB: Given your story, the wedding portrait is especially poignant (fig. 2). Nothing could be more heteronormative than a wedding portrait such as this one, with your aunt happily clutching her bouquet, smiling with her white wedding dress and veil. K, however, seems distinctly uncomfortable: (s)he's offered Hazel the left arm, but the tension in his (her?) body is palpable, and both hands seem almost clenched with anxiety. I am reminded of Roland Barthes, describing his experience in front of the camera: "I constitute myself in the process of 'posing,' I instantaneously make another body for myself."[11] Here the work for K is especially painful: the body he is making is the expected one, but the wrong one for her, for K. I look at this image with a sense of sadness and loss for both of them and what the future holds.[12]

Album Two: The Velvet Collar and Other Stories (Stephen Whittle)

Stephen Whittle has been a leading activist on trans° issues in the United Kingdom since his own transition in 1974; for the past several decades, he has been a tireless author, editor, and activist in the United Kingdom and internationally.[13] He has been with his partner, Sarah Rutherford, since the late 1970s, and they have four children together—but it was not until the passing of the United Kingdom's Gender Recognition Act in 2004, for which Whittle had been campaigning for years, that Whittle was able to marry Rutherford and legally adopt his four children. Davidmann has known Whittle for nine years and was his official wedding photographer in 2005; they have collaborated together on photographic projects, including a set of reflections (photographs and oral accounts) on Whittle's own family album (figs. 3–6).

Whittle created this album to leave behind for his children. It documents his life from an early age, his family background, and his transition. In Whittle's album, being trans° is represented as a part of life as opposed to a cause for erasure. In figure 3, Whittle is on the far left of this group of five siblings, wearing a dress with Mary Janes and a bow in his hair. He looks at his younger brother, who clutches his small hands together and gazes at the camera. But what Whittle remembers, Davidmann reports, is his brother's velvet collar. Whittle associated the velvet collar with being a boy: if one were a boy, one would get this amazing velvet collar. Whittle really coveted that collar, to him a material symbol of longed-for masculinity.

Figure 4 is a series of identity cards, which Whittle has gathered into one page on his family album. These images "queer" the traditional family album by representing not the "private" but rather the state's involvement in the production of its citizenry. Identity cards are often a site of trauma for trans° people, as they function as legal barriers, or gateways, to state (dis)services, from health care to border control. Getting the right card, with the right image, the right name, and the right initials in the right part of the card, for example, can take years. These cards validate a hard-won identity, despite one's resentment at the state for having the power to confer that identity. As Whittle wrote in relationship to a portrait that he and Davidmann collaborated on (fig. 6), "As I have travelled through the life of my own, every ongoing transition . . . it has always been the dream of being myself, whatever that is, that has sustained some semblance of sanity."[14] For Whittle, the incoherence of a family snapshot of his childhood in girl's clothing, or a page of ID cards, is an integral part of his trans° family album, as these images mark moments in his complex, gendered self-making.

The last two images pair Whittle and Rutherford across the space of thirty years, in 1978 and 2009. The 1978 snapshot shows them embracing on a floral couch; Whittle remembers that he was trying to unhook Rutherford's bra at the time, a playful gesture of desire that appears welcomed but which Rutherford was also playfully, but firmly, refusing to acquiesce to while in the company of the photographer. The snapshot is otherwise unremarkable, except to say—remarkably—that trans° people and their non-trans° partners have unremarkable moments. Paired with figure 6, however, is a portrait that Davidmann made with Whittle and Rutherford in 2009; together, the images speak to the longevity of their relationship, which has now spanned thirty-five years.

Whittle asked Davidmann to collaborate with him in the making of figure 6, *And the Bridegroom.* Whittle wanted to reference, visually, Lucian Freud's painting of the same title. Central to Freud's painting is the queer icon Leigh Bowery, lying next to his wife, Nicola Bateman.[15] In reflecting on why he wanted to emulate the painting, Whittle wrote: "With Sarah, over these 30 years, I have wanted to be the Leigh Bowery of this picture; a big man, a man with strength, a man who can fling open his body to the wider world. Having a body that contradicted me was always the problem, to her [Sarah] it never was."[16] The desire to have a portrait taken of oneself and one's life partner is in keeping with the conventions of family portraiture, as is the reiteration of an "image." For example, in figure 2 the poses that K and Hazel have taken on restate the image conventions for wedding portraiture. In contrast, in figure 6 Whittle transgresses the expectations for photographic portraits of married couples by choosing a queer icon as the image for himself. Whittle is shown to be in control, not only of his own body but also of the image that he becomes in the photograph and the image that will live on through the photograph.

Trans° Representation and the Family Album

Family snapshots represent family members, for the most part. In other words, the dominant genre of the photograph album is that of portraiture: bodies are insistently on display, in almost every image, including those of trans° family members, whether or not those bodies read as trans°. While the genre of family photography is organized around the visual representation of the (familial) body, family snapshots of trans° people carry with them a shadow history of corporeal and subjective violence to the nonnormative body that is racialized in its history. As Ben Singer has shown, since the nineteenth century photography has been central to medicine's rendering of trans° peoples' atypical embodiment as pathological.[17] K's wedding portrait, or Davidmann's portrait of Whittle and Rutherford, cannot be read outside a longer coercive history of medical and anthropological photography that has historically rendered both the nonwhite and queer and/or trans° body as the taxonomic object of a colonial, pathologizing gaze. Because of the photograph's "that-has-been" quality, photographs can connote a rhetoric of objectivity and disinterestedness that has made this imaging technology particularly suited to scientific racism and colonial power.[18] Photographs of trans° people in the family album, therefore, threaten a double violence: one stemming from the colonial, racist, and intertwined histories of medical photography and physical anthropology and the other tagged with the hetero- and cisnormative scripts of the family photograph album.

Some artists have, for these reasons and others, shifted to nonfigural representation as an approach to working with trans° material.[19] While some contemporary artists such as Zackary Drucker and Rhys Ernst continue to work with portraiture, other artists such as Emmett Ramstad and Chris Vargas challenge and subvert normative expectations that trans° subjectivity can be read through and on the body. Yet in the context of family photography, the focus of our conversation here, the body remains central: the genre of the family album is predicated on the body's visual representation and the viewer's affective relationship to the person that body represents. For this reason, family photography is especially loaded: one cannot avoid the dense histories of power, racism, colonialism, and medicine's taxonomic gaze by simply taking trans° family members out of the wedding photographs, confirmation snapshots, or family portraits. On the contrary, in some cases, as in trans° activist Raj's photograph albums archived at the CLGA, the trans° family album can function as a site of queer, utopic futurity; snapshots of trans° friends, family members, and kinship networks are central to the trans°-positive affective work that these albums perform for some viewers, including those who identify as trans°.[20]

Recent scholarship in the imbrication of race and family photography suggests new approaches in thinking through the affective work of the family snapshot. As Tina Campt has argued in her work on family photography and the black diaspora in Europe, family photographs register at multiple sensory and affective levels. They "are affect-laden objects that incite individual responses and modes of intensive engagement."[21] The fact that photographs "move us" with an affective intensity is what makes them so political. And while most scholars have emphasized the violence that such images can wreak on nonnormative family members, Campt shows how the affective work of such images can also work to produce modes of belonging, identification, and community among populations—such as the black diaspora in Europe—that may find themselves otherwise unwelcome within a prescriptively white Europe. Trans° family photographs, in other words, like other images, are polysemic; against heteronormativity, they can also work instrumentally to produce narratives of queer and trans° kinship, thereby providing sites of critical affective labor regarding trans° belonging. In Davidmann's two image sets concerning trans° family photography, we can see not only examples of violent erasure (in the K series) but also the work of family photographs in producing trans° family belonging and community (in the Whittle album).

Conclusion: Remembering and Forgetting

All family photograph albums are what Lauren Berlant and Michael Warner might call an "amnesia archive," parts of collective memory that erase uncomfortable pasts.[22] The very form of the family photograph album seeks a purging of the uncomfortable, the awkward, the painful (i.e., the queer); it is not by accident that most photograph albums are archives of bourgeois rituals designed to produce family togetherness, from birthdays to holiday celebrations, to summer vacations. The photographs that do not fit the album are the queer ones: those images that trouble the "normalcy" that this conservative form has historically sought to produce. In these two albums, we can see two different encounters with the impulse to remember and the drive to forget.

The images we have selected from K's album signify the efforts to erase an uncomfortable past: from the "to be destroyed" on figure 1 to (failed) "proof" on figure 2, a directive that could not be a more explicit call to forget a family's trans* history. In contrast, Whittle's identity cards are a queer incursion into a photographic genre that seeks to cordon off public from private, as if such a distinction is ever possible; the photographs of him and of him and Rutherford together queer a trans* narrative that often focuses on the trans* body and its transition in isolation from queer kinship networks. In creating an album that insists on remembering the complexities of his transitioning self in relationship to both family and the state, Whittle and Rutherford (and Davidmann) queer the trans* family album.

Figure 1 (*left*). *Ken. To be destroyed*. Digital print, 2013. Photograph courtesy of Sara Davidmann
Figure 2 (*right*). *Proof*. Vintage photograph by Alexanders, Artists' Colourmen, and Photographers' Studio, Edinburgh, 1954. Rephotographed. Digital print, 2013. Photograph courtesy of Sara Davidmann

Figure 3. *Stephen 1961*. Stephen Whittle family album. Rephotographed 2007.
Photograph courtesy of Sara Davidmann and Stephen Whittle

Figure 4. *Stephen Identity Cards*. Stephen Whittle family album. Rephotographed 2007.
Photograph courtesy of Sara Davidmann and Stephen Whittle.

Figure 5. *Stephen and Sarah 1978*. Stephen Whittle family album. Rephotographed 2007.
Photograph courtesy of Sara Davidmann and Stephen Whittle

Figure 6. *Stephen and Sarah 2009 (And the Bridegroom)*. C-type print.
Photograph courtesy of Sara Davidmann

Notes

1.   We use the asterisk to denote not only gender identities prefixed by "trans" but also others that complicate and/or challenge the binary gender system, such as genderqueer, cross-dresser, and others. See Avery Tompkins, "Asterisk," *Transgender Studies Quarterly* 1, nos. 1–2 (2014): 26–27. For a history of "trans" as a category, see Nicholas Matte, "Historicizing American Transnormativity: Medicine, Media, and Activism, 1964–1990" (PhD diss., University of Toronto, 2014); and David Valentine, *Imagining Transgender: An Ethnography of a Category* (Durham, NC: Duke University Press, 2007).

2.   See, e.g., Ann Cvetkovich, *An Archive of Feelings: Trauma, Sexuality, and Lesbian Public Cultures* (Durham, NC: Duke University Press, 2003); Nan Alamilla Boyd and Horacio N. Roque Ramírez, eds., *Bodies of Evidence: The Practice of Queer Oral History* (New York: Oxford University Press, 2012); Nan Alamilla Boyd, "Who Is the Subject? Queer Theory Meets Oral History," *Journal of the History of Sexuality* 17, no. 2 (2008): 177–89; and Esther Newton, "My Best Informant's Dress: The Erotic Equation in Fieldwork," in *Margaret Mead Made Me Gay: Personal Essays, Public Ideas* (Durham, NC: Duke University Press, 2000), 243–58.

3.   For a discussion of oral history interviews with LGBTQI people, privacy, and online access, see Elise Chenier, "Privacy Anxieties: Ethics versus Activism in Archiving Lesbian Oral History Online," in this issue.

4.   Diana Taylor, "Acts of Transfer," in *The Archive and the Repertoire: Performing Cultural Memory in the Americas* (Durham, NC: Duke University Press, 2004), 1–33; K. J. Rawson, "Archive This! Queering the Archive," in *Practicing Research in Writing Studies: Reflexive and Ethically Responsible Research*, ed. Katrina M. Powell and Pamela Takayoshi (New York: Hampton, 2012), 237–50.

5.   Ann Cvetkovich, "Photographing Objects as Queer Archival Practice," in *Feeling Photography*, ed. Elspeth H. Brown and Thy Phu (Durham, NC: Duke University Press, 2014), 273–96; Jennifer V. Evans, "Seeing Subjectivity: Erotic Photography and the Optics of Desire," *American Historical Review* 118, no. 2 (2013): 430–62; "Photography and Historical Investigation," special issue, *History and Theory* 48, no. 4 (2009); Elspeth H. Brown, "De Meyer at *Vogue*: Commercializing Queer Affect in First World War–Era Fashion Photography," *Photography and Culture* 2, no. 3 (2009): 253–75. For queerness as having an "especially vexed relationship to evidence," see José Esteban Muñoz, *Cruising Utopia: The Then and There of Queer Futurity* (New York: New York University Press, 2009), 63. For other recent efforts to expand the meaning of the archive to include nontraditional objects and knowledges, see Ann Laura Stoler, *Along the Archival Grain: Epistemic Anxieties and Colonial Common Sense* (Princeton, NJ: Princeton University Press, 2009); Deborah B. Gould, *Moving Politics: Emotion and ACT UP's Fight against AIDS* (Chicago: University of Chicago Press, 2009); and Nan Alamilla Boyd, "Talking about Sex: Cheryl Gonzales and Rikki Streicher Tell Their Stories," in Boyd and Roque Ramírez, *Bodies of Evidence*, 95–112.

6.   K. J. Rawson, "Accessing Transgender // Desiring Queer(er?) Archival Logics," *Archivaria*, no. 68 (2009): 123–40; Charles E. Morris III and K. J. Rawson, "Queer Archives / Archival Queers," in *Theorizing Histories of Rhetoric*, ed. Michelle Ballif (Carbondale: Southern Illinois University Press, 2013), 74–89.

7.   For recent critiques of the concept of a trans narrative, see *Everyday to Stay*, by Chase Joynt (2010), documentary short, 21 min.; *against a trans narrative*, by Jules Rosskam (2009), video, 1:1, Video Data Bank; and Beatriz Preciado, *Testo Junkie: Sex, Drugs,*

and Biopolitics in the Pharmacopornographic Era (New York: Feminist Press, 2013). For writing that works against the grain of "individual" transition by seeing trans° as an intersubjective process of becoming, see Jane Ward, "Gender Labor: Transmen, Femmes, and the Collective Work of Transgression," *Sexualities* 13, no. 2 (2010): 236–54; Susan Driver, "Queer Femmes Loving FTMs: Towards an Erotic Transgender Ethics," in *Trans/forming Feminisms: Transfeminist Voices Speak Out*, ed. Krista Scott-Dixon (Toronto: Sumach, 2006), 112–21; Tam Sanger, *Trans People's Partnerships: Towards an Ethics of Intimacy* (New York: Palgrave Macmillan, 2010); and Sally Hines, "Intimate Transitions: Transgender Practices of Partnering and Parenting," *Sociology* 40, no. 2 (2006): 353–71.

8. For the ideological work of normative family albums, see Pierre Bourdieu, *Photography, a Middle-Brow Art*, trans. Shaun Whiteside (Stanford, CA: Stanford University Press, 1996); Marianne Hirsch, *Family Frames: Narrative, Photography, Postmemory* (Cambridge, MA: Harvard University Press, 1997); Shawn Michelle Smith, *American Archives: Gender, Race, and Class in Visual Culture* (Princeton, NJ: Princeton University Press, 1999), 113–32; Laura Wexler, *Tender Violence: Domestic Visions in the Age of U.S. Imperialism* (Chapel Hill: University of North Carolina Press, 2000), 94–126; Nancy Martha West, *Kodak and the Lens of Nostalgia* (Charlottesville: University Press of Virginia, 2000); and Catherine Zuromskis, *Snapshot Photography: The Lives of Images* (Cambridge, MA: MIT Press, 2013).

9. Roland Barthes, *Camera Lucida: Reflections on Photography*, trans. Richard Howard (New York: Hill and Wang, 1981); Simon Watney, "Ordinary Boys," in *Family Snaps: The Meanings of Domestic Photography*, ed. Jo Spence and Patricia Holland (London: Virago, 1991), 30–34.

10. Color versions of the images in this article are available in the online version, doi.org/doi:10.1215/01636545-2849612.

11. Barthes, *Camera Lucida*, 10.

12. After this point in the text, we have collaborated on a jointly written narrative.

13. Stephen Whittle, *Respect and Equality: Transsexual and Transgender Rights* (Portland, OR: Cavendish, 2002); Kate More and Stephen Whittle, eds., *Reclaiming Genders: Transsexual Grammars at the* Fin de Siècle (New York: Cassell, 1999); Susan Stryker and Stephen Whittle, eds., *The Transgender Studies Reader* (New York: Routledge, 2006).

14. Stephen Whittle, text for *And the Bridegroom*, personal collection of Sara Davidmann.

15. Bowery (1961–1994) was a gay, Australian, London-based performance artist, model, fashion designer, and all-around art star in the 1980s and early 1990s; his cultural work was influential in the transatlantic avant-garde club and fashion scene in these years. In 1994 he married Bateman, his longtime companion.

16. Whittle, *And the Bridegroom*, text.

17. T. Benjamin Singer, "From the Medical Gaze to *Sublime Mutations*: The Ethics of (Re) Viewing Non-normative Body Images," in Stryker and Whittle, *Transgender Studies Reader*, 601–20.

18. Barthes, *Camera Lucida*, 115; Allan Sekula, "The Body and the Archive," *October*, no. 39 (1986): 3–65; Elspeth H. Brown, *The Corporate Eye: Photography and the Rationalization of American Commercial Culture, 1884–1929* (Baltimore: Johns Hopkins University Press, 2005); Jennifer Tucker, *Nature Exposed: Photography as Eyewitness in Victorian Science* (Baltimore: Johns Hopkins University Press, 2005).

19. For scholarship that considers recent trans° cultural production that distinguishes between

the transsexual and the transgender body in representation, see Judith Halberstam, "Technotopias: Representing Transgender Bodies in Contemporary Art," in *In a Queer Time and Place: Transgender Bodies, Subcultural Lives* (New York: New York University Press, 2005), 97–124.

20. For more on snapshot photography, trans° lives, and queer bonds, see Elspeth H. Brown, "Photography, Euphoria, and Queer Futurity: Rupert Raj's Trans° Family Albums, 1971–1988," forthcoming.

21. Tina Campt, *Image Matters: Archive, Photography, and the African Diaspora in Europe* (Durham, NC: Duke University Press, 2012), 16.

22. Lauren Berlant and Michael Warner, "Sex in Public," in "Intimacy," ed. Laurent Berlant, special issue, *Critical Inquiry* 24, no. 2 (1998): 547–66.

Archive Discipline

An Interview on the Danish Gay and Lesbian Archive with Karl Peder Pedersen

Peter Edelberg

Doing empirical gay and lesbian historical studies can be a daunting task. Gays and lesbians were often criminalized in Europe in the past, and are still today in parts of the world, creating a situation where historical sources for describing gay and lesbian lives in the past often are either lost or come in the form of criminal records. However, legal and social situations even in Western Europe differed widely from each other. When the gay and lesbian movement gained ground in Western Europe after the Second World War, homosexuality was illegal, for example, in West Germany and Britain, but legal in Denmark, France, and Sweden. Thus the ability and feeling of safety to collect archives has also differed. The Scandinavian gay and lesbian unions are some of the oldest, still running, lesbian, gay, bisexual, and transgender (LGBT) unions in the world. Founded in Denmark in 1948 by a circle of friends around the activist Axel Lundahl-Madsen (later Axgil), the union included "local" branches in Sweden and Norway, which after a few years became independent.[1]

During the summer of 2007, the Danish union of gays and lesbians experienced a severe economic crisis, and for a time people feared that the association would go bankrupt. This severe crisis made the board decide to turn over its archive to the Danish State Archives, as was proscribed in the statutes of the association. Consisting of 278 boxes, almost 30 shelf meters, or nearly 100 feet, the archive was

Radical History Review
Issue 122 (May 2015)   DOI 10.1215/01636545-2849621
© 2015 by MARHO: The Radical Historians' Organization, Inc.

a rather large collection gathered over the course of twenty-five years. After it was turned over to the Danish State Archives, all boxes were bar-coded, making them searchable and findable in the main archive database, www.sa.dk/daisy (search term: "Landsforeningen for Bøsser&Lesbiske," or "National Union of Gays & Lesbians"). This arrangement has preserved a unique gay and lesbian archive for future generations under safe conditions, and in a way that makes it accessible to all researchers who might want to use it.

While it could seem dangerous to people in some countries to leave a gay and lesbian archive in the hands of the authorities, in Denmark this is certainly the safest place it can be. Since homosexuality was decriminalized in 1933, authorities have increasingly supported and encouraged LGBT rights. Giving the archive to the state has meant an increasing level of professional accessibility, making possible history books on gay and lesbian history, which are sorely needed in Denmark.

However, the archive would never have existed had it not been for a handful of archive activists, since neither state authorities nor other LGBT activists at the time paid much thought to documenting queer lives. As a historian who has conducted empirical research into the gay community in postwar Denmark, I set out to interview one of these activists, fellow historian Karl Peder Pedersen (b. 1952), to document the story of a specific gay and lesbian archive and inspire both activists and archivists to document queer lives.[2]

The interview was conducted over mail, where I asked questions and Pedersen responded. I have translated it into English and edited the final version to include some further contextualization and explanatory remarks, and Pedersen has approved all changes.

The main Danish gay and lesbian association has had many names in its lifetime, from the National Association of Homophiles in the 1960s to the National Association of Gays and Lesbians in the 1970s. Today it is called LGBT Denmark— the Danish National Association of Gays, Lesbians, Bisexuals, and Transgender People, but thinking that the name always reflected the people in the organization would be a mistake. Bisexuals and transgender people have been part of the association since long before the title included them. While I mostly use *gay and lesbian* to describe the association, as was customary at the time, the reader should not think that it excludes bisexual and transgender people.

Peter Edelberg: *I had my debut in the gay community in 1993 when I started attending the gay and lesbian youth group in the gay and lesbian community center. At that time I was hardly aware of the archive and library. Now as a historian I have fully realized the importance of such archives. Can you tell me how the archive began?*

Karl Peder Pedersen: In the beginning of the 1980s the homosexual movement in Denmark—like all over the Western world—experienced great progress with increasing membership and expansion of activities. Thanks to this new support the movement was able to make a difference in the political arena, and in time it succeeded in procuring funds from the state, the city council, and private organizations. These funds meant that the association had the opportunity to set up a professional secretariat run by paid employees, and this situation was a major change from the past, where voluntary and unpaid activists did the office work.

Already in 1980 the association had enough funds to buy its own house at Knabrostræde 3, right in the heart of Copenhagen, and there the association fitted out offices and meeting rooms for the secretariat and for the many activist groups. One of these groups was the library group, whose goal it was to collect donations in order to build up a gay and lesbian book collection. In 1983 the collection was already voluminous and stayed open for a couple of hours every week.

Some of the donations to the library consisted of not only books but also photographs and manuscripts that really belonged in an archive. Therefore, the library group created a subgroup, the archive section. Central figures were the cofounder of the association, Axel Axgil, and his partner, Eigil Axgil. At that time, they were retiring from long and diverse careers and had chosen to move back to Copenhagen. I joined this project as a newly educated, and at that moment, unemployed historian, to which I sought to add scholarly expertise. I soon got support from my friend, chemical engineer Ib Krog Larsen, who for many years led the cataloging of the photography collection.

Both the archive and the library enjoyed good facilities at Knabrostræde 3. The house was large and spacious—a beautiful private house from the 1850s, which more recently had been split up into offices and shops. An old storage building came along with the house and was made into a café, a discotheque, and meeting rooms. The purchase of Knabrostræde 3 made the Danish gay and lesbian association visible as never before, which resulted in increased membership and easier access to public and private funds. That resulted in the association's economy allowing for the supply of practical needs, so everything was registered and kept according to professional standards.

Today most young lesbians and gays look for information on the Internet, and gay and lesbian literature is easily accessible in Internet bookstores. In the early 1990s, I remember that my local library stocked gay and lesbian literature for young adults. However, it seems there was more to your effort than just keeping a library. What was the situation in the 1980s? What was the driving force behind the work?

As hinted previously, only a small circle of people were active in the archive work. Much time was spent doing practical tasks, for example, daily photocopying of newspaper articles about homosexual issues—a task that Axel and Eigil for years carefully saw to. No major program statement was ever formulated, but although it was practically never mentioned or debated, there was no doubt we had two goals. First, [we wanted to] secur[e] historical documentation, which without our efforts would be lost. We saw the lack of historical documentation as dangerous, making "our," that is, homosexual, history impossible to recount. Without a homosexual history, future, possibly hostile, politicians in power could much more easily roll back the development [that was made] to the repression and anonymity of the past. Second, we wanted to function as documentation central for the board and activist groups of the association, providing them with concrete and precise information, when needed in the political struggle.

Karl Peder Pederson in the archive of the National Association of Gays and Lesbians.
Courtesy LGBT Denmark Library

Were you primarily an archive for the association, or did you have a wider scope,
for example, documenting gay and lesbian life outside of organizations?

During the first years, the archive group saw it as its task to contact homosexuals who were in possession of interesting source material, which we feared would be lost, in case of their death. Naturally, former chairpersons of the association and other individuals who had played a part in Danish gay and lesbian history were foremost in our minds. We succeeded in gathering material from the chairpersons Axel Axgil (1949–52), Holger Bramlev (1952–58), Per Kleis Bønnelycke (1970–77), and Henning Jørgensen Sandau (1977–86), not least thanks to Axel's personal contacts.

This collection work took time, and it led to major disappointment when a great effort did *not* lead to convincing the person to let the association's archive safeguard personal files for future generations to study. Many deeply felt the fear of being exposed to public contempt postmortem, and naturally the terrible ravaging of the 1980s AIDS epidemic did not relieve the fear, but forced many back into the closet.

All in all the archive section managed to collect material from about twenty-five persons, which is not terribly impressive. Nevertheless, it was mostly essential source material, not least the files of previous chairpersons, as this material nicely complemented the association's own files, which only went as far back as the 1960s. The collection strategy of the archive with reference to private individuals did not lead to major results for two reasons. First, we never managed to recruit many people for the archive work; second, the registration and archiving of the association's own files took up [an] increasing amount of time and soon occupied all our efforts. The employees who, in the beginning of the 1980s, had been hired for the new national secretariat had no archive experience and therefore saw a great advantage in leaving archiving to us "professionals" in the archive. Not only did we take good care of the material in locked cupboards; we also sorted and registered it, making the documents easy to find when needed. Thus the archive began attending to the staff functions of the secretariat, instead of solely archiving and cataloging, occupying—as mentioned previously—a good deal of our efforts. When the archive received documents from the secretariat, from the many elected board members, or from committees, every document had to be studied and classified, and when one received [a] larger collection of documents a very time-consuming task was at hand, as everything had to be sorted out and registered from scratch.

During the 1980s and 1990s, the National Association of Gays and Lesbians was a powerful lobby organization with a small professional secretariat and many activist groups and committees consisting solely of committed amateurs. These groups had no "archive discipline"; a very unfortunate anarchy reigned. This lack of discipline was intensified by quick replacements in these groups; for example, it was an exception if the same person chaired a group or a committee for several years. Association members typically entered this kind of work during their education or in coming out periods, and after a time the interest declined quickly. Despite expressing an understanding of the importance of keeping and documenting the history of the association, it was rarely translated into conscious action. These working conditions contributed to making the archive work difficult, since all initiative and enthusiasm had to proceed from us. That some worked against us would be too harsh to say, but often we felt ignored and had to ask each other if it was worth it to carry on.

Working in an archive enclave . . .

The gay and lesbian archive was thus fully occupied with sorting out and registering the material, which kept coming, and the institutional affiliation with the association of gays and lesbians provided secure economic conditions. This arrangement relieved the archive from securing funds from other sources, as well as having to market itself externally and seeking publicity to a wider audience. Working in the archive increasingly felt like a lonely frontier, where we did not doubt the support from the troops, but it was rarely visible or obvious. Our isolation was increasingly a problem, making it impossible to increase the number of activists. With only three to four persons—the last ten years only two—we only had time to continue the usual routine tasks and no time at all for public campaigns.

I wonder what the conditions will be for historical research of the LGBTQ [lesbian, gay, bisexual, transgender, and queer] culture of today. The "archive discipline" you mention is even more lacking today than it has ever been. LGBTQ groups grow up and disappear again without leaving any archives to speak of behind; their websites eventually deteriorate, their e-mail correspondence is lost when they buy a new computer, and their zines are rarely kept in libraries of any kind. We face a challenge in the future when we want to explain what happened in [the] 1990s and the 2000s. How was your archive used by the public and by researchers?

For many years the gay and lesbian archive in Copenhagen was open to the public every Thursday from 5 to 7 p.m., but far from every week saw visitors. Usually the visitors were university students, writing papers on registered partnership, discrimination, and such, and [they] would use our collection of newspaper clippings, which was sorted not only chronologically but also thematically. On other occasions researchers—mostly foreign—wished to use the files of the association, for example to elucidate how the association had acted in specific periods or to figure out how the association—officially and unofficially—had influenced political or administrative decisions and specific laws passed by the Danish Parliament (Folketing). Some researchers like the Swedish historian Jens Rydström and the American jurist Darren Spedale worked for weeks and months in the archival collections, as did three Danish researchers, writing a book on the history of the AIDS struggle in Denmark.[3] In the Danish researchers' foreword, they emphasized that "the extent of and degree of order in the archive has been invaluable in the research phase" and that they probably could not have written their book without the collections of the archive.[4] The archive group naturally valued and took to heart those words of praise.

During the years many have benefited from the archive collections, and on occasions we have lent out material, first and foremost photographs, to newspapers and publishing houses.

The association's own archive . . .

The main part of the 278 boxes, now housed by the Danish State Archives, contains the association's own files, that is, meeting minutes, correspondence, thematic files, personal files et cetera. One finds not only the final documents but also notes and clippings, making it possible to trace the national board's internal strategic considerations. From the beginning in 1948, foreign contact played an important part, and the association was an active player in the work of several international organizations in the 1980s. The cooperation gathering around the Nordic Council of Homosexuals was also important, and the positive influence of this council on the common Nordic parliamentary process can hardly be overestimated. The Nordic Council of Homosexuals was a cooperation between Nordic activists that started around 1980, but [it] has not been active for many years now.

Apart from the work to influence the political decisions in a gay friendly direction, the association of gays and lesbians also took upon itself to advise gays and lesbians in difficult circumstances or maybe [when they] just need[ed] contact with someone they could talk to. Most of these calls went to the telephone help lines set up by the association and have left no trace, whereas members of the national board or secretariat dealt with a number of more fundamental inquiries, in which case they created a file. Among items of special interest are letters, which the association received from homosexuals all over the world. These are kept in a separate correspondence file of the foreign committee. Some of these letters are moving testimonies to times and places when homosexuals were criminalized, persecuted, and despised to an appalling degree.

The archive must be a goldmine of gay and lesbian lives. Can you give us an example of what you can find in the archive?

In the beginning of the twentieth century, the Copenhagen police conducted a crackdown on the homosexuals of the city, and dentist Emil Aae played a leading role as an "outed" gay man. After he was released from prison, he wrote a book, describing in detail the case as he saw it.[5] The book was a shattering critique of a participating judge, and this judge filed a case of defamation against Aae. Again Aae was convicted. He recanted, [and] his book was also confiscated, which made it a collector's item among gays. The verdict made Aae so embittered that he emigrated to Hungary, where he settled down as a dentist in Budapest and died in 1926.

From a gay and lesbian perspective it was an obvious task to investigate whether any source material by or about Emil Aae was kept in Denmark. Thanks to his rare surname and the phone book, it was easy to identify three to four relevant people. One of them was found to be his grandchild, while another was an old lady, who had been married to his nephew. Both were naturally surprised to be contacted on this delicate matter, but [they] did not actually take offense that we had broken into their world and started talking about something they might have wanted to forget. As it was, the family had experienced something even worse after Emil Aae's time. During the German occupation of Denmark in World War II, one of the dentist's nephews had been a member of the Nazi party, so in 1945 when the resistance movement publicized the list of members of the Nazi party, the name "Aae" came out first. During a single generation the carriers of a respectable name had been "scandalized" twice! As a result of this contact we managed to copy a series of letters and photographs and secure them in the archive.

In a recent book on police surveillance and persecution of homosexuals in Berlin, the German historian Jens Dobler has made me aware that when it comes to sources for homosexual history one deals with a source deficit [*einer difizitären Quellenlage*]. According to Dobler, this is caused not only by the former stigmatization and persecution of homosexuals, which alerted them not to keep anything that might compromise them, but also by the fact that they did not have children, who might more or less automatically pass archival material from generation to generation. I believe that Dobler is on to a point of prime importance and [making] another strong argument for distinct gay and lesbian archives.[6]

Confidence and trust are important for any archive. Even though gays and lesbians increasingly have "come out" during the past decades, few people want their private papers publicly accessible. How have you dealt with the dilemma between documenting gay and lesbian lives and securing these persons' privacy?

If one wants to receive interesting source material from people, a decisive factor is to guarantee the donors that one will handle their donations with confidentiality and respect the terms of admission the donors set down. Luckily, the situation in modern Denmark is that most people have a liberal attitude toward this question, preferring free access to their material. We were often met with overwhelming helpfulness when we needed additional information about people and events, mentioned in the documents, which in turn enhanced the value of the material. It goes without saying that the frequent counseling files with names, addresses, and other information that make it possible to identify individuals cannot be freely available. Total openness would ruin the association's opportunity to provide this assistance in the future, and therefore the statutes of the association solemnly promised that all such files are confidential for seventy-five years. This limit is in tune with the statutes of the Danish State Archives and therefore presents no obstacle. A seventy-five-year confidentiality limit does not mean that a researcher cannot gain access to the files; in fact, a researcher usually will get access. However, access requires a special permission, stating certain conditions, for example, not passing on names encountered in the file or contacting persons whose names the researcher has found in the file.

The Danish archive law is quite unique. Usually any serious researcher can get access to extremely private material in the public archives as long as he or she promises to handle the material without disclosing individual identities. Personally,

I have gotten access to a series of court cases regarding homosexuality and prostitution in Denmark in the 1960s. Your effort has not only stored a lot of important information, but now it can actually be used. How do you see the future for the material you have gathered?

Luckily, the economic crisis in the Gay and Lesbian Union in 2007 led to the archival collection being handed over to the Danish State Archives, where it will be kept in the future. After the transfer to the Danish state, the two remaining archive activists relinquished their post and the archive was dissolved. However, this is no disaster, since the current archive production of the association is electronically stored, and paper documents are kept only on rare occasions. In that way the transfer of the paper archive of the association marks the end of an era where information was kept and archived in paper form. A volunteer archive effort encompassing twenty-five years ended in a satisfying manner for all parties concerned: The vast collection of valuable information was kept safe for future generations and searchable from anywhere in the world via the Internet. Hopefully, this increased availability means that the collections will be used by many. Every time that happens, I am sure, it will thrill the members of the defunct archive section and confirm their belief that all the trouble was worth their while!

. . . . .

Digging into the archives while I did my PhD made me rethink many of my preconceptions about gay and lesbian history. Feeling the paper the minutes of the board meetings of the association of 1948 were written on gave me a "reality shock." I realized that I had a deep obligation to these people to treat their story with care and respect. Interviewing Pedersen made me see how the archive itself had a story and was the concrete product of certain people's efforts. As historians we know these things theoretically, but realizing them is something else. Engaging with the physical archive and the persons behind it made me appreciate what I had in my hands as a historian.

Notes

A color version of the image in this article is available in the online version, dx.doi.org/10.1215/01636545-2849621.

1. Fredrik Silverstolpe et al., *Sympatiens hemlighetsfulla makt: Stockholms homosexuella 1860–1960* (*The Mysterious Power of Sympathy: Homosexuals in Stockholm, 1860–1960*) (Stockholm: Stockholmia Forlag, 1999), 630–47.
2. Peter Edelberg, "The Long Sexual Revolution: The Police and the New Gay Man," in *Sexual Revolutions*, ed. Gert Hekma and Alain Giami (Houndmills, Basingstoke: Palgrave Macmillan, 2014), 46–59; Edelberg, "The Queer Road to 'Frisind': Copenhagen, 1945–2012," in *Queer Cities, Queer Cultures: Europe since 1945*, ed. Matt Cook and Jennifer V. Evans (London: Bloomsbury Academic, 2014), 55–74.
3. Jens Rydström and Kati Mustola, *Criminally Queer: Homosexuality and Criminal Law in*

Scandinavia, 1842–1999 (Amsterdam: Aksant 2007); William N. Eskridge Jr. and Darren R. Spedale, *Gay Marriage: For Better or for Worse? What We've Learned from the Evidence* (New York: Oxford University Press, 2006); Jan Fouchard, Bent Hansen, and Henning Mikkelsen, *Bøssepesten: Historien om AIDS-bekæmpelsen blandt bøsser i Danmark 1981–1996* (*The Gay Plague: The History of the AIDS Struggle among Gays in Denmark, 1981–1996*) (Copenhagen: Borgens Forlag, 2005).

4. Fouchard, Hansen, and Mikkelsen, *Bøssepesten*, 12. Edelberg's translation.

5. Emil Aae, *Den fulde sandhed om min arrestation og fhv. kst. Kriminalretsassessor Wilckes store sædelighedssag 1906–07* (*The Whole Truth about My Arrest and Former Judge Wilcke's Great Morality Affair, 1906–7*) (Copenhagen: Universalforlaget 1909).

6. Jens Dobler, *Zwischen Duldungspolitik und Verbrechensbekämpfung: Homosexuellenverfolgung durch die Berliner Polizei von 1848 bis 1933* (*Between Tolerance and Crime Fighting: The Persecution of Homosexuals by the Berlin Police from 1848 to 1933*), Schriftenreiche der Deutschen Gesellschaft für Polizeigeschichte (Series of the German Society for Police History) 6 (Frankfurt: Verlag für Polizeiwissenschaft, 2008), 16.

Queering Archives

A Roundtable Discussion

Anjali Arondekar, Ann Cvetkovich, Christina B. Hanhardt,
Regina Kunzel, Tavia Nyong'o, Juana María Rodríguez,
and Susan Stryker

Compiled by Daniel Marshall, Kevin P. Murphy,
and Zeb Tortorici

In your own work, how has your thinking about the relationship between notions of queer and the archive shifted over time?

Susan: I hadn't thought about this question until you asked it, but in retrospect I can see that 2003 was a pivotal year in how notions of the queer and the archive shifted in my own work. At that point in my career I'd spent about a decade thinking and writing about transsexual embodiment and transgender history. I drew inspiration and lifted techniques from queer-of-color feminists like Gloria Anzaldúa and Audre Lorde to craft a narrative voice *as* a transsexual writer that functioned as a critique of objectifying and delegitimating knowledges about the mode of my embodiment and that expressed as well the counterdominant knowledges rooted in my own embodied experience. At the same time, I was immersed in archival research for a book project on trans history in San Francisco. That book remains to be written, but the research I conducted informed many of my other projects

Radical History Review
Issue 122 (May 2015)   DOI 10.1215/01636545-2849630

during those years, namely, editing *GLQ*'s transgender studies special issue (1998), writing coffee-table books on the Bay Area's queer history and the history of queer paperbacks (1996, 2000), and the lengthy process of making a documentary film about the Compton's Cafeteria riot that finally came out in 2005. What's clearer to me now than it was then was that I toggled back and forth between intensely subjective investigations into lived experience while also documenting the context in which that experience transpired and was fascinated by the interplay between the two registers. I've always been interested in the historicity of identity, in questions of how we become the particular kinds of people we are through the mutually constitutive interplay of psychical, social, and environmental forces. I should note that I was doing this work while deeply involved with the GLBT [Gay, Lesbian, Bisexual, and Transgender] Historical Society in San Francisco, initially as a volunteer, then a board member, and finally as the first paid executive director of the organization. I earned my living in those days by attending to the care and feeding of an actual, physical collection of queer historical materials and had even gotten a certificate in archival studies.

The configuration of my life started changing in 2003. Perhaps significantly, this was the year of publication for Ann Cvetkovich's *An Archive of Feelings* as well as Diana Taylor's *The Archive and the Repertoire*. Although the former is ostensibly about trauma and the latter ostensibly about performance, both works are also centrally concerned with the embodied nature of memory and with the transmission of cultural knowledge through bodily practice. Both were extremely influential for me in beginning to piece together conceptually the two halves of my working life—the archives and the body—as commensurable material expressions of assembled knowledges. More directly influential was meeting Nikki Sullivan, who introduced me not only to her own brilliant scholarship on body modification practices but also to a wider conversation within Australian feminist philosophies of the body and to bodies of continental philosophical work whose edges I'd only skirted before. I started working closely with Nikki and her colleagues in the Department of Critical and Cultural Studies at Macquarie University in Sydney in 2003, and later that year [I] left my job at the GLBT Historical Society in part to take a visiting scholar position there. I spent time in Australia nearly every year for the next decade, participating in the formation of what's now known as the Somatechnics Research Network. It was in this milieu that I began to assemble a theoretical apparatus capable of bridging affective and embodied experience with the material-discursive, the historical, and the archival. In 2010 I guest edited a special issue of *Australian Feminist Studies* called "Embodiment and the Archival Imaginary" that gestured toward these interests.

I fell in love with Maurice Merleau-Ponty's phenomenological account of embodiment as an ongoing process of becoming, rather than a mere static material existence, a process he characterizes as a sedimentation, or an archiving, of experience. This lived body materializes its historical and psychical contours over time precisely through the gestures and patterns of motion that it acquires, automates, forgets, and repeats, through the habits and habitats it enacts and occupies by means of a *habitus*, which Pierre Bourdieu tells us is nothing other than "history turned into nature, i.e. denied as such."[1] As Gaston Bachelard noted in *The Poetics of Space*, "We are the diagram of the functions of inhabiting" the spaces where we have lived intimately. "The word habit," he says, "is too worn a word to express this passionate liaison of our bodies, which do not forget," with the unforgettable spaces of our inhabitation.[2] And yet as Henri Bergson reminds us in *Matter and Memory*, we remain capable of initiating voluntary motor actions that introduce the potential for change and creative expression that emanate within but depart from received patterns of movement. There is more than a prescripted social choreography, in other words; there is an improvisational ontological dance, which is inherently queer or trans to the extent that it crosses and disrupts old patterns and bends our movements, both personal and collective, toward new and previously unrealized ways of being.

Juana María: This resonates so deeply with me. In doing the work that became *Queer Latinidad*, I really didn't have a theoretical foundation for thinking about archives, even as the differences among activist, legal, and digital archives and their relationship to identity practices were at the heart of what I termed discursive spaces. *An Archive of Feelings* and *The Archive and the Repertoire* were both published the year my book came out, so they were simply not available to me. (Timing is everything!) In writing about Proyecto ContraSIDA por Vida, I remember having to work against the academic assumption that I needed to do ethnographic work; instead, I was interested in the ephemera—flyers, notes, objects, images, manifestos, party debris, art—that folks at Proyecto were producing at an almost manic pace. Folks were dying every day, so the urgency to preserve and remember was palpable, particularly for queer and trans folks of color. In the daily heartbreak of the AIDS epidemic, documenting racialized sexual difference, producing creative queer forms of memorialization and self-representation was/is about producing materials for the streets, for the funders, and for each other. The many folks at Proyecto elevated that form.

Curiously, for that project I had originally wanted to look at a group of Latina lesbians and bisexual women doing local political work, a group I had been centrally involved with in San Francisco, but when I presented the idea to them—they went into panic mode, wanting to control and dictate what I was able to write, and that was not going to work. Queer archives are all about the soiled and untidy—about leaving your dirty *chonies* [underpants] on the kitchen table. Because communities of color are so often under attack, marked as a collective hot mess of excessive, irrational, unorganized bodies and behavior, we have reasons to worry about what we make available to the public for consumption. But the queers and queens that were dying at Proyecto mostly just wanted to be remembered; they wanted to leave a beautiful trace. And they did.

In the new project, *Sexual Futures, Queer Gestures, and Other Latina Longings*, I try to draw out how the archives of colonialism, slavery, and state violence become lodged and also activated in our archives of gesture, sensory memories, language, cultural histories, and sexual fantasies. I am working with phenomenology and performance studies, but also with law and public policy. I wanted to open up the tension between the ephemeral and the sedimented in order to explore how the racially gendered abjection that characterizes the archive might get deployed as a resource for the political projects, but also for our own erotic pleasures. So what is the psychic residue of history, how does that become embodied, and how does it inform our meaning-, erotic-, and world-making practices? Because I was interested in how these traces inflect sex, the question of archive—of representing archives of feelings, of desire, of erotic imaginings—became both the theoretical impulse and the methodological challenge of the project.

Regina: In a probably apocryphal story, when an FBI [Federal Bureau of Investigation] agent asked legendary bank robber Willie Sutton after his capture in 1933 why he robbed banks, Sutton replied, "Because that's where the money is." Trained as a historian in the 1980s, I was encouraged to think of archives in terms similar to Sutton's (though without his dry wit): as places where the sources are. But even before the "archival turn," it was difficult to spend much time in archives without coming to the realization that they were less depositories of documents than themselves historical agents, organized around unwritten logics of inclusion and exclusion, with the power to exalt certain stories, experiences, and events and to bury others. Michel Foucault, Jacques Derrida, Michel-Rolph Trouillot, and others have underlined the archive's normative, normalizing power, but I wonder, too, if there's something queer about archives: in their unruliness masked by orderliness, their excess and eccentricities, their sometimes erotic charge, the way they spark and frustrate our desires (as self-conscious as Anjali's work has made me of the desires I bring to the archives).

Thinking more self-consciously about the relationship between notions of queer and the archive came later for me. In the late 1990s, when I started working on what became *Criminal Intimacy*, people would ask me how I could possibly find sources to write about prison sexual culture. There is no archive devoted to the subject, of course, and so I assembled one from an against-the-grain reading of a wide range of sources, including nineteenth-century prison reports, mid-twentieth-century sociology, autobiographies, popular films, and more. Since so much of the archive available to queer historians is authored by people who judge, police, condemn, and punish nonnormative sexuality and gender, the methodology of reading against the grain is perhaps the key methodological strategy of queer history, as it is for other histories of marginalization. Jennifer Terry's 1991 article, "Theorizing

Deviant Historiography," continues to inspire and guide me in that method and also stands as an early meditation on the challenges of the queer archive.

In my current project, on the encounter of queer and gender-variant people with psychiatry and their negotiation with attributions of mental illness in the twentieth-century United States, I've taken Ann Laura Stoler's work as a provocation to think about what reading *along* the grain of the archive might yield—in this case, the psychiatric archive and its pathologizing accounts of sexual and gender difference. If I don't mine this archive for instances of queer resistance and redemptive counternarratives, I'm forced to reckon with its arguably more overarching story: of remorse, self-loathing, shame, humiliation, and pain. To borrow Ann Cvetkovich's evocative concept, this is an archive of feelings, a record of the psychic costs of stigma and social exclusion often erased in institutional or official archives and often inaccessible to us as historians. Doing justice to that archive is an enormous challenge to me.

Anjali: I work primarily on histories of sexuality in mid- to late nineteenth-century British and Portuguese colonial India. I belabor the specific geopolitics and periodization of my work, not to gesture to its limitations and/or fixed sets of expertises but rather to emphasize the inescapable centrality of the imperial archive (as idea and institution) within such formations. Simply put, interrogations of archival form and content have been and continue to be rather axiomatic within colonial and/or postcolonial scholarship. My engagement with archival hermeneutics thus began more through my work within critical area studies (i.e., South Asian studies) than with any specific turn in queer studies. In fact, for many years, it seemed surprising to me that queer studies had not engaged more robustly with the archival challenges posed by the Subaltern Studies Collective, for example (which included interventions from formidable feminist scholars such as Indrani Chatterjee, Kamala Visweswaran, Susie Tharu, and Gayatri Spivak, in case we tend to simply think of the collective solely in terms of the big gents: Partha Chatterjee, Dipesh Chakrabarty, Gyanendra Pandey, et al.!), where the expansion of the archive was constitutive to the very unsettling of colonial epistemologies. Queer studies provided me with critical tools to think through questions of subject formation and historiography, but, for a large part, I struggled to find a way to bring those questions to the specificities of locations such as South Asia.

One key difference was that archival debates within queer studies in the Euro-American academy (at least till about a few years ago) relied primarily on a search-and-rescue model, or savage-to-salvage model, where the lost histories of the past were recuperated and reinstated within more liberatory histories of the present. Rather than render sexuality's relationship to the archive through such a preferred lens of historical invisibility (which would presume that there is something about sexuality that is lost or silent and needs to "come out"), I began to be more interested in exploring sexuality's recursive traces within the colonial archive against and through our very desire for access. If my first book on colonial British India signaled the failures (pleasurable or otherwise) of such recuperative forms within histories of sexuality, my current work in Portuguese India reaches beyond the grammar of failure and loss toward an archival poetics of ordinary surplus. More broadly, I am now more interested in thinking through how the absence and/or presence of archives secures historical futurity, and what proceeds from an unsettling of that attachment, from a movement away from the recursive historical dialectic of fulfillment and impoverishment. I am, for example, currently reading archives produced by a collectivity of *devadasis* [a compound noun, coupling *deva*, or god, with *dasi*, or female slave; a pan-Indian term, (falsely) interchangeable as sex worker, courtesan, or prostitute]. The archives, from mid-nineteenth-century colonial Goa, are exhaustingly plentiful (over one hundred years of materials), continuous to this day, and surprisingly accessible, all archival forms that run counter to our expectations of archives as lost, erased, and/or disappeared.

Tavia: The origin story of my relation to the archive (no doubt as fictive as any other origin story) lies in my undergraduate exposure to the work of Foucault, and specifically the essay "Nietzsche, Genealogy, History." I have never really deviated from the formative impression Foucault gave that what I should expect from the archive is the estrangement of myself and others, or that I could call that estrangement queer. So, in possible contrast to Anjali's experience, I first encountered historical "search and rescue" missions always already undermined by Nietzsche's and Foucault's corrosive irony. Persuasive arguments against using the archive to reach and somehow repair historical injury have recently been made in queer studies by Heather Love and in black studies by Saidiya Hartman. I like to imagine that I have always accepted such arguments as axiomatic, much as I like to believe that the argument against the "ruses of memory" in my first book were aligned with such a perspective.

This origin story does not really answer the question, which I might paraphrase as follows: How has my relationship to the archive "changed over time"? Change over time (and space) is the historical sine qua non, so I'll try to be answerable to it, in two ways, both of which may be a little to the side of history *proper*, but ways that might still be of some use to an *improper* history, which I still think queer history is or could become.

The first answer is pedagogical. I have taught a course on "queering the archive" for a decade now, following the "Jessica Seinfeld" tactic of hiding nutritious vegetables in more appetizing dishes (shredded carrots in meatballs and so on.). The appetizing dishes in this case were the contemporary topics that my students— mostly in performance and cultural studies—brought to the class, and the blended vegetable was the historical sensibility I hope they left with. By presenting the archive not as an intimidating, dry-as-dust array of institutions and protocols but rather as a chaotic array of objects that fairly pulse with weirdness and surprise, I tried to sidestep the use of history for salvage purposes. Instead, at the risk of pandering to their narcissism, I encouraged students to enter the archive phenomenologically, to move and be moved by the past as they encountered its sensuous fragments, and to build narrative, speculative, and creative accounts accordingly.

The change over time here has only been that the task of queering the archive has gotten easier as the archives I work with have themselves moved toward promoting themselves as exciting, accessible, and, well, queerer destinations (alongside libraries, museums, and other institutions tasked with neoliberal reinvention). As queering the archive has gotten easier, however, I of course have begun to suspect that it is becoming too easy and that some kind of corrective, such as the "reading along the grain" proposed by Regina (via Ann Stoler), might be called for, in order to better grapple with the enduring significance of archival power in the era of its partial transition into a space of ludic exploration and flexible self-fashioning. What kinds of metanarratives does the archive continue to encode that may actually be fostered by our routinized epistemological doubt as to its hidden efficacy? The emergent interdisciplinary literature on the Anthropocene is one area where this important question is being asked, and queer historicist scholars like Dana Luciano are providing necessary interventions in that field as it takes shape.

The second answer is more speculative and perhaps a little banal. The digitization of archives has radically changed the experience of researching in archives and thereby transformed the stakes of making the kinds of genealogical arguments about the past that I cut my intellectual teeth on. Genealogy is no longer, as Foucault stated, "gray, meticulous, and patiently documentary."[3] It can also now be in vivid color, slapdash, and instantaneously aggregative. Think of a genealogical topic today (say, "passing women") and a cornucopia of digitized primary material, much but not all formerly classifiable as "ephemera," can be at one's fingertips. This accelerationism has rapidly expanded and popularized archival research (now often just "searching") from a specialist pursuit to an almost ubiquitous activity. But the towering irony of that is that it is communicative capitalism that has brought us Foucault's "great carnival of time where masks are constantly reappearing."[4] Are we already past the tipping point when the primary commonsense usage of the word *archive* refers not to an institution housing documents but to the ubiquitously accessible location where digital copies of one's e-mails, MP3 files, videos, et cetera, one's so-called data double, are stored? I think my students are already there. What will it mean for them to encounter the traditional archive as a back formation from this new digitally native sense of the archive as information retrievable through metadata and algorithms? I speculate that as the sheer quantity of historical information (across time and especially space) has expanded, queer subjectivities are poised between, on the one hand, a sharp rejection of the past (for its manifest failings in relation to the ongoing autopoiesis of new gendered and sexual subjects) and, on the other, an uneasy embrace, really, an immersion in a kaleidoscopic range of past subjectivities, historical and fabulated. It is this latter tendency, actually, that seems to be increasingly hegemonic, which presents the classic opportunity/danger dyad for historical scholarship.

Christina: Although I probably should not admit it, I have always had a queer relationship to the "archive" insofar as I am a hoarder. (The stigma attached to collecting tendencies such as mine means that no matter how imaginative we may be here, *archive* must be placed in scare quotes.) I have long lived among boxes and piles of paper, disks, videos, files, and other formats of information. An object of both repulsion and fascination for many, including, most recently, audiences of The Learning Channel and other networks dedicated to health-based television programming, hoarding is—as Scott Herring argues in his new book *The Hoarders: Material Deviance in Modern American Culture*—a queer relation to material culture and its accumulation. And it was from the bottom of my own collection of flyers, notes, objects, images, and other ephemera that Juana María so perfectly describes that I began to think about doing the historical research that would become my first book, *Safe Space: Gay Neighborhood History and the Politics of Violence.* As a graduate student, activist, and committed denizen of nightlife venues, I had amassed a large collection of materials charting debates about and innovative responses to the politics of safety and gentrification in New York and San Francisco neighborhoods. I was eager to better understand how LGBT [lesbian, gay, bisexual, and transgender] identities had become so bound up with ideas of injury shared by the rational choice criminology restructuring US cities, as well as how activists and other collectives had imagined alternatives. This backward process—of anchoring historical research in the present—is, of course, not the *proper* way to write history. But my approach was shaped by Foucault's concepts of archaeology and genealogy that, as for Tavia, had influenced my own training from the start. (It was also archaeological in a more literal sense, as I would sort the layers of papers copied from archives and other sources that would accumulate and mix on my floor.)

   This is, then, to repeat Tavia's reminder of the ever-fictive (or fantasy) nature of origin stories, as I locate my long-standing relationship with queerness and the archive in a different self-professed pathology. But it is also to express a kind of wariness about offering a queer relation to the archive as necessarily that different from a range of other practices that go under other names or as that which somehow escapes the shortfalls that have been diagnosed as constitutive of more traditional archival approaches, the latter of which I will confess to quite enjoying (perhaps because, as Regina notes, even traditional archives can have queer qualities). I am struck by—and my own story here might serve as an example of this—how often queer projects repeat the same recuperative drive that Anjali describes, as they are routed into new forms of visibility and institutionality even if in the name of perversity, marginality, or shame.

From the perspective of your work, what types of things are being referenced when people describe queer studies as having experienced an "archival turn"? Do particular uses of archival materials, techniques, or knowledges in effect periodize particular practices in queer theory?

Ann: As these issues and the enthusiasm they have generated indicate, there is a queer archives movement with tremendous vitality right now. As universities and public libraries acquire their collections, grassroots and community-based archives have crossed over into mainstream visibility and institutional legitimation. Moreover, it is not just scholars but also activists and artists who are working in archives and redefining what we mean by archival research and practice. And in addition to the creation of LGBTQ [lesbian, gay, bisexual, transgender, and queer] archives, there are efforts to "queer" the archive, that is, to return to conventional archives from the vantage point of radical and alternative forms of archival practice, research, and exhibition. These are only some of the many good reasons to declare an "archival turn," but I would also suggest that this groundswell of recognition and institution building is the result of work that has been going on for quite some time, and to privilege this moment of visibility can run the risk of erasing a lot of invisible labor behind the scenes.

It's also gratifying to see others acknowledge *An Archive of Feelings* as a point of reference for the archival turn especially since my own archival turn was somewhat accidental (although the accidental encounter is, of course, a form of queer archival method). As Susan notes, *An Archive of Feelings* is centrally concerned with trauma, and, like others who've told their origin stories, I came to the concept of the archive by way of theoretical critique—in my case of trauma as unrepresentable and hence creating trouble for the archives. Having gone to graduate school in the 1980s, my foundational texts for the archival turn predate queer theory. One of them is Gayatri Spivak's "Can the Subaltern Speak?" (and the Subaltern Studies project that Anjali mentions), in which a provocative fusion of critique and archival research generates alternative accounts of colonialism. Another is Toni Morrison's *Beloved*, which turns to fictional ghosts to grapple with the affective and practical challenges of slavery's compromised and absent archives. Like Tavia, I currently find indispensable Saidiya Hartman's recent writing with and about the archive, which builds on *Beloved* and other so-called postslavery novels, to explore the limits and the necessity of the archive for a history of racism's enduring present.

My route to what I call "actually existing" archives (in a nod to Marxism's ambivalent relation to the real) was thus quite circuitous, but, once I got there, the lure of collections like the Lesbian Herstory Archives as both utopian horizon (a place for all lesbians to touch their herstory) and lived reality (a house in Brooklyn filled with all kinds of crazy stuff) was irresistible. My encounters with LGBT community-based and activist archives complemented my oral histories with lesbian AIDS activists, another kind of research method that went against the grain of my training in theory and literature by getting me into messier encounters with real people and with questions of what counts as evidence or archive. Many of the women I interviewed, such as Polly Thistlethwaite, Maxine Wolfe, and Jean Carlomusto, had ties to the Lesbian Herstory Archives and articulated very direct connections between AIDS activism and archive activism. I'm intrigued to see not only how many of us were driven to the archive by the demands of activism and community-based history projects, especially AIDS-related ones, but also how the archive sometimes provided relief from the demands of oral history and ethnography, which often privilege the live encounter as activist method.

Also worth mentioning since it has come up in other comments is the relation between performance studies and the archival turn. My oral history and archival research was facilitated by a guest teaching gig in performance studies at New York University among a cohort that included José Esteban Muñoz, Diana Taylor, and Fred Moten, and in the context of the debates inspired by Peggy Phelan's claims for the ontology of performance as disappearance. José's "Ephemera as Evidence" was foundational for the concept of the "archive of feelings," as was Lauren Berlant's use of the term *archive* to talk about evidence and method in cultural studies.

Although the "archival turn" can be understood as cultural studies' theoretical reframing of what historians call the archive, I would emphasize that, through that process, cultural studies has also come to new archival practices. My own archival turn is thus a double one—initially conceptual but ultimately actual. And so much has happened since *An Archive of Feelings* that I'm now working on the sequel!

Regina: The "archival turn" in queer studies has intensified a kind of thinking in the field about crucial questions: the vulnerability and often absence of documentation of queer life, the places beyond official archives where we might locate such documentation, the relationship of grassroots archives to official archives, the possibilities of what Jack Halberstam calls "silly archives," the importance of what Ann Cvetkovich calls an "archive of feelings," the elusive archive of traces, ephemera, innuendo, gesture.

I'd locate the beginning of important thinking about the queer archive, though, before the archival turn. The ONE Institute archive was founded out of an audacious ambition to create a new field of homophile studies in the late 1950s. I think, too, about community-based gay and lesbian history projects in the 1970s, and about Jonathan Ned Katz's extraordinary *Gay American History* (1976), in which he combed archives for evidence of queer life over the course of four centuries. Katz's documentary projects were not just about culling sources (although his work has been an extraordinary gift to scholars since) but were also early reflections on the queer archive—on where we might locate it, what we might read as queer, and on its possibilities and limits.

Anjali: In many ways, the "archival turn" in queer studies mirrors the broader shifts in the field itself. If, for example, affect studies, trans/studies, postcolonial studies, to name a select few, have radically shifted the parameters of what and who constitute the "subject/s" of queer studies, so also have they transformed our understanding of what stands in for the idea of the archive. We continue to expand our understanding of archival forms, across genres, periodizations, species, but less so, I would submit, across geopolitics. Even as we mobilize the historical and locational transactions enabled through the sign of geopolitics, some troubling analytical turns persist. In many ways, "geopolitics" continues to be more about territorial demarcation, linguistic affiliation, demographic enumeration, divergent temporality and less an epistemology that interrogates the very persistent demand for those formations. The challenge here is to ask what does the turn to geopolitics bring to queer analyses of the archive and vice versa, even in its providential failures? I am, for instance, currently coediting a special issue with Geeta Patel called "Area Impossible," and we are exploring just such a conversation. What's become obvious for us as we navigate the architecture of the issue is how US-centered our conversations around archives still are (to wearily make that argument yet again!) and how rare it is to see discussions of archival forms that reach back beyond the nineteenth century.

Tavia: In addition to the tendencies and developments above, I would also argue that the archival turn in queer studies cannot be fully grappled with without also reckoning with the shift in meaning of *archive* and *archiving* wrought by technology. Without being technologically determinist, it is certainly possible to point to the "real subsumption" of archivally oriented queer scholarship, to adopt the Marxist terminology. Whereas earlier efforts at queer archival formations—the ONE Archive and Jonathan Ned Katz's pioneering documentary histories—were hardly even subject to "formal" subsumption, being after all volunteer efforts conducted outside even nascent neighborhood gay economies, the cognitive labor through which digital archives are produced and interpreted is thoroughly colonized by capitalist rationality and valorization. The Google corporation's move to digitize every book ever published is still the most salient event through which to think the real subsumption of the archive and processes of archival interpretation. Those of us trained before these tools became ubiquitous are deskilled by them, even as those for whom they are second nature may lack any sense of an outside or limit to the content, and, more importantly, the form, of the information they encode. For queer studies, I think this means specifically the partial banalization of our claims to exclusion, suppression, or disappearance, as what we confront instead is a superfluity of indifferent and undifferentiated access to the past: queer, straight, and everything in between and beyond. That such access is demonstrably *not* a replacement for the kinds of radical historicist projects that emerged within queer social movements and queer academic praxis is the most pressing reason that an "archival turn" in queer studies is on the pressing intellectual agenda.

Juana María: To echo Tavia, rather than exclusion we are entering a moment of such intense saturation of images, text, and video that our relationship to documentation and the archival is transforming. I have become curious to witness those situations that actively elude the archive, that refuse the allure of documentation and cherish the ephemeral qualities of the live. Those moments where you really did have to be there, a return to the "Event," but also the secret, the intimacy of friendship, the play party, the club, the digital exchange. I have been attending more events where photography, posting, or tweeting is not allowed, and I see it as a way to respect the integrity of the collective experience that wishes to remain unruly, that wants to dissolve into the night. There is an impulse to Snapchat the archive, to make the records of foreclosure, debt, prison, surveillance, institutionalization disappear. At the same time, places like YouTube and Twitter have become vital repositories for documenting everyday violations and using these as evidence to demand reparations, creating a collective archive of systemic state abuses that contest dominant forms of mass media and the soul-crushing logics they promote. That the contradictory potential of these digital forms captures the "corrosive irony" of previous archival forms should therefore not surprise.

Do you feel there is a necessary tension between inclusion and critique?

Ann: Celebration and critical caution are both important when assessing the "archival turn." The successful work of inclusion has brought us to an interesting crossroads where it is useful to maintain a critical perspective that is alert to blind spots, absences, and the operations of power, especially given the origins of national archives in forms of state power and surveillance. The archive can become an extension of neoliberal and homonational strategies when inclusion is about assimilation and equality and not about alternative and absent voices or transformative knowledge. The goal is not just stand-alone buildings and collections but critical engagement with existing practices.

   I would suggest that the critique of the archive and the creation of counterarchives exist in a necessary, and ideally productive, tension with each other. We need both—a passion for alternative collections and ongoing attention to absences that can't be filled. We want a queer archive, not just an LGBT archive—not just inclusion but transformation of what counts as an archive and innovative approaches to an engaged public history that connects the past with the present to create a history of the present.

Juana María: Yes! I am reminded of Roderick Ferguson's work on governmentality that crystallizes the paradox that surrounds the queer archival project: "institutionalization is founded on divisions between legitimacy and illegitimacy."[5] That is the risk, so we need to remain attuned to our own affective attachments to forms of recognition and be willing to challenge how legitimacy is established and the forms of power it serves and upholds. Our response to risk needs to be about generating promiscuous forms of knowledge production, responding with activist creativity and intellectual agility rather than efforts to conserve or canonize.

In understanding ourselves through alternative logics of making sense that are often viewed as irrelevant, irrational, and illegitimate, queer others have had to create methodological practices for what José Esteban Muñoz terms "queer evidence: an evidence that has been queered in relation to the laws of what counts as proof."[6] And, sometimes, we just have to resist the impulse to offer proof and allow ourselves to dwell in the realm of unknowing and nonsense.

Christina: Following Anjali's earlier comments about what has not been included in queer studies' shifts in recent years, I would add that the historiography of LGBT social movements has had a tenuous relationship with queer theory and has held onto what appear to be many conventional understandings of the archive. One reason has been an understandable defensiveness, as scholars who have long adopted imaginative, suspicious, and tenuous approaches to archiving and to writing history, often with limited resources, have found their efforts ignored and then replicated or assumed to be restricted to literal preservation or transcription, when in fact their practices have always been engaged with critique.

In addition, as Ann and others have shown, LGBT community-based archives emerged out of social movements. One result has been that collecting and processing tendencies reflect the dominant parameters of that movement, not only in demographic but also in ideological terms. As might be self-evident, they tend to collect the materials of organizations founded in the name of LGBT individuals and so identified goals. This has by no means been static; archivists and others have worked hard to expand the terms of inclusion, to represent, albeit slowly, those individuals in the margins of a mainstream movement, most especially along race and gender lines. Many archives have also sought to recognize queer politics as they take form in a US-centered antiassimilationism, perhaps best represented by groups like Queer Nation. But other political cultures that might also be described as queer are not always found within LGBT-identified archives. For researchers who hope to historicize the kind queer politics described by Cathy Cohen—a politics that centers analyses of race and attends more to the interlocking structures of normativity, power, and kinship than modes of sexual or gender identification (without dismissing so-called identity politics)—it requires looking for sources outside LGBT-designated archives.[7] This is in part about exclusion—multi-issue groups are often sorted into archives along the same vexed terms of movements themselves (e.g., debates about identity and the Left, or, more importantly, what is *the Left*?)—as well as about suspicion—radical or systematically ignored groups rarely trust their papers to institutional *or* community-based archives. But it is also to say that this kind of social movement history requires scholars not only to queer their analytic but also to queer their research practice. Where and how might one research critiques of normalizing sexual relations outside lesbian and gay identification or ways in which nonnormative gender has been the grounds for varied forms of radical political affiliation? This requires a critical analysis of the geopolitical, to return to Anjali's discussion earlier, not only to capture what might be called queer internationalisms (and their others) but also to engage the very different forms of legibility social movements have taken around the world.

This has been a pressing concern for me in my most recent research. *Safe Space* was organized squarely around the history of US LGBT-identified social movements, and it tells a story about how activism against violence became a key means by which normative LGBT identity was slowly and unevenly disaggregated from forms of vice and deviancy otherwise associated with racialized poverty in the city. My current research looks at those left out of that vision; namely, I am trying to write a *queer* left social movement history that focuses less on LGBT subjects per se and instead on how a range of individuals on the outsides of normative leftist social movements in the United States have been variably taken up or ignored, and it traces this alongside the entwined dynamics of social services and social movements in the post–World War II city. The project begins by thinking about some of the uses of the category of the so-called *lumpenproletariat* so reviled by Karl Marx and invested with potential by Frantz Fanon and others and then looks at a series of collective projects including antipoverty groups, harm reduction strategies, and antiprison organizing. Some repositories are obvious here, but others less so.

What are your reflections on practice as theory?

Ann: A key principle that stems from this tension is that we can't know what a radical or queer archive is in theory and instead need to work it out in practice. I say this as someone who has been shaped by theoretical critique, including Derrida's deconstructive claim that the archive never reaches its goal, postcolonial critique's insistence that the subaltern cannot speak, and Afropessimism about the impossibility of retrieving the experience of the lost and disenfranchised. Many of us remain perennially suspicious of institutionalization, of knowledge claims, of dreams of liberation through archival collection. Although it can be tempting to think so, the archive cannot necessarily redeem us from the past or guarantee our survival into the future.

At the same time, for those in the humanities who are steeped in critique, it has been very meaningful to take up archival practice as a research method, to see critical ideas about incomplete and partial archives as tools that can lead to practical decisions about what kind of archives to collect and preserve and, even more importantly, what to do with them. To this end, I have found it useful to develop a practice of ethnographic fieldwork in both alternative and institutional queer archives—to study not just the items in the archive but the material history of their archivization.

What about the connection between affect and activist artists?

Ann: In looking for how the critical impulse can be fused with practice, I have been especially inspired by the model of queer activists and artists, and especially the combination of the two together. When activists work with or create archives they do so with an eye toward preventing them from becoming a dead memorial, and they make them come alive by connecting them to the needs of the present. Working creatively with archives, artists are unafraid to make use of their very personal, subjective, and affective investments in the archive and thus produce alternative scholarship and activism through a mixed method that is not just aimed at factual knowledge.

Central to this queer archival method has been attention to the affective power of archives—that they are collected out of affective need, generate complex affective responses (both positive and negative), and enable affective approaches to history, including the scholarship on queer temporalities so generative of late within queer theory. I have been gratified to see my own concept of "an archive of feelings" gain traction not only among scholars but among artists; Tammy Rae Carland, for example, used it as the name for her exhibition of photographs of objects that had affective meaning for her. Inspired by her work as well as that of artists such as Zoe Leonard, Barbara Hammer, Catherine Lord, Ulrike Müller, Allyson Mitchell, and Alexis Pauline Gumbs (just to name a few), I have embarked on a new project that picks up where *An Archive of Feelings* left off in exploring the current state of LGBTQ archives as well as the creative practices they have generated.

Juana María: *An Archive of Feelings* remains such a pivotal text for me; it gave language to the affective flows among artists, activists, and academics in such a compelling way, not because they are organically conjoined, but precisely because so often they are not. Part of what made that work so transformational for me was sensing [Ann's] embodiment of vulnerability; in that text (and others) Ann allows us to see the seams (and tears and sweat) of her practice. As academics, we are always already archivists, making editorial decisions about inclusion, representation, value, and pitch. And it is this articulation in her work of what an ethical queer archival academic *practice* might look like (and feel like) that touched me so deeply.

Tavia: I resonate with what Juana and Ann have said. Part of the phenomenological turn I have been privileged to witness and foster in my students has been in seeing them develop, alternately and in tandem, a queer praxis and a queer poetics of the archive. At the same time, I sense that praxis, or struggle, and poetics, or making/production, remain in tension within queer circles today. Praxis-oriented activists are not in automatic congruence with poetics-driven artists. To the contrary, their happy meeting often seems like an ephemeral miracle. I don't believe in their conciliation, personally, and one of the biggest dangers that Roderick Ferguson alerts us to, in his useful theorization of the "will to institutionality," is that we will seek to make them so. The drive to merge queer activism, theory, and artistic production, I would go so far as to argue, is part of the flattening out of counterpublics we can associate with communicative capitalism and neoliberalism. José Esteban Muñoz's recent theorizing of the incommensurable is equally pertinent here. It returns us in a different way to his early theorizing of ephemerality in the queer archive, which has had a deserved influence among artists as well as researchers. The incommensurable for Muñoz points to differences that cannot be subsumed under a single term (much as queer ephemerality cannot be fully appropriated to the logic of the archive) but that can nevertheless be shared out. The incommensurable points to the spaces between us, across which we touch and are touched. It sounds a little poetic, but that is my preferred image for how queer activism and art can encounter each other without becoming each other.

How has archival theory engaged postcolonial and indigenous critique?

Juana María: Where to begin? For ethnic studies scholars in the United States, official archives have often been encounters of indescribable psychic violence, torture, mutilation, and horror. While African Americans have often been erased from accounts of US history, cataloged instead in property records, juridical encounters, and chronicles of imprisonment, Native Americans have suffered the unabated brutality of romanticized archival *mis*representation, memorialization as murder. In the bloody archives of slavery and colonialism, even as we witness the psychic perils of expurgation, we already have evidence of the dangers of "museumization." Through anthropology, law, photography, and exhibition practices, Native Americans have served as the quintessential dead subjects of the official archives of "Americanness." And generations of scholars like N. Scott Momaday, Gerald Vizenor, Shari Huhndorf, Beth Piatote, J. Kēhaulani Kauanui, and so many others have been instrumental in reimagining the relationship between official archives and the living subjects that escape their grasp.

　　For diasporic African people and other racialized groups there has long been a move toward reimaging the relationship between materiality and memory and creating alternative archival forms that fill the spaces of exclusion. This lineage includes folks like Arturo Alfonso Schomburg, Zora Neale Hurston, Toni Morrison, and queer of color scholars like José Quiroga, Jafari Sinclaire Allen, Deborah Vargas, Mireille Miller-Young, Omise'eke Natasha Tinsley, and so many others. Their work points to how genres like slave narratives, *rumba* (Afro-Cuban rhythms and dance), folktales, *corridos* (Mexican ballad or folksong), and porn also constitute archival forms of knowledge. However, these genres are not just engaged in transmitting social histories; they also function as inspired projections of other ontological possibilities. As methodological models, these academic histories of archival engagement become resources we can turn to, not just because queers are also part of these racialized records, but because scholars of race have already produced such a rich theoretical reservoir that considers the limits, risks, and imaginative possibilities of archival engagement.

Tavia: For those of us working in black studies as well as queer studies, it is hardly possible to begin without addressing Saidiya Hartman's statement that "the archive is a grave."[8] In the face of the evidence Juana has just presented, and the generations of radical scholarship in ethnic studies, indigenous studies, black studies, and colonial/postcolonial studies she cites, who could doubt this claim? And yet as scholars like Rinaldo Walcott and Christina Sharpe have argued, taking death as a point of departure (rather than as an ultimate horizon) has as yet unforeseeable possibilities for black queer studies. In the realm of queer theory, this entails a complete reconstruction of the problematic identified with the work of Lee Edelman, for whom queerness is inexorably the cultural figuration of the death drive. Edelman scrupulously eschews a racial analysis he seems to associate with identitarianism, but the strand of negativity that runs through current black studies is very far from encoding identity logics. To the contrary, it posits that the slave, in whose afterlife we are shadowed, is *anterior* to the human around which identity, rights, and so on coalesce. We cannot be posthumanist (let alone postracial), because we are not yet human. The living death of slavery is a structuring antagonism and perpetual spur to a black speculative drive that exceeds the terms of history's destruction of the body (perhaps another way in which black studies has led me beyond my formative reading of Foucault). The radical strand of black testimony that runs from Olaudah Equiano's praxical documentation of the *Zong* massacre to M. NourbeSe Philip's poetic reconstruction of it may count as so many insurrectionary instances of this black fabulation.

Anjali: I concur with all that has been said and would add just one wrinkle to the story. The incursions of postcolonial and indigenous critiques need to be equally understood through the shifting parameters of what each of those terms (*postcolonial* and *indigenous*) means within geopolitical formations. And this is not to make the obvious point about multiple histories or temporalities; rather, it is to point to broader epistemologies of postcoloniality and indigeneity than the ones currently in circulation. Simply put, what does indigenous critique signify in the postcolonial space of South Asia? Is it fungible with Dalit critique or debates around scheduled castes and tribes? I am always wary of the summoning of postcoloniality and/or indigeneity as the desired alterity, without a clear understanding of how the terms emerge and create archival forms that demand radical exclusions rather than inclusions (as is the case in India, for example). Archives are, after all, always in situ.

Ann: I proposed this as a topic for discussion because, in my view, the project of combining postcolonial and indigenous critique and queer critique more substantially in theory and practice remains unfinished business. (Anjali's *For the Record* is an important benchmark here.) The current moment of archival activism represents an opportunity to create new alliances on the ground, but I find that LGBT archives are still not always actively considering their relation to the racialized histories of colonialism and slavery that Juana María and Tavia have very eloquently articulated as foundational for any radical, and hence queer, archive. Moreover, the degree to which museums and archives have absorbed the critical frameworks we have been describing is uneven, and the limits of recovery work that many of us take for granted are not always part of public histories, which frequently remain celebratory, redemptive, or "postracial." The messy gaps in the process whereby our scholarship gets taken up can be, in yet another spin on the archival turn, the site of ethnographic research.

Of late, I have been drawn to indigenous perspectives, inspired in particular by revisionist work in Canada's national and regional museums and new forms of cultural sovereignty for archives and museums such as the return of artifacts to their ancestral homes. Indigenous frameworks that question notions of open access or the paper document and the archive's intimate connections to property, ownership, and land claims have important implications for queer archives. The archival turn ultimately requires the thorough rethinking of what counts as knowledge and method. By approaching the land as living archive, transforming schools, and embracing the digital, indigenous resurgence is actively creating new cultures from the archive rather than exclusively mourning past violence or lost traditions.

As an interdisciplinary space, queer studies can often be characterized by ongoing territory disputes that reflect tensions between particular disciplinary knowledges and methodologies. Can engagements with the archive and the archival in queer scholarship be understood in these terms?

Regina: I'd like to think that an engagement with the archives and things archival would have the power to bridge territory disputes and tensions between disciplines in queer studies, or if not to bridge them, then at least spark real conversations across those different disciplinary spaces that I wish happened more often. A wide array of scholars from a range of disciplines and interdisciplines have become interested in the archive. This discussion in *RHR* is itself evidence of a conversation across disciplinary knowledges and locations, one that I hope is enriched by a theoretical engagement with "the archive" as a discursive field and a material engagement with archives.

Anjali: I have always been slightly bemused by the constant celebration or dismissal of interdisciplinarity within queer studies, particularly when it comes to the diversified holdings of queer archives. To return to a point I made earlier about periodization and geopolitics, such questions of interdisciplinarity often seem beside the point within histories of colonialism and sexuality. If one were to take the case of colonial India, for example, interdisciplinarity emerges more as a ruse of the colonial state, rather than a disruptive reading practice. What we need, now more than ever, is a genealogy of interdisciplinarity as concept and practice within and without Euro-American archival forms. For me, queer archival forms demand reading practices that are meandering, ragged, and unfamiliar; no blueprints here for a studied interdisciplinarity!

What types of key limits or liabilities do you observe in the expanding uptake of the archival in queer scholarship?

Regina: Sometimes I worry (along with others) that *the archive* referenced by the "archival turn," understood as a universal metaphor for memory structures, information storage, and knowledge production, might become so expansive as to include nearly everything and that, as a result, it will lose any relationship to what I'm tempted, with some embarrassment, to call "real" archives. I'm drawn by calls like Jack Halberstam's to understand the queer archive as a "complex record of queer activity" that might include ephemera of events, shows, meetings, and collective memory or José Esteban Muñoz's insistence that we track evidence of the queer in innuendo and gossip, in "traces, glimmers, residues, and specks of things."[9] At the same time, I hope that some strands of the conversation about archives remain tethered to material archives, broadly construed, and engaged with the practices of working with, in, and sometimes against them. Among my favorite moments in Susan Stryker's wonderful film *Screaming Queens: The Riot at Compton's Cafeteria*, for instance, is when Susan is on camera in the archive, reminding us of the kind of material engagement with archival documents—fragmentary though they may be—that led her to recover that story of trans and queer resistance.

Christina: I share Regina's sentiments here—both her investment in "real" archives, and her embarrassment about using that term. I also like the formulation "actually existing" archives that Ann used earlier in this discussion. I find contradiction useful, not only as an analytic for understanding capitalism but also as a method for *bothness*—that we can claim identities and critique the structures of their consolidation, write narrative history but also redirect its assumed end-point trajectories, take up a critical poetics and craft an earnest polemic. This is not to insist that these things can or should be the same, but I want to suggest that to only oppose them is to resolve rather than sit within or work with their differences. I very much agree with Tavia that it is important to resist "conciliation" and, following José Esteban Muñoz, to consider what happens in the space of incommensurability.

Archival work is inevitably about selection: which collection to engage, open, or assemble. And this process is followed by further editing processes of sifting, sorting, and prioritizing key pieces for analytical focus. What sorts of archives do you think should compel the interest of contemporary queer studies?

Regina: I am drawn in my work to subjects who are not always legible as "LGBT" and who sometimes stretch the limits of what we might think of as "queer." In *Criminal Intimacy*, I explored forms of same-sex sexuality in prison dismissed as "situational" and therefore often treated as empty of meaning for an LGBT history that was primarily interested in questions of identity. Among the challenges of my current project on queer and gender-variant encounters with psychiatric "treatment" is its inclusion of subjects not easily assimilable into narratives of queer history and as a consequence often marginal to the enterprise of LGBT history: reluctant subjects, afraid that they're homosexual; unpalatable subjects, attracted to young children; unheroic subjects, debilitated by shame and self-loathing. My interest in this collection of sexual and gender dissidents springs less from an impulse of inclusion than from an interest in a history of disavowal—a kind of strategic disaffiliation that might result from the promptings of gay activists to conceive of homosexuality beyond the mental hospital and psychiatrist's office and by historians who often followed suit.

In my current project, I'm also thinking about the ways in which my conceiving of the sources I'm using as a queer archive might keep me from recognizing other things about it—for instance, its status as a disability archive or an archive of racialized encounter.

While this project and projects past have been utterly indebted to LGBT archives, my interest in these dissident subjects has made me think about the liberationist origins of so many of those collections and the ideas about gay and lesbian identity that shaped (and shape) their accession priorities and collection practices. The archival turn proposes that we ask how documents come to be archived in the first place, in whose interest they have been preserved, and how the documenting of particular events and processes (and not others) shapes what can be known about the past. What kinds of queer or LGBT subject is privileged in those archival collections, and who is left out? How do accession policies understand and define queerness? What stories do LGBT archives put into motion, and what stories do they make difficult to know and to tell?

Christina: In my new work, I am also interested in how the idealization of recovery in LGBT social movements and archival projects functions not only as a bringing into visibility but also as a normalizing aspiration to the healthy and self-realized self. This is in line with Regina's new work on psychiatric institutions, and her framework of "disavowal" is very powerful to me as a way to think about the politics of representation. In *Safe Space*, I featured many activists whose forms of outsiderness might cast them as the ideal vanguard of radical queer politics today—people who adopted nonconventional gender, exchanged sex for money, and lived on the economic and social edges of dominant society. But many of them also refused some of the ideals held by radical movements then and now including those of self-determination or communitarianism, be that by acting in ways others considered irrational or against their own self-interest, embracing combativeness and materialism, working not only against but also for the police, shaming others who lived as they did, or adopting racism or sexism in everyday speech or exchanges, all practices that trouble these figures' neat integration into LGBT social movements *and* archives. The merging of social services and social movements in this history has often offered recovery (from addiction, mental illness, or other things understood as unhealthy) as solution, or it has provided an expanded framework for prideful identification. And as social movement history is often imagined as an aggregation of individual actors, it also assumes that those actors understand themselves as part of this political story. What analytics and methods, then, might the logic of nonrecovery offer?

Anjali: One of the first things that the newly elected Hindu-right government did in India a few months ago was to destroy a cherished collection of archival materials. These materials were government records of a key period in Indian history and had little (if anything) to say about queer bodies or subjects. Yet their destruction (alongside the growing rise in censorship) is a continuous reminder of the fragility of archives and access in so many parts of the world. Thus, even as LGBT archives in India are now beginning to emerge (especially online), the destruction of printed materials and cherished collections that interrogate India's so-called Hindu past is on the rise. All this to say, I worry less these days about the visibility of what we understand as queer archives and despair more about the disappearance of the very large, messy archives that we worked so long and hard to supplement! Such issues have particular import for those of us who work in the historical archive and in regions of the world where digitization or online access is not even within the realm of possibility.

Notes

1. Pierre Bourdieu, *Outline of the Theory of Practice* (Cambridge: Cambridge University Press, 1977), 78.
2. Gaston Bachelard, *The Poetics of Space: The Classic Look at How We Experience Intimate Places* (Boston: Beacon, 1994), 15.
3. Michel Foucault, "Nietzsche, Genealogy, History" in Paul Rabinow, ed., *The Foucault Reader* (New York: Pantheon, 1984), 76.
4. Ibid., 94.
5. R. A. Ferguson, "Administering Sexuality; Or, The Will to Institutionality." *Radical History Review* no. 100 (2008): 158–69, doi: 10.1215/01636545-2007-027.
6. José Esteban Muñoz, *Cruising Utopia: The Then and There of Queer Futurity* (New York: New York University Press, 2009), 65.
7. Cathy J. Cohen, "Punks, Bulldaggers, and Welfare Queens: The Radical Potential of Queer Politics?" *GLQ* 3, no. 4 (1997): 437–65.
8. Saidiya Hartman, "Venus in Two Acts," *Small Axe* 12, no. 2 (2008): 2.
9. Judith Halberstam, *In a Queer Time and Place: Transgender Bodies, Subcultural Lives* (New York: New York University Press, 2005), 170; José Esteban Muñoz, "Ephemera as Evidence: Introductory Notes to Queer Acts," *Women and Performance: A Journal of Feminist Theory* 8, no. 2 (1996): 10.

Who Were We to Do Such a Thing?
Grassroots Necessities, Grassroots Dreaming

The LHA in Its Early Years

Joan Nestle

In memory of Allan Bérubé, 1946–2007

In memory of Georgia Brooks, 1943–2013

[The colonized] draw[] less and less from [their] past. The colonizer never even recognized that [they] had one; everyone knows that the commoner whose origins are unknown has no history. Let us ask the colonized [herself]: who are [her] folk heroes, [her] great popular leaders, [her] sages? At most [she] may be able to give us a few names, in complete disorder, and fewer and fewer as one goes down the generations. The colonized seems condemned to lose [her] memory.
—Albert Memmi, *The Colonizer and the Colonized*, 1967

We had rituals too, back in the old days, rituals born out of our Lesbian time and place, the geography of the fifties. The Sea Colony [a working-class lesbian bar in New York City] was a world of ritual display—deep dances of Lesbian want, Lesbian adventuring, Lesbian bonding. We who lived there knew the steps. . . . But the most searing reminder of our colonized world was the bathroom line. Now I know it stands for all the pain and glory of my time,

Radical History Review
Issue 122 (May 2015)   DOI 10.1215/01636545-2849939
© 2015 by MARHO: The Radical Historians' Organization, Inc.

and I carry that line and the women who endured it deep within me. Because we were labeled deviants, our bathroom habits had to be watched. Only one woman at a time was allowed into the toilet because we could not be trusted. Thus the toilet line was born, a twisting horizon of Lesbian women waiting for permission to urinate, to shit.

The line flowed past the far wall, past the bar, the front room tables, and reached into the back room. Guarding the entrance to the toilet was a short, square, handsome butch woman, the same every night, whose job it was to twist around her hand our allotted amount of toilet paper. She was to us, an obscenity, doing the man's tricks so we could breathe. The line awaited all of us every night, and we developed a line act. We joked, we cruised, we commented on the length of time one of us took, we made special appeals to allow hot-and-heavy lovers in together, knowing full well that our lady would not permit it. I stood, a fem, loving the women on either side of me, loving my comrades for their style, the power of their stance, the hair hitting the collar, the thrown-out hip, the hand encircling the beer can. Our eyes played the line, subtle touches, gentle shyness weaved under the blaring jokes, the music, the surveillance. We lived on that line; restricted and judged, we took deep breaths and played.

But buried deep in our endurance was our fury. That line was practice and theory seared into one. We wove our freedoms, our culture, around their obstacles of hatred, but we also paid our price. Every time I took the fistful of toilet paper, I swore eventual liberation. It would be, however, liberation with a memory.
—From "The Bathroom Line," Joan Nestle, in *A Restricted Country*, 1987

I have been lucky enough in my own life to have participated in the beginning moments of a people's movement from private history to public discourse. I remember the early meetings in Boston, Manhattan, Maine, San Francisco, [Buffalo,] and Toronto, where a handful of [gay] men and women gathered to share their discoveries and to agonize over how to find the money to continue [their work], how to best share [these discoveries] with the communities they were documenting and how to balance the need for anonymity—a survival tactic of our people for so long—against the delight of revelation. I remember the flickering slide shows, capturing the lost faces and communal streets of other gay times, and the stunned recognition of the audiences, meeting for the first time with their own public story. In those days, we were not always sure that this fledgling idea of lesbian and gay history would find a home in the world.
—Joan Nestle, from the introduction to *A Fragile Union*, 1998

Wars pound at my heart as I write this, images of lifeless Palestinian children being dug out of ruins, other bodies held hostage in farmers' fields, extreme nationalistic movements carving out who will survive and who will be driven into exile and the smug weapons-dealing power brokers reaping billions while pretending to be sad at the state of the world—always the push of unsettled histories, unresolved inequities. This uneasy terrain of invasion, diminution, and attempted erasure has been my background for all the conscious years of my life, let us say from 1950 until now, a time parallel with my queer fem coming out into the working class butch-fem bars of New York City and in 1974, the co-founding of the Lesbian Herstory Archives, born at the juncture of gay liberation and the women's liberation movement.

I know how to live in the shifting terrain of the margin, for there we knew more than the intruders, but I move very cautiously into the new territory that is being offered. Perhaps younger women will feel more at ease, more trusting of this new place, but they will not have the same memories, the same fears of betrayal, the same sense of comrades left at the border who could not cross over. How do I remain true to Maria, the bartender from Barcelona, who protected me from police entrapment in the early 1960s, or to Rachel, the lesbian whore who lay in my arms dreaming of a kinder world, or the butch women I saw stripped by the police in front of their lovers? These actions happened in marginal places, the reserves on which we were allowed to touch or dance or strut until someone decided enough of these freaks and took our fragile freedoms away. But this old country, as James Baldwin called his historical ghetto—the Jim Crow–ridden American South—is a complex and paradoxical place. I never want my lesbian daughters to find each other in bars where police brutality is rampant, to dance in a public place where a bouncer measures the distance between the partners to make sure no parts of the body are touching. I never want their nipples and clitorises measured by doctors convinced that lesbians were hormonal abnormalities, as was done in the 30s and 40s, and yet, while I know that living in the pre-liberation queer ghetto endangered my life, remembering it gives me life.
—From Joan Nestle, "The Will to Remember: My Journey with the Lesbian Herstory Archives," 1998

In the past ten years or so, it has been fashionable to show the faults of the liberatory impulse, to see it as a false narrative of beginnings and endings, but as I look over my lesbian queer archiving life, I can see how deeply the sense of what Didier Eribon called the daily insult to the gay self—I would add the working-class gay woman's self—propelled my involvement in the project called the Lesbian Herstory Archives (LHA). Throughout the late 1950s and 1960s we had taken to the streets to question the House Un-American Activities Committee and its punishing of deviant thinking, the brutalities of racial injustice, and the futility of war. This belief in committed group protest, in the collective power to refuse designated hatreds, this touch between endangered bodies—holding one another against the push of Ronald Reagan's mounted police, the feel of Mr. White's hand holding mine as we marched through Selma on the road to Montgomery, the shared water-soaked bandannas held to eyes seared with tear gas as we sat in front of the Pentagon, the push of women's bodies as we packed the streets of New York City marching for abortion rights—these grassroots moments of protest and creation were the roots of my archival dreaming. We asked no permissions to announce our desires for change; we had no training except the lessons of life based on racial, gender, and class hierarchies, but living on the borders of the acceptable had shown me the richness of difference, the comradeship of the obscene. It was always the primacy of the endangered body and then the question, how do you imagine a grassroots site of appreciation for the shamed and the derided, for the defiant and the lustful?

Forty years later, the uniqueness of the LHA still stands: its grassroots base; its refusal of governmental funds; its demystifying of the archives profession; its determination to keep *lesbian* as the all-inclusive noun; the collective ownership of its building, which functions as a community cultural center, funded through small donations from many; its collective structure where consensus still rules—thus the building, the means of organization, its lesbian centeredness, makes the LHA its own kind of artifact. None of us in the founding collective were professionally trained archivists or librarians. Judith Schwarz, who joined us in the late 1970s, came the closest—she was a pioneer in the field of records management. None of us taught or attended queer / lesbian, gay, bisexual, and transgender (LGBT) studies in traditional universities, but I did attend Jonathan Katz's class in gay history at the Alternative University in New York City. We were a band of independent "scholars" sharing our work often under the gaze of more professional gatherings like the Berkshire Women's History Conferences or the National Women's Studies gatherings. Sometimes we acted like the working-class kids we were. I remember one particular beautiful summer night on the campus of Smith, or it could have been Bryn Mawr, Madeline Davis and I decided to strip and plunge into the lake that so beautifully framed the campus. We had waded far offshore, when our landed buddies started telling us to get out, but their shouts were drowned out by the roar of campus security vehicles screeching to a halt on the shore, and, in no time at all, Madeline and I, large women both, were bathed in a merciless spotlight and called to attention by the loudspeakers announcing that we had broken college rules—they kept the light on us for that very long walk back to shore and proper decorum. There were many moons that night.

The 1970s

The Sheer Joy of Collectivity

The apartment turned into a silk-screening factory for our first and only T-shirt, printed with the word *lesbian* in over forty languages, with photographer-artist Morgan Gwenwald directing us, dozens of women working in every nook and cranny, washing lines draped through every room, festooned with T-shirts hanging out to dry. All of us learning a different aspect of the task, the great bustling of bodies in motion, of wonder at what we were creating. Turning inexpensive white cotton T-shirts into an international singing of the word *lesbian* in all its variety.

The Sheer Sexuality of It

Welcoming visitors to a private home that was a people's public space, the seduction of formality into comfort, my fifties fem self opening to the stranger, the researcher, the new volunteer, taking them in as I placed bowls of fruit before them, as I piled up the subject files they would need, as I took them on the tour of the archives-apartment, intimate living space transformed for that time into offered sites of desired resources, my bedroom, the audiovisual room of the collection, my bed heavy with bodies intent on studying the offered images, the erotics of it all, the fulfillment of want and longing for a touchable past.

The Sheer Grassroots Socialism of It All

Apartment 13A, the biggest living space I had ever had, giving home to my broken mother, my lover, and myself and still room for collective undertaking. Resources shared from purloined office materials, from the salaries of our daily jobs, from the boxes of materials left in front of the door, from the hands of travelers from across the seas who wanted to see this new thing, a lesbian archive. For the "At-Homes," where lesbian cultural workers presented their creations to overflowing crowds, everything free, sometimes we had to have a second showing, with women filling up the 1928 tiled hallway as they waited their turn. The kindness of neighbors in this rent-controlled building on Ninety-Second Street, New York City, in the grips of a depression, the well-off not wanting to live above Seventy-Second Street, the city "dirty and filled with danger" as the 1970s have been described, "unwanted" people photographed in dark doorways—whores and drug dealers deplored in the right-wing newspapers—three sex workers lived on the same floor of the LHA when we found the apartment, interracial couples abounded in the building, a safe place for the different, and no one questioned the steady stream of gender-questioning people through the doors of 215. A crack in the economics of a city allowed many grassroots collective undertakings to come to life. Womanbooks on the corner, a constant flow between this pioneering resource and the LHA. How marginalities can speak to marginalities, again below the gaze of the Nationally Valued.

The Sheer Generosity of It All

Volunteers flooding the apartment on work nights, after long days of survival work, staying late, filing, talking, planning, welcoming, opening mail, preparing mailings, pasting up exhibits to be loaned, logging in journals, shelving books, Deb Edel always finding more room just when the apartment said no more, and then after endless hours, out into the night for long subway rides back to Brooklyn, Queens. Keys left downstairs, materials left out on the archival table for researchers' use, the whole apartment theirs, nothing ever taken. I come home from teaching, never knowing who will be in the house, friends made for life. Artists bring their work, share their skills, always adding to the knowledges we need. The collection grows because of a community's appreciation at being seen, heard, housed. The interplay between generosities, moments of respite from struggling to survive in the city. From our newsletter, July 1980: "Georgia Brooks, a member of the collective, facilitated a weekly discussion group for Black Lesbians about Black Lesbian culture. Bibliographies and reading material were handed out on a wide range of topics including poetry, short stories, journal writings and individual authors such as Ann Allen Shockley, Audre Lorde and Lorraine Hansberry. This study group will be repeated this fall and more will be added!"

The Sheer Comradeship of It All

Around the country, gay history projects begin reaching out to one another. Sitting in a circle on the wooden floor in the early days of the San Francisco Lesbian and Gay History Project—listening to Allan Bérubé telling us of his work on passing women in California's gold rush years, seeing his groundbreaking work "She Also Smoked Cigars . . . ," the delight Allan emanated touched us all; Eric Garber's face flushed with excitement as he outlined his thinking about the gay Harlem Renaissance; Maida Tilchin talking about her work with the 1960s paperback covers, again bodies shaped by a kind of mutual lust for the historical knowledges that seemed to be waiting for us just beyond the diurnal; John D'Emilio, Amber Hollibaugh, Gayle Rubin, Estelle Freedman, and Martha Vicinus; Judith Schwarz sharing her work on the women of the Heterodoxy Club of New York City in the early twentieth century, a work engaged in after grueling hours of paid labor in the records libraries of legal firms; Pat Gozemba and the men and women of the Boston Lesbian and Gay History Project. The wonderful larrikin feeling that we had as we followed leads, shaped lines of inquiry, met in other countries, visiting Jonathan Katz in his old West Village apartment, where his black-and-white cat, seemingly always a kitten, strolled over the shoe boxes filled with thousands of index cards, the tracking of desire and punishment that would become *Gay American History*; attending our first workshop on how to do oral histories where Deb and I stood with Paula Grant, Elizabeth (Liz) Lapovsky Kennedy, and Madeline Davis, our backs leaning against the hard walls, Liz and Madeline already deep in their study of the working-class butch-fem community of Buffalo, New York. Bert Hansen calling us to say that, on his way home from work, he had found boxes of file folders with some papers still in them spilling out into the gutter in front of a Village apartment house, and knowing we always needed folders, he wanted to bring them over. This was how we found the 1920 love letter written to the labor educator Eleanor Coit, by Alice, the young woman who so loved her: "This is a 'very quiet' letter, Eleanor dear, and you won't read it when you are dashing off somewhere in a hurry, will you—please." Helping one another without the possessive territoriality that so often marks academic endeavor. That was to come later, but now we laughed and worked and wondered at it all. The LHA has a photograph of a group of us, queers all, the sun hitting our faces as we took a break from the "Sex and the State" conference in Toronto. Before the world of academics and archival professions, there was Allan Bérubé, his mustache thick and smiling, an independent scholar who sang of class, history, and queer desire. It is his body I see now, in his just-right-fitting blue jeans, his flannel shirt, and his welcome, the twinkle in his devoted eye. These people, these projects, were the golden riches of my time.

The Sheer Womanness of It All, the Sheer Lesbianism of It All, All the Variations of Woman and Lesbian Welcomed

Again the photographs of this history so carefully posted now by Saskia Scheffer on the LHA's website, so far from the boxy, disk operating system–running computer we started with—a series of heads and upper bodies of women to be found at the work nights, visitors' weekends—twenty, thirty LHA visitors, many previously unknown to one another, all bodies pressed into a momentary intimacy to fit in the camera's frame. I look now from my new geography so far away from those 13A rooms, at one of these fading group images, looking back at the first decade of the LHA, and call out their names as best as I can remember—Pamela, Julia, Sahli, Georgia, Valerie, Lucinda, Linda McKinney, Vicky, Polly, Alexis, Clare, Nancy, Beth Haskell, Irare, Amy Beth, Sam, Jan Boney, Ruth Pardo, Sabrina, Mabel Hampton, Deb Edel, Judith Schwarz, Morgan Gwenwald, Paula Grant, Arisa Reed, Leni Goodman, Saskia Scheffer, Maxine Wolfe, Teddy Minucci, Desiree, and multitudes more—, and now new generations taking the LHA into another kind of archival imagining—Shawnta, Flavia, Hailey, Heather, Rachel, Kayleigh, Collete—and always Deborah Edel.

The Sheer Complexity of It All

The LHA was born in my eyes as an anticolonization project, what we called in the 1970s, lesbian separatism. A cultural, political undertaking to put us back into history, but always in our full complexity. Not in the service of lesbian purity but to provide one place where all who entered were for that time Lesbians. *Lesbian* becoming the noun that stood for all possibilities of queerness, for all possibilities of deviations.

Lesbian sex workers, my comrades from the bars, were in my hands of inclusion. Not a role-model lesbian history, not an archives of safe stories, always my own undertaking of keeping in the archives the tensions of lesbian difference, as we participated in the creation of lesbian feminist New York culture. This was the one place in my life where I stood for a Lesbian-specific world, and even though through the years, some of my queer archiving mates were uncomfortable with this specificity—Jonathan, Bert, Allan, Martin, Seymour, John—our early mates helped in all the ways they could. In 1992 when the LHA was holding a celebration in the Prospect Park pavilion to commemorate the opening of the new building, on a blistering hot day, amid two hundred women, I looked up to see John Preston coming toward me, two suitcases hanging by his sides, his face bathed in sweat, John in the last months of his struggle with AIDS, and with whom I was doing a book on relationships between gay men and lesbians, had detoured from his train trip back to Boston to be part of the celebration—"I know how much the archives mean to you," he said as he bent down, and I strained upward for our lips to meet. Here we were, at this moment, the two pornographers, as we laughingly said, embracing amid hundreds of dancing lesbian feminists. I have never forgotten how much it cost John to make that pilgrimage that afternoon. The LHA through its own kind of generosity brought into my life a multitude of inclusions.

The Sheer Politics of It All

Unfettered by institutional connections, we carried our LHA banner into the streets in support of a larger politic, first in antiapartheid demonstrations, then in reproductive rights marches, in the Washington march against America's intrusions into Central America, wherever we felt that seeing the words "Lesbian Herstory Archives: In Memory of the Voices We Have Lost" would refuse an absence, would remind others of the hidden history of lesbian activism. No one ever asked us to step out of the line of march. The sheer politics of refusing to have a board of directors or a letterhead with "famous" names, our search to find a social justice bank that would take a risk with us when, after twenty-five years, we had outgrown 13A and needed a permanent home, and the politic of honoring our commitments. The forty-year-long commitment to never allowing lack of money to deprive a woman from public LHA events. The politic of never wanting to be a national archive, that shifting thing of Nation, which in its generality, hides its specific exiles. Believing in regional lesbian archives that were also community centers, safe spaces for unsafe discussions, always creating cultures of place, believing in the internationality of the lesbian self: "Send us something in the language you make love in." The books standing on the shelves in the alphabetical order of authors' first names, to deny the power of patriarchy, we used to say. The archives as artifact.

The Sheer Struggles of It All

To accommodate all the needs of full-time work, then the work of the LHA—another full-time job, to rise in the morning and go to bed at night in full view of all that needs to be done. To raise the money to ensure best archival practices, then and still now.

October 5, 1981

The morning when I went to walk Perry before going off to work and found a death threat outside our door on a pile of sex magazines. "To the two female faggots . . . I hate fags of both sexes and my campaign of terror against you has just begun. You'll be hearing from me again and again and again. [Suggested sex acts for many lines.] Signed, Jack the Ripper, the real one." We made the letter public in *Womanews*; many volunteered to be a protective brigade. We and the collection survived.

. . . . .

August 13, 2014

Trying to finish this written journey before we head off on one of our exhausting necessary trips, back to New York for the LHA's fortieth-anniversary celebration, for work on my history of the LHA while it was in its first home, to see dear, dear friends separated from me now by continents, by twenty-three hours of flying, by aging body.

There is no end to my thoughts about queer archiving, though. No end to the LHA, but new questions, new uncertainties about what we thought it all meant and what the future seems to be about. When Daniel visited the other day, I said to him that in the past we were worried about exclusion from history, and now I worry about inclusion—as more and more gay people turn to the right, as we are welcomed into the national fold, as we are no longer the unwanted deviant but are now courted for our votes, for our domesticities, for our support of national agendas of security—I am speaking in an American context, but in Europe, too, the coalitions of the queer- and the migrant-hating have grown stronger. I have read the phrase, the activist archives, used to describe our projects of reclamation, the archives as a partner in the liberation of a people. But some of the most important collections in the LHA to me are the documents of our failures, or our own exclusions, of the complex face of gender and sexual differences. Queer archives of the future perhaps will give evidence that it is harder to live with a history than without one. The traceable arc of the public choices made, the markings of who we left at the border, the futility of thinking such words as *lesbian* or *man* or *woman* have fixed meanings.

The archiving that calls to me now, and perhaps always did, is the archiving of dissent. Times of war always call for unified fronts, and this is an endless time of war, an endless time of the policing of the borders. The queer archives must be a border crossing in all directions. I am saying good-bye now, this seventy-four-year-old Jewish working-class fifties fem lesbian-feminist who once helped bring a lesbian archive into being and who is now the archived. What did my over forty years of work with the LHA teach me—to question orthodoxies, the Nation's and within our own communities; to refuse allotted places; to move into unknown waters with comrades on either side; to take on huge statements of no; to collectively say yes to previously unthought-of equities; to take pleasure in new decipherings of old conversations; to compose homes in exile; to find the songs of the exiled who perhaps need another kind of body; to look always for the national absences; to keep alive the markings of the disappeared.

. . . . .

From My Haifa Journal, May 2007

Hannah and Dalia, our friends in Haifa, made us see with their eyes, and so we saw through the landscapes to deeper histories. When we first traveled the roads between Tel Aviv and Haifa, our eyes fell off the scrub hills, but Hannah asked us to look again. "See those prickly pear cactuses?" and she slowed the car down so we could focus our gaze. "Every time you see a cluster of them, you are looking at the ruins of a Palestinian home. The farmers used the plants to form natural corrals for their grazing animals and also ate the fruit born at the tip of the rounded leaf." We started to look deeper, longer, and soon we could see the tracings of another people, a recently displaced people. Stone foundations started to appear, buried in the living scrub. May you all have friends—and archives—that make you see again.
—Joan Nestle, Melbourne, August 2014

Rüstem Ertuğ Altınay is a doctoral candidate in the Department of Performance Studies at New York University. Ertuğ's primary fields of research are the politics of gender and sexuality in Turkey, with a focus on artistic and everyday performance, visual practices, fashion, and queer historiography. His essays have been published in various peer-reviewed journals and edited volumes.

Ben Power Alwin is founder and executive director of the Sexual Minorities Educational Foundation, Inc., a federal 501(c)(3) nonprofit organization. He is curator of the Sexual Minorities Archives, a forty-year-old national collection of LGBTQ literature, history, and art located in Northampton, Massachusetts. He holds an MA in sociocultural processes from Governors State University, Illinois, and a BA in American literature from the University of Illinois, Chicago. He has lectured on transgender issues at the Five Colleges in western Massachusetts and at Syracuse University, University of Connecticut, Western New England University, and Yale University, among others, and has taught local LGBTQ history at Historic Northampton and at numerous Pioneer Valley history talks and Northampton, Massachusetts history walks. He wrote for *On Our Backs* magazine in 1989 under the name Bet Power and published a trans autobiographical piece, "My Wonderful Askewness" in *Crossing Sexual Boundaries: Transgender Journeys, Uncharted Paths* (2006). He is working on a children's book about gender identity and expression from a cat's perspective entitled, *Max Talks about His Person.*

Anjali Arondekar is associate professor of feminist studies at the University of California, Santa Cruz. Her research engages the poetics and politics of sexuality, colonialism, and historiography, with a focus on South Asia. She is the author of *For the Record: On Sexuality and the Colonial Archive in India* (2009), winner of the Alan Bray Memorial Book Award for best book in lesbian, gay, or queer studies in literature and cultural studies, Modern Language Association, 2010. She is currently working on two book projects: "Abundance: On Sexuality and Historiography" and "Lyrical Summonings: Sexuality and South Asia."

Elspeth H. Brown is associate professor of history at the University of Toronto, where her research focuses on histories of gender, sexuality, photography, and capitalism in the twentieth-century United States. She directs the LGBTQ Oral History Digital Collaboratory and is completing a scholarly history of the modeling industry in the twentieth-century United States, from 1909 to the 1970s. www.elspethbrown.org.

Elise Chenier is associate professor of history at Simon Fraser University and founder of the Archives of Lesbian Oral Testimony (alotarchives.org). She has authored numerous articles on various aspects of gender, sexuality, and race in Canada and is currently working on a book tentatively titled *Outlaws to Inlaws: Same-Sex Marriage in the United States from 1940 to 1980* about which she blogs at echenier.wordpress.com/.

Ann Cvetkovich is Ellen Clayton Garwood Centennial Professor of English and professor of women's and gender studies at the University of Texas at Austin. She is the author of *Mixed Feelings: Feminism, Mass Culture, and Victorian Sensationalism* (1992), *An Archive of Feelings: Trauma, Sexuality, and Lesbian Public Cultures* (2003), and *Depression: A Public Feeling* (2012). She has been coeditor, with Annamarie Jagose, of *GLQ: A Journal of Lesbian and Gay Studies.*

Sara Davidmann is a visual artist / photographer. For fifteen years she has taken photographs and recorded oral histories in collaboration with people from UK trans*/queer communities. Her work is internationally exhibited and published, and she has received numerous awards for her work. She is a senior research fellow in photography at the London College of Communication, University of the Arts London (UAL), and member of the Photography and the Archive Research Centre. In 2013 she launched the UAL Gender and Sexuality Research Forum. www.saradavidmann.com

Peter Edelberg, PhD, is currently external lecturer at the University of Copenhagen. He is the author of *Storbyen trækker: Homoseksualitet, prostitution og pornografi i Danmark 1945–1976* (*The City Pulls: Homosexuality, Prostitution, and Pornography in Denmark, 1945–1976*) (2012) as well as several articles on gender and sexuality.

Jen Jack Gieseking is a cultural geographer who researches the co-productions of space, identities, and justice in digital and material environments. S/he is working on her second book, *Queer New York: Geographies of Lesbians, Dykes, and Queer Women, 1983-2008.* Jack is postdoctoral fellow in the Digital and Computational Studies Initiative at Bowdoin College. S/he is co-editor of *The People, Place, and Space Reader*, and can be found at jgieseking.org or @jgieseking.

Christina B. Hanhardt is associate professor in the Department of American Studies at the University of Maryland, College Park. She is the author of *Safe Space: Gay Neighborhood History and the Politics of Violence* (2013).

Robb Hernández is assistant professor of Latina/o literature at the University of California, Riverside. His book project, *Finding AIDS: Archival Body/Archival Space and the Chicano Avant-garde* examines alternative archive formations, curations, and collecting practices generated through the AIDS crisis in Latino artist communities. His monographs, *VIVA Records: Lesbian and Gay Latino Artists of Los Angeles* and *The Fire of Life: The Robert Legorreta—Cyclona Collection* were published by the UCLA Chicano Studies Research Center Press.

Kwame Holmes is assistant professor of ethnic studies at the University of Colorado-Boulder. He is currently serving as postdoctoral fellow at the Center for African American urban studies and the economy at Carnegie Mellon University.

Regina Kunzel is the Doris Stevens Chair and professor of history and gender and sexuality studies at Princeton University. Kunzel's most recent book is *Criminal Intimacy: Prison and the Uneven History of Modern American Sexuality* (2008).

Daniel Marshall is a senior lecturer in the Faculty of Arts and Education, Deakin University, Melbourne. His current research focuses on queer youth histories, contemporary queer youth cultures, archival theories, and queer methods. He has published essays in *Continuum: The Journal of Media and Cultural Studies*, the *Journal of Bisexuality*, and *Sex Education*, and in edited collections including *After Homosexual: The Legacies of Gay Liberation* (UWA

Press), *Zombies in the Academy: Living Death in Higher Education* (Intellect Press) and *Bodies of Evidence: The Practice of Queer Oral History* (Oxford University Press). For a decade he has worked as a volunteer at the Australian Lesbian and Gay Archives. He has a PhD in cultural studies from the University of Melbourne.

Cait McKinney is a PhD candidate in the Communication and Culture Program at York University. Her dissertation research traces a cultural history of digital and online media through lesbian feminist information activism, beginning in the early 1970s. Cait's writing has appeared in *TOPIA: Canadian Journal of Cultural Studies, Shift: Graduate Journal of Visual Culture*, and *No More Potlucks*. caitmckinney.com

K. Mohrman, a PhD candidate in American Studies at the University of Minnesota who is specializing in Mormon and critical gender and sexuality studies, is currently working on completing a dissertation tentatively titled "Exceptionally Queer: Mormon Peculiarity and the History of US Sexual Exceptionalism."

Kevin P. Murphy is an associate professor of history and chair of the Department of American Studies at the University of Minnesota. He is the author of *Political Manhood: Red Bloods, Mollycoddles, and the Politics of Progressive Era Reform* (2008), coeditor of the *RHR* special issue "Queer Futures" (2008), and cofounder of the Twin Cities GLBT Oral History Project, which published the book *Queer Twin Cities* (2010).

Joan Nestle's most recent work is a special issue of *Sinister Wisdom*, coedited with Yasmin Tambiah on the theme of lesbians and exile (no. 94, fall 2014). Freed from formal affiliations, she supports the Australian Lesbian and Gay Archives and the Women's History Archives in Melbourne, far from where she started—the Bronx, NYC in 1940—and stands with Women in Black in monthly protests against the Israeli occupation of another people's future. She has just returned from joining in LHA's fortieth anniversary celebration in New York City. May our archives be not fortresses of protected memory but buzzing with the possibilities of uncertainties.

Mimi Thi Nguyen is associate professor of gender and women's studies and Asian American studies at the University of Illinois, Urbana-Champaign, and author of *The Gift of Freedom: War, Debt, and Other Refugee Passages* (2012). Her following project is called *The Promise of Beauty*. She has also published in *Signs, Camera Obscura, Women and Performance*, and *positions*.

Tavia Nyong'o is associate professor of performance studies at New York University. The author of *The Amalgamation Waltz: Race, Performance, and the Ruses of Memory* (2009), Nyong'o is completing a study of memory and fabulation in black performance and another on sense and sensitivity in queer aesthetics and politics.

Karl Peder Pedersen was granted his MA in history from the University of Odense in 1978, an MA in geography from the University of Copenhagen in 1981, and a PhD in 1991 from the University of Copenhagen. He was head of the Gay and Lesbian Archive from 1984 to 2007 and is currently archivist and senior researcher at the Danish State Archives. He recently published his doctoral thesis on police and crime investigation in nineteenth-century Denmark, *Kontrol over København: Studier i den sene enevældes sikkerhedspoliti 1800–1848 (Control over Copenhagen: Studies into the Secret Police in Late Absolutist Denmark, 1800–1848)* (2014).

Anthony M. Petro is an assistant professor of religion at Boston University, where he is also affiliated with the Program in Women's, Gender & Sexuality Studies. His research examines the history of religion, sexuality, and health in the United States. Petro's forthcoming book is called *After the Wrath of God: AIDS, Sexuality, and American Religion.*

K. J. Rawson is an assistant professor of English at the College of the Holy Cross. With Eileen E. Schell, he co-edited *Rhetorica in Motion: Feminist Rhetorical Methods and Methodologies* (University of Pittsburgh Press, 2010) and his scholarship has appeared in *Archivaria, Enculturation, Present Tense, TSQ,* and several edited collections. He recently began work on the *Digital Transgender Archive,* an online digital repository of transgender-related historical materials.

Barry Reay holds the Keith Sinclair Chair in History at the University of Auckland, New Zealand. He has published extensively in early modern and modern social and cultural history and is the author or editor of thirteen books, including *Sexualities in History: A Reader* (2001), *New York Hustlers: Masculinity and Sex in Modern America* (2010), *Sex before Sexuality: A Premodern History* (2011), and *Sex Addiction: A Critical History* (forthcoming).

Juana María Rodríguez is a professor in the Department of Gender and Women's Studies at the University of California, Berkeley, where she is also part of the graduate group in theater, dance, and performance studies. She is the author of *Sexual Futures, Queer Gestures, and Other Latina Longings* (2014) and *Queer Latinidad: Identity Practices, Discursive Spaces* (2003) and is developing a third project that considers the relationship between knowledge production and visual representations of racially sexualized subjects.

Susan Stryker is associate professor of gender and women's studies and director of the Institute for LGBT Studies at the University of Arizona. The author and editor of numerous articles, anthologies, and books on queer and transgender topics, she currently serves as general coeditor of *TSQ: Transgender Studies Quarterly.*

Zeb Tortorici is an assistant professor in the Department of Spanish and Portuguese Languages and Literatures at New York University. He received his PhD in history from the University of California, Los Angeles, and has published essays in *GLQ, Osiris, Ethnohistory, Journal of the History of Sexuality, History Compass,* and *e-misférica* and in edited volumes including *Queer Sex Work* (2015). He is coeditor, with Martha Few, of *Centering Animals in Latin American History* (2013) and is editing "Sexuality and the Unnatural in Colonial Latin America."

Robert Summers has published papers on queer art, aesthetics, embodiment, and relationality. Summers has chaired panels and given papers nationally and internationally. His first published work on Vaginal Davis, "Vaginal Davis *Does* Art History," is in *Dead History? Live Art?* (Chicago University Press, 2008). He is currently working on a project that interlaces Aby Warburg's way of (un)doing art history, practitioners of queer/freak art, and queer temporalities and spatialities—which will culminate into a book.

Jeanne Vaccaro is a postdoctoral fellow in gender studies at Indiana University. She received her PhD in Performance Studies at New York University, and her work on transgender performance and politics appears in *GLQ, The Transgender Studies Reader II, Women and Performance: A Journal of Feminist Theory* and *TSQ.*

DOI 10.1215/01636545-2849962

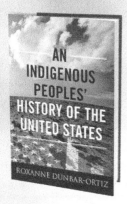

 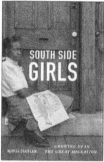  

Printed and bound by CPI Group (UK) Ltd, Croydon, CR0 4YY

09/06/2025

14685756-0002